H0805

A Quality Transformation Success Story from StorageTek

Also available from ASQC Quality Press

An Approach to Quality Improvement That Works, Second Edition
A. Donald Stratton

Breakthrough Quality Improvement for Leaders Who Want Results
Robert F. Wickman and Robert S. Doyle

Incredibly American: Releasing the Heart of Quality
Marilyn R. Zuckerman and Lewis J. Hatala

A Quality System for Education
Stanley J. Spanbauer

ASQC Total Quality Management Series
Richard S. Johnson

Principles and Practices of TQM
Thomas J. Cartin

*Benchmarking: The Search for Industry Best Practices
that Lead to Superior Performance*
Robert C. Camp

The Whats, Whys, and Hows of Quality Improvement
George L. Miller and LaRue L. Krumm

Root Cause Analysis: A Tool for Total Quality Management
Paul F. Wilson, Larry D. Dell, and Gaylord F. Anderson

To receive a complimentary catalog of publications,
call 800-248-1946.

A Quality Transformation Success Story from StorageTek

A. Donald Stratton

ASQC Quality Press
Milwaukee, Wisconsin

A Quality Transformation Success Story from StorageTek
A. Donald Stratton

Library of Congress Cataloging-in-Publication Data

Stratton, A. Donald
   A quality transformation success story from StorageTek/A. Donald
Stratton.
      p. cm.
   Includes bibliographical references and index.
   ISBN 0-87389-251-8
   1. StorageTek (Firm)—Management.   2. Computer storage device
industry—United States—Management—Case studies.   3. Data tape
drives industry—United States—Management—Case studies.   4. Data
disk drives industry—United States—Management—Case studies.
   5. Total quality management—United States—Case studies.
   I. Title.
HD9696.C64S677   1994
658.5'62—dc20   93-37658
                                                      CIP

© 1994 by ASQC

10 9 8 7 6 5 4 3 2 1

ISBN 0-87389-251-8

Acquisitions Editor: Susan Westergard
Project Editor: Kelley Cardinal
Production Editor: Annette Wall
Marketing Administrator: Mark Olson
Set in Times by Linda J. Shepherd.
Cover design by Daryl Poulin.
Printed and bound by BookCrafters, Inc.

ASQC Mission: To facilitate continuous improvement and increase customer satisfaction by identifying, communicating, and promoting the use of quality principles, concepts, and technologies; and thereby be recognized throughout the world as the leading authority on, and champion for, quality.

For a free copy of the ASQC Quality Press Publications Catalog, including ASQC membership information, call 800-248-1946.

Printed in the United States of America

   Printed on acid-free recycled paper

 ASQC
Quality Press
611 East Wisconsin Avenue
Milwaukee, Wisconsin 53202

TO TANNER DAY

Contents

Foreword

Since 1990 Storage Technology Corporation has used a set of broad objectives to provide direction for Excellence Through Quality (ETQ), our home-grown quality initiative. Each fall the Quality Advisory Group plots month-by-month strategy to attain the objectives that have been set for the coming year. The document they produce is known as the Excellence Through Quality Roadmap.

Do we take the roadmap seriously? Without question. Despite the volatility of the high-technology industry in which StorageTek operates, we have remained steadfast in our pursuit of roadmap objectives. Over the last three years, the roadmap has become gospel. Word among the management team is unequivocal: "If you want something done, get it on the ETQ Roadmap."

The story of *A Quality Transformation Success Story from StorageTek* by Don Stratton is actually StorageTek's roadmap to quality improvement.

As the architect of ETQ, Don has implemented at StorageTek what he describes as the *five change mechanisms*. His recommendations for using the five change mechanisms are born of real-world experience. Likewise, my endorsement of the five change mechanisms comes from firsthand knowledge of the benefits they can bring.

When Don writes about the importance of "management communication," his words are backed by a corporate record of consistency that is difficult to match. Since 1989 ETQ has been the first item on the agenda of every quarterly all-managers meeting. Since 1989 every monthly issue of *StorageTek News* has brought home the importance of quality to our 10,000 employees worldwide.

Don's emphasis on education parallels a corporatewide emphasis on quality education at StorageTek. We completed delivery of our three-day quality core course to 10,000 employees to help them understand teamwork, leadership, and continuous improvement. Now we are teaching management how to coach and nurture those teams for maximum benefit. Phase II courses, following core training, relate to team dynamics, career coaching for managers, and gathering and using data effectively. At StorageTek, education also requires the involvement of suppliers and customers.

The change mechanism—management network—starts at the top. I chair the highest level process improvement council. Our executive vice presidents, vice presidents, and directors chair their own process improvement councils. A worldwide network of quality officers keeps us focused on key business processes, and managers implement ETQ with the aid of workbooks designed by and for StorageTek people.

Our nine-step quality improvement process (QIP) is taught in detail during core training. QIP opportunities are now part of the budget process. We use QIP to reduce cycle times, and it is embedded in our management training. Twenty percent of every employee's annual review is an assessment of improvement in the processes that affect his or her job.

The fifth mechanism, rewards and recognition, is the glue that holds QIP together. We have an annual Chairman's Quality Award for cross-functional and departmental teams, using the Baldrige award criteria as our model. Applications are scored by a board of examiners and a board of judges performs site visits. The highest level council makes the final selection.

The winners of the Chairman's Quality Award are honored for their achievements. When a team from Puerto Rico is invited to come to Denver for the sole purpose of being recognized for its quality improvements, the message is clear: Quality counts.

Other aspects of our reward and recognition plan involve experiments in gainsharing, self-managed work teams, and separating merit from appraisal. Active involvement in ETQ is a prerequisite for promotion to management, and the top 40 executives in the company now share management by objectives, one of which is implementing ETQ.

In the introduction Don offers a challenge to universities and colleges to do more to place quality improvement as a respected discipline, one worthy of degree-level recognition. I agree with this. I also applaud those who are working with colleges and universities to get them up to speed on this subject. We are in the embryo stage of helping the University of Colorado, and Don is leading the charge.

I also wrote the foreword to the second edition of Don's first book, *An Approach to Quality Improvement that Works.* I would like to give you an update on the key issues mentioned at that time.

There is "no instant pudding." I hope that by this time most of us are sick of hearing this. Deming was right; you can't expect to see overnight results. I encourage top levels not to become impatient about the "bottom line." Meaningful results will occur over time if you keep at it. It doesn't take a decade, and I think we started to accrue results the minute we started down the quality path. Some of these results were obvious and others quite subtle.

The CEO must lead the effort and be the champion. I have chaired the highest level quality council for three years. We have concentrated on the five change mechanisms mentioned earlier. This was important for us because we had more than one or two balls in the air at one time.

Something interesting is beginning to happen. In the past Don had the most to say about the status of the five change mechanisms. Now the executive vice presidents have taken ownership, and they are making major contributions. These contributions are not aimed only at the groups they are in charge of, but they apply to the entire organization. It's great to see teamwork start at the top and emanated throughout the company.

Quality cannot be delegated. I discussed this issue at a seminar sponsored by George Washington University in 1992, led by Dr. J. M. Juran and Dr. A. Blanton Godfrey of the Juran Institute. I talked about how I delegated quality improvement in the past and why it didn't work. Don talks about our La Chaumière experience in chapter 2. In retrospect I think that was the turning point because I took charge. This must be done and maintained over time.

It is a painstakingly slow process. It took us two years to train 10,000 employees in six different languages. It took us one year to write the strategy. Because of executive- and manager-level movement, sometimes we took two steps backward until these people got on board. At one time I thought there would be an end to this journey. Now I'm convinced there is no end.

Key business processes must be defined and owners determined. We have made good progress on this one! We first thought we had some 60 key processes. We broke the 60 down to eight. Now we are concentrating on two: product creation and product delivery. All employees can fit themselves into either of these two processes. Last week our top team concurred on the subprocesses that make up the two key processes. The major elements of the subprocesses and the key metrics will give us an idea of how we are doing over time.

A specific cross-functional group needs to be the catalyst and guide the effort. Don talks about the five-year quality improvement team that became the quality advisory group (QAG) and has been meeting weekly for over four years. The QAG consists of managers, directors, vice presidents, and also includes field representatives via a speaker phone. The QAG wrote the original strategy which is still viable and continues to advise the highest council and the councils where they are members.

The quality effort must be pervasive and cover the entire organization. We knew this from day one. Our manufacturing group was practicing quality improvement but the rest of the company thought it was not involved. Over the last four years we have gone from 50 teams in manufacturing to over 1000 today throughout the company. Our annual chairman's quality award has included manufacturing, support groups from the field, customer service, and metrology. Most employees at StorageTek are members of a team.

Do not put up with the cry for more budget. This is the way we should be doing our jobs in the first place. We are not there yet on this one, but some good things are beginning to happen. During the budget process we are hearing things like what kind of training we need, how many facilitators, how many application specialists, and what kind of reward and recognition we need to build into the budget. This means quality improvement is beginning to be embedded in how we do things.

Potential savings are enormous. These start to accrue the minute you start down the quality improvement path. We have had many team successes over the last four years starting with no savings to enormous savings. The team effort story I like the most involved a group in our tax accounting area. The team used a problem-solving tool that Don brought to StorageTek, and while using this process it discovered that StorageTek had overpaid taxes to the State of Colorado. The team met with state tax people, convinced them with the data, and the state agreed to pay back over 200,000 dollars plus interest per year over a three-year period. The savings I am most proud of was the decrease in external cost of quality from 31 percent of revenue to 5 percent. This saved over 250 million dollars and, most importantly, changed the way we do business. We no longer "fix in the field." Our flagship product, known as the library, has now shipped over 5000, and our customers are truly delighted. We plan on introducing 14 new products this year that will achieve the same satisfaction in the eyes of our customers. This is where it counts!

At StorageTek, quality improvement has gone beyond theory to become part of everyday business. When a new challenge arises, our people share a common set of tools and techniques for meeting it head on. The result of our quality initiative is not merely a common vocabulary but a basic shift in corporate culture. We are now quality driven.

As I write this, we are in the midst of the steepest ramp of new products in our corporation's history. We have great ambitions. We also have great confidence that we will achieve them because of the quality processes that are in place at StorageTek.

This book is filled with ideas and techniques that any company can use to implement total quality improvement.

Ryal Poppa
Chairman, President, and Chief Executive Officer
Storage Technology Corporation

Acknowledgments

I would like to thank all those members of quality action teams and quality resolution teams that have believed in me, used the tools, and worked to implement quality improvements, both small and large, throughout the company. You will read about my feelings on the issue of gradual improvement and breakthrough improvement later on.

The idea for writing this book came from two consultants from the Praxis Group. Upon hearing the StorageTek story of success in quality improvement and knowing I had already written a book, they suggested this one. I'm glad!

I am also grateful for the support of StorageTek's top management team, headed by my manager, Ryal Poppa, CEO, chairman, and president. When we first started the effort I met weekly with the top management committee made up of Poppa's direct reports. This group now meets monthly on quality issues.

I am also indebted to the Quality Advisory Group which now has 15 members. This group represents the entire company and meets once a week to address and make decisions on major issues. I'm also grateful to our many account reps throughout the world that understand the value-add that quality improvement brings. Hundreds of account reps, worldwide, have turned quality into a secondary marketing strategy at StorageTek.

I appreciate the thorough work of the Quality Press reviewers. One reviewer suggested a change in title, which I used. The advice of Judith Keller-Hargrave, Phil McNichols, and David Reid is greatly appreciated. The piece written by Jim Parry, Division of Forestry in Florida, entitled Quality Action System Facilitator Manual is included in the appendix. Barb Kelley's work in transcribing the manuscript is also appreciated.

Introduction

Dr. W. Edwards Deming went to Japan in 1950 and taught the Japanese how to use statistics as a tool to monitor and make improvements in their business processes. Only later did Deming develop his 14 points for management to use in the new economic age, and only one of these 14 points relates directly to the use of statistics. The point here is that the 14 points evolved over time and are aimed mainly at the Western style of management that Deming is trying to transform.

In a most recent Juran IMPRO seminar, Dr. J. M. Juran, another well-known expert, was asked the question, "If you could do anything different, in looking back on the history of quality improvement, what would it be?" What he said was that he wished we would have concentrated on building infrastructures for quality improvement and organizing for quality the same way we organize for finance.

Here are the two giants in the world of quality improvement saying almost the same thing: We must evolve from techniques of improvement to putting in place an infrastructure that will ensure improvement.

We should move from talking about tools to talking about our cause, advised Jamie Houghton, chairman of Corning Glass, at one of the ASQC quality congresses in the year he presided as chairman of National Quality Month. This is indeed a very significant change, and one that will cause quality improvement to catapult to a top priority in every American industry during the 1990s.

In my first book, *An Approach to Quality Improvement That Works*, I discussed in detail a technique for quality improvement. The technique involved a combination of two well-known disciplines: cause and effect and force field analysis. I discovered this technique while working at AT&T. I had managed a project in the 1970s with 18 people spread across the United States: six people in New York, four in Baltimore, four in Denver, and four in California. During the first month of the project, I realized that everything was out of control, and I called my friends at the corporate education center for help. I spent two days with the experts and came away with the knowledge of how to use Dr. Kurt Lewin's discipline of force field analysis to manage that project. This entire effort is documented in my first book.

A decade later I was exposed to Dr. Kaoru Ishikawa's discipline of cause and effect. It was that pressure, I believe, that helped me through the thought process that led to using cause and effect to analyze another problem, get to the root causes, and make high-level recommendations in a short amount of time. Force field analysis goes much farther in exploding each cause that describes the problem areas and the action that needs to be taken to solve problems. When making a presentation to the AT&T management team just two days later, they were amazed with the thoroughness of the analysis and immediately began to realize that this technique was extremely powerful.

Shortly after that experience I was placed in charge of implementing quality improvement efforts in our southern region involving work with installation and engineering personnel throughout a nine-state area. In seven years I worked with 75 small groups throughout AT&T with major emphasis on network systems. I personally facilitated the use of cause and effect and force field analysis, and reached improvement in a relatively short time. I wrote articles on the subject for *Quality Progress* magazine and finally a book, *An Approach to Quality Improvement That Works,* that was published in the late 1980s.

People at StorageTek, headquartered in Denver, Colorado, read the articles and book and called me with an interesting job offer. My feeling at the time was that this would be a very risky move; I had worked for AT&T for 31 years. Several factors helped me decide to accept the StorageTek offer. One was the thorough understanding of CEO Ryal Poppa of what quality improvement was about and his intention to use it to help move the company into the 1990s. He was not after a short-term fix. He knew that meaningful quality improvement would happen over the long run, and I was confident of his knowledge and direction during the interview process. The other factor that led me to accept the challenge was that at that time StorageTek employed 9000 people, 5000 in one location. This was very different from working in a company with over 300,000 people and coping with the autonomy of each individual region and location. When I first started with AT&T at the Kearney Works, located in New Jersey, that one location employed 14,000 people. The opportunity of working in a company that I consider small, with the right kind of leadership from the top, was an opportunity that I didn't want to turn down.

In the first 16 months at StorageTek I worked with 42 small groups using the cause and effect/force field analysis (CE/FFA) technique. In all of this work at AT&T and StorageTek as well as at the Florida Motor Vehicle Agency, the Florida Division of Forestry, and Lockheed in Atlanta, and exposing executives to the technique in major seminars given in Brazil, Oklahoma State University, North Carolina University, the University of Colorado, and Georgia State University, I find that there is one common thread. The CE/FFA technique is an extremely powerful communication tool. It allows participation of an entire group. It allows groups to meet periodically and to pick up where they left off without any trouble. It allows groups to focus on achieving action items, and it enables small groups to better communicate their ideas to higher management. In all my experience, I have not yet experienced management as anything other than cooperative because of the thorough analysis that the CE/FFA technique provides.

Now, after working as the lead quality person in a reputable corporation and implementing quality improvement throughout that corporation, I know that we must put an infrastructure together with the guiding principles that will help it work. As Frank Gyrna of the Juran Institute said in a recent *Quality Progress* article, "What we really need is a chief quality officer equivalent to the chief financial officer in every company throughout the United States." It is at that level that the necessary influence can be leveraged and the necessary actions put in place to make quality improvement happen throughout the entire corporation. I also believe that the education function in the corporation should be part of this—the entire education function, not just part of it. Everything that we teach in our courses—production, engineering, marketing and sales, management development, or quality—needs to tie directly to the overall quality improvement thrust. I have this responsibility at StorageTek.

This book is aimed primarily at top management levels throughout American corporations. Many companies are now on the right path and are doing the right thing in terms of quality improvement as evidenced by those that have won the prestigious Baldrige award. The great majority, however, are still far behind and need to catch up. It is these companies that this book will help the most. I am aiming primarily at CEOs and officers and directors of corporations throughout America. Managers and quality practitioners who have an intense desire to move forward faster will also benefit from this book. I am speaking from the platform of real-life experience and working in a company where the results of implementing quality improvement are extremely impressive.

I would also like to offer a challenge to every college and university in the United States. Everything I have learned about quality improvement I have learned "on the run." I have attended the seminars, read the books, practiced quality improvement by trial and error, and talked and corresponded with the renowned gurus of quality improvement. This has taken a decade. The challenge I propose is for college and universities to develop a graduate-level and undergraduate-level degree program in quality improvement. The field is wide open as to what this should include. In addition to a sound knowledge of statistics, one needs to master and understand how real change takes place; how to communicate both up and down in the organization; how organizations really work; and to develop a full appreciation for and hands-on experience of the power of a cross-functional approach. We need to start teaching about reward and recognition, and we need to move away from the methods of the 1950s. We're in the 1990s, folks!

We have taken a shot at these things at StorageTek over a period of five years, and we have made remarkable progress. We are not, however, raising the victory flag. We have a long way to go in continuing to change the culture. We have a four-year plan to change reward and recognition, and we are currently into year two. We are continuously redefining our key business processes and assigning executive leadership. Although we have earned ISO 9001 registration from the British Standards Institute, we continue to work diligently to keep it. Beyond that we intend to apply for the Baldrige award. All this will take another five years. So please do not take from this book the notion that we know it all. We don't. We are learning continuously what works and what doesn't. We want to share this with you.

Deming said, "What is needed is a transformation of the American style of management." This is what this book is all about. Transformation requires a total ongoing effort aimed at doing things differently, such as putting the external customer as first priority; incorporating a connected, viable training for all employees, starting at the top; involving management in a new role of coaching and teaching; involving everyone in effective problem-solving methods; communicating as never before the values and beliefs of the corporation; rewarding and recognizing in new ways.

As in my first book and its subsequent edition, I do not dwell on what's wrong. I want to share with you what works and what needs to be done to make the phrase "Made in the USA" one we can be proud of again.

Chapter 1
Beginnings

Background of StorageTek

StorageTek was founded in 1969 in Boulder, Colorado. Four men, who at the time were working at IBM, decided to go into business on their own. With $75,000 of their own money and $225,000 in venture capital, Jesse Aweida, Zolton Herger, Juan Rodriguez, and Tom Kavanagh opened up shop in a small office above the Aristocrat Steak House. The business they started was the manufacture of high-performance drives for storing computer data on magnetic tape. Rodriguez is given credit for designing the marketable advantages into StorageTek's first tape drive. He developed a way of automatically compensating the read/write capabilities of the tape drive to enable it to read tapes of various qualities. Later StorageTek added disk drives to its product offerings.

StorageTek issued its first public stock offering in 1971. At its peak in 1981 the stock was worth more than $40 a share. Annual sales reached $1 billion in 1982.

In 1982 StorageTek began shipping its new high-density disk drives in volume. IBM, its primary competitor, was having some difficulty with its current disk drive, and StorageTek aimed to take advantage of this and ship as many of its own disk drives as possible. This seemed like an opportune time and a good strategy. Hindsight proves, however, that this turned out to be devastating for StorageTek in the long run. In an effort to ship as much product as possible, StorageTek neglected to maintain a sound quality standard. This resulted in the huge and unforeseen cost of repairing the drives in the field and losing a good portion of its customer base.

Two other ventures in the early 1980s were also becoming a source of strain on StorageTek. A development effort to produce a state-of-the-art version of a mainframe computer using high-speed semiconductor technology cost the company considerable dollars. Failure to achieve a marketable optical laser device put an unbearable strain on the company's cash reserves. IBM, in the meantime, was continuing to introduce new devices and to reduce prices. StorageTek could not cope.

By the summer of 1983 StorageTek had lost $120 million. In October 1984 the company laid off approximately 1300 people at its headquarters. The same month StorageTek filed for reorganization under chapter 11 of the Federal Bankruptcy Code. The dream of building a company that could compete with IBM in all areas, including large mainframe computers, had ended. In 1984 Jesse Aweida stepped down from his duties and gave way to new leadership. This provided the opportunity for the company to regroup and emerge from this period as a new and viable organization.

In January of 1985 Ryal Poppa joined StorageTek. Prior to joining StorageTek, Poppa was chair, president, and CEO of BMC Industries in Saint Paul, Minnesota. He joined BMC in January 1982, when the company had revenues of approximately $85 million. Under Poppa's guidance BMC strengthened its position as a major manufacturer and supplier of electronic components and systems for high-technology industries. Through a series of acquisitions, and expanded research and development, BMC's product line grew substantially to over $350 million by 1984.

Before BMC, Poppa was chair and CEO of Pertec. Pertec manufactured computers with a business of approximately $185 million. He assumed the role in 1973 and within seven years increased the size of its operations and markets by six times.

In just over two years Poppa was able to lead StorageTek out of chapter 11 and back into profitability. This the fastest turnaround of any company in the history of high-tech industry. In the summer of 1987 StorageTek emerged from chapter 11 protection as a new and viable company, with a strong new product line and bright prospects for the future. A new management team was installed that focused its strategy on four product categories: tape, rotating magnetic disk, solid-state magnetic disks, and high-performance printers. In 1988 Poppa began to search for a person to lead the corporation in the area of quality improvement. The search was led by Harris Ravine, at that time the executive vice-president, customer satisfaction. I am proud to have been selected as that person and started work with StorageTek on August 1, 1988.

After joining StorageTek and after talking to quite a few people at many levels throughout the company, I learned certain facts concerning the past. There were those who could remember seven prior quality initiatives that had failed. One of the strategies was to latch onto a quality guru and do a lot of chest pounding and flag waving to get people's attention to do a better job. All of the initiatives had been patterned after one guru. Most of the big names were involved at one time or another in the attempts to turn StorageTek into a quality-conscious company. In the days prior to chapter 11, the heroes had always been gunslingers, meaning the rewards went to rugged individualists who climbed the ladder by putting out fires. Another devastating bit of information was that I was at least the seventh person to serve as quality vice-president over the last decade. The thought had been that if quality was bad, fire the quality vice-president and get another one. It became apparent that quality had always been delegated to the quality office and that most people in the company did not feel any responsibility toward improving the processes for which they were responsible. I exclude the manufacturing people somewhat because they, of course, were the only ones involved in use of quality circles and statistical process control (SPC) to help improve processes to any extent.

Determining a Baseline

StorageTek was engaged in several improvement efforts. The systems development discipline was involved with design for manufacturability, cycle time reduction, and the program management process. Manufacturing was involved in implementing SPC and just-in-time (JIT). Field engineering had formulated a five-year strategic plan and was investigating two productivity improvement strategies and alternate delivery mechanisms. All were important and all were making some gains; however, unlike other companies that had embarked on a total quality improvement effort, the above initiatives failed on two crucial criteria. First, they were not organizationwide, and second, they were not systemic. The initiatives had, for the most part, been functionally formulated and were being functionally executed.

In late 1988 highest level management decided that a group with a crossfunctional mix should be put together to analyze the situation and make recommendations that would aid StorageTek in creating an integrated approach and an improvement plan for the entire company. The group consisted of employees from corporate quality, corporate education, organizational development, human resources, and supplier quality. The group consisted of 10 people with over 60 years of experience in StorageTek. The group met once or twice a week for several months to hammer out a baseline of where the company was concerning total quality effort and to develop recommendations based on the group's analysis. It decided to use the CE/FFA technique (see chapter 4 for the CE/FFA description) to help them better understand the various forces that were driving in negative directions so that positive forces could be developed. The charter of the group, approved by the highest executive levels, is as follows:

> To develop a corporate strategy for achieving a total quality culture that defines and integrates the processes and systems necessary to continuously improve individual and organizational performance.

The first thing the group did was analyze the corporate operating principles in terms of their intent versus actual practice. The following is a summary of that analysis of the five operating principles of StorageTek, including people, practices, quality, accountability, and action. You will see the words *today* and *future*. *Today* refers to the 1988 time frame. Many of the characteristics under *future* have been accomplished.

The second thing the group did was to use the CE/FFA method to further analyze why certain specific conditions exist. Many of the driving forces have now been implemented. The results of this study follow.

People

People are the key to StorageTek's success. Individual recognition and advancement will be based upon performance that supports StorageTek's commitments to our customers and investors.

Today	Future
Individual versus group rewards	Balanced and aligned rewards
Dependence on management information	Using knowledge and creativity
Reliance on a few, however brilliant	All employees as intellectual resources
Consume human resources	Develop human resources
Reliance on external expertise	Value internal expertise
Exchange relationship	Ownership, commitment, and pride
Compliance	Empowered partners

Practices

We will act with integrity to ensure credibility in our relationships with our customers, investors, fellow employees, suppliers, and those communities in which we operate worldwide.

Today	Future
Employees focus on personal success	Responsibility for success of peers
Functional isolation	Disciplines without boundaries
One best way	Multiple solutions through employee involvement
Value status quo	Critical thinking and new approaches
Fear, skepticism	Trust

Quality

Our standards of quality will ensure our competitiveness. We will sacrifice short-term gain for reliability and excellence in serving our customers' needs.

Today	Future
Inspection/detection	Prevention
Little q	Big Q
Schedule versus quality	Schedule and quality
Short term	Long term
Product	Total organization process improvement

Accountability

Our business will be managed to achieve planned growth and long-term profitability. We will grow by building upon demonstrated strengths and meeting customers' needs.

Today	Future
Individual versus group goals	Integrated structures and systems
Price	Cost
Focus on internal competition	Focus on external competition
Selected communication	Clear milestones and published results

Action

Each of us will participate in and contribute to the cost-effective, timely resolution of challenges and opportunities that continuously improve our customer commitment.

Today	Future
Verbal commitment	Active involvement
Functional programs	Integrated systems
Reactive	Proactive
Individual action	Group involvement
Act when told	Act as necessary
Learning not part of the "real" job	Learning, development valued as an investment
Action within comfort zones	Risk taking, innovation

CE/FFA Study

The following is the result of the CE/FFA study. As far as the driving forces were concerned, the group divided those among management and worker in terms of who would be responsible for implementing. Of the 89 driving forces, 90 percent fell in the management category and 10 percent in the worker category. For management items, the group felt that responsibility for implementation would fall as follows: corporate officers—37 percent; middle management (including VPs and directors)—41 percent; and lower management—22 percent. Seventy-eight percent of the driving forces were aimed at director levels and above and in this particular company, these were significantly high levels. These were extremely significant data, especially when considering the high volume of activity required. In some ways, of course, this was not a surprise, given the massive type of change that needed to take place. The only people in the corporation that could drive it would be those who are at the highest levels.

I. Level of Shared Vision Is Still Too Low

Restraining Forces

1. High degree of secrecy
2. Low level of trust
3. Believe don't need to know
4. Officers disagree about what it is
5. Not clearly defined and communicated
6. Think it is shared
7. Sharing information widely not part of current management style
8. Don't understand importance of having a shared vision

Driving Forces

1. Publish and communicate the vision (1–6) (management—executives)
2. Increase level of participative management and educate on importance of participative management (1–4, 6–8) (management—all, corporate education, human resources)

3. Officers go through goal deployment process (4–8) (management—executives, human resources, corporate education)

4. Officers' responsibility to share it, ensure that people know it and understand it (1–4, 6–8) (management—executives)

5. Live it—"walk the talk" (1–8) (management—executives, all)

6. Education on importance of shared vision (1, 3, 7, 8) (management—middle, corporate education)

II. The Level of Executive Action Involvement Is Too Low

Restraining Forces

1. Responsibilities delegated inappropriately

2. Always managed this way

3. They don't understand the value of their involvement

4. Schedules

5. Work force expectations

6. Value external customers at expense of internal customers

7. Don't know how to do it

8. Think they are doing it

9. Safety of the office

10. Lack of role models

Driving Forces

1. Role clarification (2, 3, 5, 6, 8, 10)

2. Executive development (2, 3, 6, 7, 8, 9, 10)

3. Provide examples of benefits of change (1–10)

4. Hearing from other executives (1, 3, 6, 7, 8, 10)

5. Commit more proactive time (3, 5, 9)

6. Increase employees' responsibility/opportunity for getting management involvement (1, 2, 3, 5, 6, 7)

7. Reward active involvement (1–10)

8. Increase focus on internal customer satisfaction (2, 5, 6, 7)

9. Listen to your experts (2, 3, 6, 7, 10)

10. Practice cross-functional involvement (2, 3, 6, 7, 8, 9, 10)

11. Practice management-by-walking-around (7, 8, 9, 10)

12. Model leadership behavior (1–10)

Note: All driving forces above require executive action.

III. The Level of Short-Term Thinking Is Too High

Restraining Forces

1. Push for short-term return on investment

2. American management mind-set

3. Schedule versus quality mentality

4. Short-term life cycle of product

5. Not fully understanding customer expectations

6. Short-term goals/rewards

7. Imbalanced resource allocation

Driving Forces

1. Change reward structure (1, 2, 6) (management—all)

2. Reduce time to market (4) (management—all)

3. Instill schedule *and* quality mentality (3) (management—all)

4. Increase awareness through expanded customer survey (5) (management—middle, lower, corporate quality)

5. Increase investment in prevention functions (7) (management—all)

IV. The Level of Employee Involvement Is Too Low

Restraining Forces

1. Not encouraged

2. Management believes it knows best

3. Lack of participative management philosophy

4. Inadequate resources allocated for solutions

5. Fear

   6. Involvement not always rewarded

   7. Most employees not given time to be involved

   8. Little encouragement of risk taking

   9. Employees don't know how

  10. Many recommendations not acted upon

  11. No incentive for employees

Driving Forces

1. Shift value set: that employees have good ideas (2, 5, 6, 7, 8, 9, 10, 11) (management—all, worker)

2. Publicize successes (1, 5, 6, 8, 10) (management—all, worker)

3. Communicate benefits of employee involvement (1, 5, 6, 8, 10, 11) (management—executives)

4. Make employees' intellectual resources strategic corporate asset (2, 8, 11) (management—executives, middle)

5. Internal network of peer consultants (1, 3, 7, 9) (management—middle)

6. Create/expand and enhance formal mechanisms (1, 3, 6, 7, 8, 9, 10, 11) (management—middle, lower)

7. Reward employee involvement (1, 3, 5, 11) (management—all)

8. Reward participative management (1, 2, 3, 5, 7, 8, 11) (management—executives, middle)

9. Commit time for employee involvement (1, 3, 4, 8) (management—all)

10. Train employees how to do it (1, 3, 5, 7, 11) (management—all)

V. The Level of Little or No Functional Integration
Restraining Forces

1. Lack of cohesiveness among disciplines

2. Lack of goal integration among disciplines

3. Lack of integrated rewards

4. Concern for self-preservation

Driving Forces

1. Enhance and expand cross-functional product teams (1, 3) (management—all, worker)

2. Goal deployment among disciplines (1, 2) (management—all, human resources)

3. Recognition and reward for teamwork (1, 2, 3) (management—all)

4. Improve communication (1, 2, 3) (management—all, worker)

5. Reward risk taking (4) (management—all)

VI. Reward Systems Not Aligned with Each Other or with Corporate Objectives

Restraining Forces

1. Current systems don't address specific functional needs

2. Unclear philosophy (mixed messages)

3. Individual versus group focus

4. Lack of interfunctional coordination of informal rewards

5. Unclear corporate objectives

6. Inconsistent application among management

7. Management's fear of losing control

8. Management's fear of change

9. Reliance on traditional systems

Driving Forces

1. Design and commit to a consistent, balanced corporate reward philosophy (1, 2, 3, 4, 6) (management—executives, middle, human resources)

2. Hold managers accountable for managing to the system (2, 4, 6) (management—all, human resources)

3. Examine current systems for alignment with corporate goals (3, 4, 5) (management—executives, middle, human resources)

4. Educate in situational-participative management (6, 7, 8) (management—middle, corporate education)

5. Experiment with new systems (1, 3, 7, 8, 9) (management—middle, human resources, organization development)

6. Design systems that meet specific functional needs (1, 4, 9) (management—middle, human resources)

VII. The Level of Skepticism in the Work Force Is Too High

Restraining Forces

1. Too many dead messengers (5)
2. Too many failed programs (2, 3, 8)
3. Change structure instead of fix problems (2, 3, 4, 8, 9)
4. Distrust of management (1–10)
5. Low credibility of management (1–10)
6. Employees don't help each other succeed (1)
7. Employees don't feel respected (1, 5, 7, 9, 10)
8. Lack of candid, honest, open communication (2, 4, 5, 6, 9)
9. Lack of shared vision (2, 3, 4, 6)
10. Reliance on outside experts rather than inside experts (5, 7, 10)
11. Lack of constancy purpose (2, 3, 8, 10)
12. Performance problems are transferred (2, 3, 9)
13. History of riffs
14. We behave like employees are not valuable resources (1–10)
15. People perceive things have not changed (2, 4, 5, 6, 9, 10)
16. Inconsistent rewards (1, 3, 4, 10)
17. Reward for the wrong things (1, 3, 7, 10)
18. The way we treat temps (7, 8)

Driving Forces

1. Reward teamwork versus individual competition (management—all)
2. Communicate the vision and live it (management—all)
3. Be consistent in actions and decisions (management—all)

4. Show us—don't just tell us (management—all)

5. Listen to hard messages (management—all)

6. Improve our communication process (management—all)

7. Empower employees through education and involvement (management—all, worker, corporate education)

8. Coordinate inter- and intrafunctional activities (management—executives, middle)

9. Hold people accountable for poor performance (management—all, worker)

10. Improve implementation and management of rewards (management—all, human resources)

VIII. Education and Development Is Not an Integral Part of the Business

Restraining Forces

1. Unclear link between corporate performance and education

2. Short-term versus long-term orientation

3. Resource allocation

4. Management's fear of losing a good employee

5. Employee development is low priority

6. Employee development is not a core value

7. Learning and education is not rewarded

8. Education is not modeled by top management

9. Management not active in education process—not-my-job syndrome

10. Lack of career development plan, philosophy, etc.

11. Education opportunities not equally available to all levels of employees

Driving Forces

1. Align education curricula to job responsibilities (1, 2, 3, 11) (management—middle, corporate education)

2. Conduct training impact evaluation (1, 2, 3) (management—corporate education, middle)

3. Allocate appropriate resources for education (1, 2, 3, 6, 11) (management—all)

4. Reopen career development process (1, 2, 4, 5, 6, 10) (management—middle)

5. Develop and implement formal plan to follow up and reinforce classroom instruction (1, 2, 5, 6, 7) (management—middle, lower, corporate education, human resources, organization development)

6. Expand technical excellence program (5, 6, 7, 10) (management—corporate education, middle)

7. Raise profile of executive involvement in education process (1, 5, 6, 8, 9) (management—executives, corporate education)

8. Develop process and reward active involvement in education process (4, 5, 6, 7, 8, 9) (management—all, corporate education)

9. Develop executive leadership program (2, 5, 6, 8, 9, 10) (management—corporate education, executives, middle)

10. Target intact work groups including managers (1, 5, 6, 9, 11) (management—middle, corporate education, human resources, organization development)

11. Hold managers accountable for employee training and development (1, 4, 5, 6, 7, 8, 11) (management—all)

IX. The Level of Performance Accountability Is Low

Restraining Forces

1. Inaccurate criteria in goal setting

2. Inconsistent reward system

3. Favoritism

4. Safer to do nothing

5. Hard to replace people

6. Inconsistent management review

Driving Forces

1. Goal deployment to ensure relevance and objectivity (1, 2, 3, 5, 6) (management—all, worker, human resources)

2. Align reward system (1, 2, 3, 6) (management—all, worker, human resources)

3. Increase participative management (1, 2, 3, 4, 5, 6) (management—all)

4. Reward risk taking (2, 4, 5) (management—all)

5. Employees review manager (1, 2, 3, 4, 5, 6) (management—all, worker, human resources)

Summary Data

Eighty-nine Driving Forces

Management	90%
Worker	10%

Management

Corporate officers	37%
Middle management (vice president, director)	41%
Lower management	22%

The group made a presentation on the CE/FFA diagram, as well as on the operating principle directions that were cited earlier. The meeting went fairly well—fairly, because it appeared as though the executives had not experienced this kind of session before. It was not pleasant to hear all of the negatives in terms of the restraining forces. It was not pleasant to discover that operating principles were not shared throughout the corporation. There was no question that in due time the officers, after examining and evaluating the quality information, agreed that something needed to be done to move the corporation in the direction that the last task force had recommended.

Two months later, the chair recommended forming another group to chart the course for the company in the area of total quality improvement. This will be discussed in detail in chapter 2.

Summary

So here we have a company founded in the late 1960s that did quite well through the 1970s, but ran into real trouble in the early 1980s. I might say that whatever has been said or will be said in this book is in no way a reflection on the founders of StorageTek. They were entrepreneurs in every respect of the word and did a great service in bringing the right product into the marketplace at the right time. The major mistakes were overextension and lack of attention to quality. The new management team, led by Ryal Poppa, addressed these two areas very early on. Poppa's vision was one of focusing primarily on the data storage and retrieval business, with the idea that specialists beat generalists any day of the week. He also knew and appreciated the value of a quality product and quality services inside the company in every aspect of the business and chartered the company to follow this course. There is no better place to start the quality movement than in a company with this kind of history and this kind of leadership.

Chapter 2
Planning and Beginning
Education and Strategies

La Chaumière Report Card

A significant event in the history of StorageTek quality improvement effort was a meeting that the chair scheduled at a retreat setting. La Chaumière is a small restaurant, near Boulder, Colorado, that the chairman rented for an evening meeting. At this meeting he told the 22 top officers of the company that the quality improvement activity throughout the company did not meet his expectations. He reminded them that all of the company's operations needed to be high quality, not just those directly related to the product line. This was a major philosophical change for our management. He let the managers know that a strategy was coming, and he told them his expectations. A significant part of this session was a report card that the chairman used to grade various important activities concerning quality improvement. These included executive direction setting, executive involvement, manager attitude, employee attitude, the level of meaningful activity, progress toward self-sufficiency, learning to use the basic tools, and results achieved or expected. These activities equated to a *D–* grade when summed up. The chair went over this and stated very clearly that he wanted to reach the *A* level over time.

The La Chaumière meeting could be characterized as the beginning of serious movement toward quality improvement at StorageTek. Prior to that meeting, company officers told me that unless they heard the chairman's opinion concerning the many activities that were beginning to take place in the area of quality improvement, they would not cooperate. They felt that this was an added chore and an added function, a task that had not been budgeted for, and so on. The feeling of these officers changed immediately when hearing the seriousness of the chairman's tone and the depth of knowledge he had about the subject. Exactly one year later the chairman revised the report card to *B+* based on significant improvement over the year.

Educational Experiences

The top 22 officers of the company attended a one-day, off-site meeting where they heard extensive discussion of Deming's 14 points. This included comments by me (these will be elaborated in chapter 3), a presentation by a quality action team headed by a corporate officer, and comments and in-depth discussion with Bill Scherkenbach of General Motors. This session was well attended and participation was excellent. The participants had a genuine interest in learning ways to manage in the new economic age.

After this meeting, many of the top people attended Deming's four-day seminar; this included members of the Five-Year Quality Improvement Team. Some came back so enthused that they visited with the chairman and recommended Deming's book, *Out of the Crisis,* and advised taking his 14 points very seriously. In addition, our top people, as well as members of the quality action team, began to attend national quality meetings to learn what other companies were doing. In addition, the chairman and other high-level executives networked with their counterparts in companies with successful quality improvement track records. They were keenly aware of and interested in what customers had to say about their involvement in the effort.

Five-Year Quality Improvement Team Formulation

A group that became known as the Five-Year Quality Improvement Team was formulated to examine practices at StorageTek and at other companies, and to develop an overall quality improvement strategy for the corporation. This cross-functional team was chartered by the CEO and sponsored by the highest level corporate management committee. It was chaired by the vice-president of corporate quality and included representatives from each major operating function in the company. Each representative was a senior manager at the director or vice-president level within the function represented. Each person was interviewed by the vice-president of corporate quality prior to being appointed to the team.

The group followed the well-documented, four main categories in the life of any team: form, storm, norm, and perform. In the forming stage, it was necessary first to find people who were interested and willing to spend the time. The group met each Monday from 10:00 A.M. to 1:00 P.M. There were many assignments given to subgroups that required an extensive amount of time taken from the normal job activities.

We were careful in the early stages to select people who were willing, interested, and ready to participate. We did not require specific knowledge in the quality improvement area because this was not possible at that particular time in the history of the company. We ensured that the people selected attended the major quality improvement seminars conducted throughout the nation and read extensively the books and literature on the subject.

There were several changes that had to be made after the third or fourth meeting, based on the interests and the activity of the members of the team, both in the meetings and outside the meetings. At least three of those changes were made within a very short time. Within the first month the group heard the results that were discussed, in an earlier chapter, concerning the work of the last task force. This was a real eye-opener for all the members and they were very satisfied with the thoroughness of the analysis and the information that it contained. It provided a guideline for action throughout the life of the group during the following year.

During the storming stage, there was much discussion concerning attendance at the meetings, the agenda, whether we were on track, not why we hadn't formulated a time line for action, and so on. These were typical activities for the storm stage but, nevertheless, had to happen in order to move forward. Very early on the group decided that it was not possible for everyone to attend, and that attendance would be nondelegable. The way the group decided to handle this was to formulate a buddy system whereby pairs of people would keep each other informed in case of absence, either in written form, by e-mail, or by word-of-mouth. Minutes of these meetings were published but, by necessity, had to be brief and summary-type minutes rather than in-depth detail.

During the norm stage, the group latched onto the Baldrige award criteria and really got to work, in terms of first understanding it and then applying it to the StorageTek culture. The group split up into subgroups. Each subgroup took a section of the Baldrige award criteria and worked on it to make sure that it applied to the various disciplines within the StorageTek operations. It was felt that the Baldrige award criteria was a well-thought-out document and that it served well as a guide for the group to formulate the overall strategy.

During the perform stage, most of the work took place by subgroups writing the different sections of the strategy, based on the elements of the Baldrige award criteria. The only change that this group made to the basic elements was to separate education from the human resources section, because that is the way it is handled at StorageTek. The content of the elements was altered to fit the StorageTek culture.

A Logo Is Developed

The Five-Year Quality Improvement Team, after deciding to use the Baldrige award criteria, looked at the overall strategy and developed the title and a symbol. This is shown in the logo below. The words

emphasize continuous improvement and process improvement, with a never-ending view of both internal and external customers, in addition to total employee involvement, meaning all 9000 people in the company and use of the nine-step quality improvement process. All of these ideas are embedded in the symbol with the words Excellence Through Quality (ETQ) in the middle of the circle.

The elements can be broken down as follows:

Leadership—This defines the role of senior management and management throughout the corporation, in creating and sustaining a clear and visible quality value system.

Quality planning—This integrates the quality improvement planning into all business planning processes.

Information and analysis—The importance of information and analysis to achieving improvement and quality and the identification of specific programs that will achieve our objectives.

Human resources utilization—Specific program that will allow StorageTek to develop and use the full potential of its people to achieve quality improvement.

Education—The plan for educating employees in quality improvement concepts and techniques.

Quality assurance of products and services—The systematic approaches that must be used by StorageTek to improve the total quality in products and services.

Quality results—Methods to develop key processes, product, and service quality measures.

Customer satisfaction—The system and processes necessary for identifying customer needs and expectations.

Although the team was called the Five-Year Quality Improvement Team, the members realized that developing a specific roadmap for anything beyond three years was not advisable. The following is the roadmap, which is very detailed, that was developed for the first year, and then the second and third years.

Strategies for Implementing Quality Improvement

Here are the strategies that were developed by the Five-Year Quality Improvement Team for each of the elements of the strategy mentioned previously.

Strategies for Leadership

All senior officers and executives will be role models through actions consistent with the principles of Excellence Through Quality.

Specific management actions to be taken include the following:

- Lead quality improvement teams focused on a critical business process.

- Work with quality officers to ensure that annual quality plans are developed, approved, and implemented.

- Participate actively in the ETQ training and education program.

- Develop quality objectives and measurements, and review progress in meeting these objectives.

- Benchmark best-of-class products and processes.

Senior management will define and communicate the company's quality principles to all employees.

Specific management actions to be taken include the following:

- Communicate through corporate publications and management meetings that achieving ETQ is a continuous process.

- Describe the expectations for ETQ to all StorageTek employees.

- Issue communications that clearly demonstrate that quality is the overriding consideration in how we behave as an organization and as individuals.

- Provide the time and resources for all StorageTek employees to be trained in ETQ.

- Publish a new StorageTek quality policy and ensure that it is understood by all employees and suppliers.

- Promote quality awareness to external groups (customers, suppliers, stockholders, business organizations, community groups, and so on).

Senior management will participate in and demonstrate leadership in the use of the quality improvement and problem-solving processes.

Specific management actions to be taken include the following:

- Actively use the quality improvement process during planning sessions, proposal evaluations, and other strategic business reviews.

- Ensure that all employees have a clear definition of their customers' requirements, and the means and resources necessary to meet those requirements.

- Recognize managers for learning, teaching, and using the quality improvement process.

- Implement the problem-solving process at the senior-management level.

Management will foster teamwork and obtain feedback from employees on the management style and behavior changes that are required to support Excellence Through Quality.

Specific management actions to be taken include the following:

- Hold regular communication meetings to inform all employees about the state of the business and the progress of ETQ.

- Emphasize teamwork through the creation of cross-functional teams to work on common problems.

- Use the management network measurement matrix to obtain and act on feedback from peers and employees regarding the implementation of ETQ.

Senior management will use appropriate forms of recognition and reward to encourage practices in support of Excellence Through Quality.

Specific management actions to be taken include the following:

- Provide recognition of individuals and team members for activities in the support of ETQ.

- Ensure that active involvement in ETQ is a key criterion for selecting individuals for promotion to management.

- Ensure that clearly defined quality improvement objectives are included in employee performance appraisals.

- Reflect the importance of ETQ by placing a significant weighting on its implementation and use in the guidelines of bonus incentive plans.

- Recognize the accomplishments of problem-solving teams.

A corporate officer process improvement council will be created to provide top-level leadership for achieving Excellence Through Quality.

The corporate officer process improvement council will consist of the corporate officer group. As part of the ETQ management network (described in the following section), the corporate officer process improvement council will drive the implementation of ETQ and ensure that resources are allocated and prioritized for high-level, cross-functional improvement projects.

Strategies for Quality Planning

Quality planning, establishing short-term and long-range goals, and allocating resources to attain these goals will be fully integrated with formal business-planning activities.

Specific management actions to be taken include the following:

- Integrate the implementation of ETQ into the strategic plan.

- Define quality goals for the operating plan.

- Provide resource support to implement ETQ in the operating plan.

- Develop quality improvement goals and measuring techniques throughout the organization.

The Excellence Through Quality management network will drive the implementation of the process and ensure that the required resources are allocated.

Excellence Through Quality Management Network

The management network consists of a series of process improvement councils starting at the very top. The chair presides over the highest level council and officers at executive vice-president, vice-president, and director level chair their own councils.

The Quality Advisory Group (QAG) advises the highest level council. Each member of the QAG is also a member of their functional process improvement council.

We also have quality officers worldwide in every division and subsidiary throughout the world.

Corporate Officer Process Improvement Council

The council is composed of the corporate management committee chaired by the CEO and vice-chaired by the vice-president of corporate quality. The corporate officer process improvement council will lead ETQ and ensure that all StorageTek management consistently and continually demonstrates commitment to the quality improvement effort.

Roles and responsibilities include the following:

- Incorporate the ETQ strategy in product, strategic, and operating plans and activities.
- Drive implementation plans to achieve ETQ.
- Provide the proper role model and leadership through participation in quality improvement projects.
- Develop quality objectives and measuring techniques, and review progress during all operating reviews.
- Participate in the ETQ training and education program.
- Promote continuous quality improvement through appropriate recognition and rewards.
- Set priorities and allocate resources for corporatewide improvement opportunities.

Five-Year Quality Improvement Team

Each corporate officer process improvement council member will appoint a quality officer(s) to support the execution of ETQ as a member of the Five-Year Quality Improvement Team. The Five-Year Team has the primary responsibility of designing the corporate strategy to achieve ETQ. The Five-Year Team will actively support the corporate officer process improvement council in driving the implementation of ETQ.

Functional Staff Process Improvement Councils

Chaired by the functional head and made up of all direct reports, the functional staff process improvement councils are responsible for managing the installation and operation of ETQ in their functional areas. Each team will include a quality officer(s) to provide support in the planning, coordination, and implementation of ETQ. The quality officer supports management as it engages in continuous quality improvement. Caution must be taken, however, that management's tasks and responsibilities are not delegated to the quality officer. The functional staff process improvement council will be responsible for prioritizing and providing resources for quality improvement projects elevated by department process improvement teams in the ETQ network. Investment for identified improvement opportunities will be included in the regular budgeting process. If a project calls for cross-functional participation, a quality action team will be established with membership from the appropriate functions. Problems not resolvable at the functional level due to lack of resources or cultural differences will be referred to the corporate officer process improvement council.

Roles and responsibilities include the following:

- Develop functional unit plans to achieve ETQ.
- Ensure widespread use of the quality improvement and problem-solving processes.
- Review and measure function progress in achieving continuous quality improvement.
- Develop functional quality objectives and measuring techniques.
- Promote and communicate support for ETQ.
- Provide guidelines for department process improvement team meetings.

Department Process Improvement Teams

All managers will act as leaders of their department process improvement teams. Teams will be composed of the manager and all direct reports to ensure total employee involvement in the quality improvement effort. Regular quality improvement meetings will be held and will include agenda items such as identifying improvement opportunities and quality barriers, monitoring and reviewing defects, participatively developing corrective action plans, and training in problem-solving methods. Quality improvement meetings should be conducted in an open and participative environment in accordance with operating guidelines provided by the functional staff process improvement council. These guidelines should address issues such as the frequency and duration of meetings, criteria for the selection and approval of improvement projects, availability of resources, and the tracking and reporting of progress. Department-level problems and improvement opportunities will be addressed by quality action teams using the participative problem-solving process. Problems identified that cannot be solved by department-level quality action teams due to lack of resources, capability, or cultural barriers will be referred to the functional staff process improvement council.

Corporate Quality Office

The corporate quality office, under the direction of the vice-president of corporate quality, will provide support to the management network in implementing ETQ.

Roles and responsibilities include the following:

- Monitor the corporatewide implementation of ETQ.

- Assist and support the department process improvement teams and functional staff process improvement councils.

- Assist in identifying training and education needs.

- Serve as technical consultants on quality improvement tools and techniques.

- Assist management in defining quality goals and measuring techniques for ETQ.

- Ensure that quality improvement and problem-solving processes are in place and used throughout the company.

- Participate in the development of recognition and reward systems in support of ETQ.
- Audit the chairman's quality award which is explained in chapter 4.

Quality Officers

StorageTek has 32 quality officers worldwide in every region and subsidiary throughout the world. These quality officers help implement quality improvement throughout their divisions. They vice chair the divisional and subsidiary process improvement councils.

Benchmarking will be used as a key planning tool for meeting customer requirements.

Specific management actions to be taken include the following:

- Provide education to key employees on the benchmarking process.
- Develop an implementation plan for the collection of benchmark data.
- Implement benchmarking throughout the organization.
- Define improvement goals based on benchmark analysis.
- Develop action plans to achieve and maintain competitive superiority.

Strategies for Information and Analysis

Information systems required to manage for quality improvement will be identified and prioritized.

- Align and focus the mission of the management information system (MIS) steering committee to allow it to prioritize information systems that support quality improvement. We must educate the committee about quality techniques and strategies to allow it to function in this role. Approval for priority will be given by the MIS steering committee to projects that meet the following criteria:
  - Identify investments through the quality improvement process.

- Spend for prevention.
- Identify data systems that have potential for cost-of-quality reduction.
- Identify cross-functional quality improvement data projects.

All data systems will meet specific criteria.

- Design data systems to ensure data accuracy, validity, timeliness, consistency, standardization, and accessibility. The data systems will be organized so that a minimum of three years of trend information can be generated.

All information systems will meet specific criteria.

- Design information systems that will help identify opportunities or problems, determine root causes, and develop countermeasures and remedies. Methods will be included to analyze data and verify that countermeasures have produced the required results. Information systems will be designed with particular emphasis on the graphic presentation of quantitative information.

Methods will be defined for improving the integration of information systems.

- Address information systems (IS) issues, including infrastructure (hardware, operating systems, data base management systems, language, and so on), data, applications, and organization in the corporate architecture process.

Strategies for Human Resource Utilization

Balanced reward systems will be instituted to ensure that all employees are recognized on the basis of quality improvement, team accomplishment, individual contribution, and corporate profitability.

- Using an interdisciplinary task force, determine the most effective methods for rewarding and recognizing employees consistent with the principles set forth in the leadership section.
- Revise the performance appraisal process to reinforce the values of quality, teamwork, and participative management.

A formal human resource utilization planning process will be integrated into the corporate business and quality plans.

- Continue the 1989 effort to integrate the human resources division strategic plan with the corporate strategic and business plans.

- Establish a process to define future skill requirements and the methods for the work force to attain the needed skills.

- Integrate vertical and horizontal career planning into staffing requirements and employee expectations.

- Develop an effective job rotation process.

- Continue to support affirmative action programs.

Continuous improvement in the quality of work life will be ensured through the implementation of programs in health, wellness, environmental concern, morale, and safety.

- Define and communicate each employee's responsibilities for safety and the environment.

- Continue to reinforce the importance of health and wellness in the work place.

- Reinforce the value of continuing education as an element of employee wellness.

Systems that value employees as the critical resource and asset of StorageTek will be instituted to attract and retain a high-quality work force.

- Form a network of interdisciplinary task teams to recommend programs that will help the corporation hire entry-level people and develop them into long-term StorageTek employees.

- Implement the elements of the human resources 1989 strategic plan on attracting and retaining employees.

- Continue to design and implement alternative work design systems which further empower employees to act.

- Implement a tuition reimbursement program for employees enrolled in selected accelerated degree programs.

Strategies for Education

All StorageTek employees will be trained in the skills, knowledge, and practices required to achieve Excellence Through Quality.

To achieve consistency in the application of the processes and tools of quality improvement, all StorageTek employees will be trained in a basic core curriculum. The framework of the core is presented in Figure 2.1. There are four elements of the core structure: orientation, which focuses on organizational direction and constancy of purpose; skills and knowledge, which focus on quality concepts, tools and methods; team effectiveness, which focuses on interpersonal competence and practices; and an application session of the quality improvement process. The core is supplemented by additional functional requirements and management practices. This approach accommodates unique needs while creating a common language and approach to quality improvement.

Specific management actions to be taken include the following:

- Establish a cross-functional education committee to develop a core program that will create a common, understandable language and set of tools.

- Train all StorageTek employees in the core skills, knowledge and practices required to achieve ETQ.

- Embed into the management development curriculum the management training required to support continuous improvement.

- Ensure that functional requirements, in addition to the core, are identified and planned for.

A top-down implementation strategy will cascade the core training program throughout the organization using intact, project-focused work groups.

Specific management actions to be taken include the following:

- Develop a top-down implementation strategy involving employees worldwide.

- Develop course materials for the core curriculum.

- Align the education strategy with other systems that influence how people perform their work (for example, awards, recognition, goals).

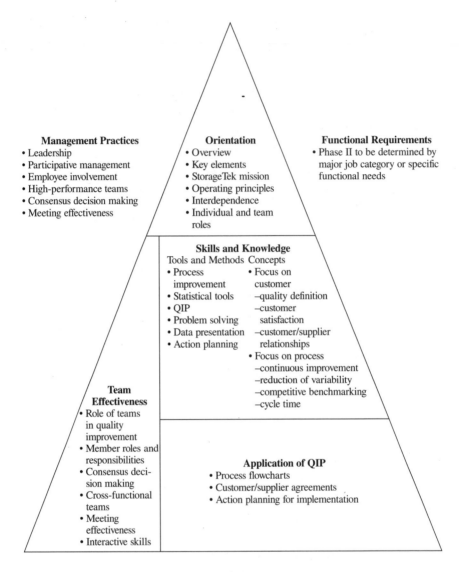

Management Practices
- Leadership
- Participative management
- Employee involvement
- High-performance teams
- Consensus decision making
- Meeting effectiveness

Orientation
- Overview
- Key elements
- StorageTek mission
- Operating principles
- Interdependence
- Individual and team roles

Functional Requirements
- Phase II to be determined by major job category or specific functional needs

Skills and Knowledge
Tools and Methods   Concepts
- Process improvement
- Statistical tools
- QIP
- Problem solving
- Data presentation
- Action planning

- Focus on customer
  –quality definition
  –customer satisfaction
  –customer/supplier relationships
- Focus on process
  –continuous improvement
  –reduction of variability
  –competitive benchmarking
  –cycle time

Team Effectiveness
- Role of teams in quality improvement
- Member roles and responsibilities
- Consensus decision making
- Cross-functional teams
- Meeting effectiveness
- Interactive skills

Application of QIP
- Process flowcharts
- Customer/supplier agreements
- Action planning for implementation

Figure 2.1. Achieving Excellence Through Quality.

The education capacity of the organization will be self-sustaining.

Specific management actions to be taken include the following:

- Select and train facilitators to lead functional education implementation efforts.

- Assign corporate quality consultants to provide training and support in the application of statistical problem-solving tools.

- Develop methods of measuring and continuously improving the impact of education on work groups and organizational performance.

- Increase partnerships with public education institutions to influence and ensure that curricula supports business needs.

- Strengthen relationships with StorageTek business partners by extending corporate processes that will be developed and used to ensure that new products and services are designed to continuously meet or exceed customer expectations.

Strategies for Quality Assurance of Products and Services

Corporate processes will be developed and used to ensure that new products and services are designed to meet or exceed customer expectations continuously.

- Use feedback mechanisms such as customer advisory boards and user forums for all major products.

- Include technical/professional managers in FORUM, GUIDE, and SHARE (uscr groups), customer awareness sessions, and international symposiums.

- Identify internal and external customer expectations clearly and the corporate ability to meet those expectations through the use of the quality improvement process.

- Provide the resources required to conduct competitive product comparisons.

- Embed the quality improvement and design for manufacturability processes in the program management process.

- Use the quality improvement process in conjunction with the program management process and design for manufacturability to reduce cycle times.

- Establish control over key technologies.

Systems will be developed to measure, evaluate, optimize, and maintain the capability of critical processes for new and existing products.

- Implement the nine-step quality improvement process functionally and cross-functionally in every process as appropriate.
- Use SPC and design of experiments to control and improve work processes.

Consistent process measurement philosophy and methodologies will be established.

- Ensure through the education process that the concept of variation is clearly understood as the corporate philosophy for improving quality.
- Drive the reduction of variation as a methodology for quality improvement using statistical process control techniques.

An audit process will be established to assess quality assurance systems and the quality of products and services.

- Conduct systems and products and services audits using corporate quality and internal audit.
- Establish that the elements of the systems audits are competitive benchmarking, the quality improvement process, and documentation.
- Establish that the elements of the products and services audits are competitive benchmarking, products and services objectives, and feedback methods.
- Translate audit findings into system and process improvements through the quality improvement process.

A standardized quality documentation system will be developed to define our systems and processes accurately.

- Establish documentation requirements for work processes, process flowcharting and customer/supplier agreements.
- Establish documentation standards based on the StorageTek quality policy, corporate quality manual, functional quality manuals, and the nine-step quality improvement process.

- Establish methodologies to stay current with changes in technology and quality improvement practices.

- Revise corporate practices and procedures on data retention to support the ETQ process.

The current system for quality assurance of internal support functions will be upgraded.

- Set internal product and service standards based on competitive benchmarking.

- Use customer/supplier agreements as the principal means of quality assurance.

- Use the quality improvement process and reduction of variation to assess quality improvement.

The current system for assuring the quality of purchased materials, products, and services will be improved.

- Develop and expand supplier advisory boards in new and existing product development.

- Establish long-term supplier partnerships by stabilizing supplier production orders and awarding contracts for the life of a product.

- Expand quality improvement training and assistance to the supplier base through StorageTek's supplier assistance organization.

- Continue to recognize top quality suppliers at the annual supplier symposium.

Strategies for Quality Results

Quality results will be based on the requirements and expectations of our customers.

The ultimate quality result is a satisfied customer (internal or external). Since perceived quality is seen through the eyes of the customer, the level of satisfaction can be defined only by that customer. The quality improvement process furnishes the method by which a measurement(s) can be determined. By systematically applying the nine-step process, we can focus on both the customer and the process. The aspects of customer-perceived quality, therefore, will be addressed automatically because the customer becomes the prime source of information for process improvements.

Trends in quality data will be used to identify improvement opportunities.

Quality metrics of current work processes must be linked to the needs of the customer. Identifying and understanding trends in the data from these metrics will enable StorageTek to focus the appropriate resources on the most important improvement or problem areas.

The corporation will emphasize process rather than only results.

In the past, quality programs have centered primarily on results. The major emphasis of any improvement process, however, should be on the consistent and effective use of the process. Monitoring or measuring results without knowledge of the process that produced those results creates an environment in which all problems are considered to be special-cause variations. This will lead away from real quality improvement by fostering and supporting a "firefighting" mentality (waiting for failures to happen rather than preventing their occurrence in the first place). Since the data provided through the identification and measurement of process failures and variations are focused on both the process and the customer, they will help direct the appropriate actions for real and sustained quality improvement.

Corporate measurements will be used to track quality improvement and not to provide goals for individual functions.

Management runs the very real risk of turning functional goals into management by objectives (MBO), which in turn creates an environment where the numbers become more important than the actual improvements themselves. As a result, we begin to manage the numbers instead of the processes. However, data at the corporate levels are essential to measure the overall effectiveness of quality improvement activities. We must use these data to understand where we are at any point in time relative to historical data, current competitive data, and future targets. Caution must always be used to drive toward real process improvements and not imaginary "numbers" improvements.

Reducing cycle time within processes is a key strategic goal.

Cycle time refers to the time it takes a product to go from design to general availability and, in a more generic sense, the speed with which a process delivers an output. To understand and reduce the cycle time of a process, a baseline or current level of performance must be determined. Once a process baseline is established, corrective action can be taken using current resources to improve process performance. Once the current process has been optimized, further improvement may require innovation through the addition or modification of resources. The nine-step quality improvement process will be used to drive the reduction of process cycle times. The implementation of this process provides a baseline of current work processes and promotes process improvements and innovations resulting in a reduction to the cycle time of the process.

Strategies for Customer Satisfaction

New methods to understand customer needs and expectations will be developed, and current methods will be improved.

Specific management actions to be taken include the following:

- Use the quality improvement process to identify internal customers and their requirements.

- Expand the use of customer advisory boards to provide direct customer input and feedback for major new product families and strategic product directions.

- Expand the use of FORUM (StorageTek's user group) to gain information on improvements to current product performance, expand customer interaction and gain insight into future requirements.

- Continue to refine the marketing customer visit program to include an ETQ focus.

- Develop a system that provides information and analysis of *customer satisfaction* and use the information to improve our processes to avoid customer dissatisfaction in the future.

New guidelines for managing customer relationships will be created and existing guidelines improved.

To ensure that we achieve exemplary customer services, we must improve the methods we use to obtain information from our customers and communicate information to them. First, we must review the communication pathways available both for customers and for StorageTek employees. Once we establish the best possible communication paths, we must ensure that customers and employees understand how to use them effectively. Second, we must create a process that customers and employees can use to review and enhance communication paths and create new ones.

Specific management actions to be taken include the following:

- Continue the use of customer surveys, both internally and externally, with an emphasis on improving the quality of the information gathered through the surveys.

- Develop an account management model that describes how we deal with our external customers. Training in the model and its concepts and principles will be provided to all personnel who interact with external customers.

- Define a long-term strategy and implementation plan for the development of a common customer information data base.

The systems and methods that StorageTek uses for determining customer satisfaction will be reviewed and documented and new systems implemented where inadequate or no systems exist.

Current methods of measuring and determining the level of customer satisfaction must be reviewed for accuracy and objectivity. Methods to translate measurements into a cost-of-quality figure and to drive quality improvement back into our processes will be developed. Concepts such as Xerox's Customer Satisfaction Index will be evaluated and considered for incorporation at StorageTek.

Specific management actions to be taken include the following:

- Define, through the quality improvement process, the processes for using customer data to improve quality.

- Review the account management model to ensure that we comply with customer needs rather than simply meet industry standards.

- Use external sources of information about our customers and their levels of satisfaction with StorageTek.

- Define a process for the review of warranties and guarantees and our compliance in terms of customer requirements.

- Define and implement a formal customer complaint analysis and action process.

- Continue the customer awareness program.

- Design and implement an assigned executive program.

Communication processes with customers, employees, and suppliers will be defined and improved so that all parties involved in any customer/supplier relationship become effective participants.

Specific management actions to be taken include the following:

- Define and implement standard methods for providing feedback to customers regarding failed products, response to complaints, and response to product improvement ideas.

- Educate all personnel involved in external customer relationships in account management concepts.

- Define and develop a method to communicate to the customer exactly what to expect from StorageTek.

- Develop and implement techniques to monitor the effectiveness of our customer communication.

- Define and implement a customer contact standards and measurement system.

Summary of Requirements

The Five-Year Team wrestled with the subject of the kind of actions that would be required by all levels of management to support implementing ETQ throughout the entire corporation. The following list of 14 actions was documented as part of the ETQ strategy.

1. All levels of management will be expected to act as role models and promoters of ETQ. They must act as leaders in removing the fear and barriers that rob people of their pride in their work and commitment to quality.

2. Managers will communicate the importance of and participate in the training of the quality improvement and problem-solving processes. They will demonstrate leadership by their commitment to use these processes.

3. Supported by their respective quality officers, functional heads will be responsible for implementing ETQ.

4. Functional officers will establish a quality management network to plan, monitor and promote ETQ throughout their organization.

5. Employees at all levels must consistently practice the nine-step quality improvement process.

6. Management will establish measurement systems that are a credible, timely source of analyzed information.

7. Management will sponsor and use various methods of obtaining feedback from employees on the management style and behavior changes that are desired to support ETQ.

8. Existing and future reward and recognition systems will be used to promote ETQ.

9. Training is the most important change agent in the early implementation phases of ETQ. The core training modules will be taught to every StorageTek employee. This training will take place within intact work groups led by their managers.

10. Educational emphasis will be focused on quality improvement, participative management, employee involvement, and team building.

11. Management must ensure that tools and techniques supporting continuous quality improvement are used to produce products and services that meet customers' demands.

12. Emphasis throughout the corporation must be on the use of processes to achieve improved results rather than only the results.

13. Cost-of-quality estimates will be used to identify and prioritize quality improvement efforts. Cost of quality should not be allowed to become another detailed measurement system nor a leverage point to create short-term gains.

14. Managers will support the idea that everyone is a customer and supplier. Communication processes with customers, employees, and suppliers will be defined and improved so that all parties involved in any customer/supplier relationship become effective partners.

Chapter 3
Deming's 14 Points

The following are Deming's 14 points; he also refers to them as the 14 obligations of top management. I will discuss each of these in detail based on readings and experiences that I have had in the implementation process.

1. Create constancy of purpose toward improvement of product and service.

I believe that one of the major thrusts of this particular point is to establish within a company a long-term view. It is more important for a company to be in existence 10, 20, or 30 years from now than it is to reach the next quarterly dividend. In the United States, because of the ways we are organized and driven by the financial community, we must pay attention to the quarterly reports and the annual numbers. Deming is trying to stretch our vision to answer the question, "Will the company be in business 10 years from now?"

Perhaps another way of looking at this is to ask the more immediate question, "Is the company delighting customers?" I first heard the word *delight* used in the business world from Colby Chandler, former CEO of Kodak, who was chair of National Quality Month and also a spokesperson at one of the Annual Quality Congresses. I am not sure if he invented this use of the term, but it is the first time that I heard it and since then I have heard many companies use it. The Coors Company in Golden, Colorado, has used it often; AT&T's Universal Card service group lists it as a key phrase; and StorageTek uses it regularly.

The concept of delighting customers is that it's just not good enough to have satisfied customers anymore. Worldwide, world-class companies are definitely satisfying customer needs. The company that will be here in the long term is the company that is delighting customers. Its product or service is so good that customers go around telling others about it and encourage others to do business because of their pleasant experiences with the product or service. This, as in other Deming points, seems simple and just plain common sense, but the more we understand the simple, common-sense terms and philosophies espoused by Deming in these points, the better off we will be.

Deming reminds us that only top management can establish the constancy of purpose necessary to know and exceed the customer's needs and expectations. Once these three characteristics of intent, a goal, and a vision are known and communicated, constancy of purpose can take place.

Constancy of purpose at StorageTek is embedded in what is known as its Operating Principles. (These principles are first referenced in chapter 1.) The Operating Principles state that StorageTek is dedicated to serving its customers worldwide by continuing to be the preferred provider of high-performance information storage subsystems and supporting services and by adhering to the following principles:

Quality—Our standards of quality will ensure our competitiveness. We will sacrifice short-term gain for reliability and excellence in serving our *customers'* needs.

People—People are the key to StorageTek's success. Individual recognition and advancement will be based upon performance that supports StorageTek's commitments to our customers and investors.

Accountability—Our business will be managed to achieve planned growth and long-term profitability. We will grow by building upon demonstrated strengths and meeting customers' needs.

Action—Each of us will participate in and contribute to the cost-effective, timely resolution of challenges and opportunities that continuously improve our customer commitment.

Practices—We will act with integrity to ensure credibility in our relationships with our customers, investors, fellow employees, suppliers, and those communities in which we operate worldwide.

2. Adopt the new philosophy.

Deming suggests here that we realize we are in a new economic age. This is the age of world competitors vying to produce products and provide services throughout the world. This is far different from the luxury we had in the 1950s and 1960s of not worrying too much about world competition. We could build automobiles that lasted only three years, and it wouldn't matter because we bought new ones when the old ones broke. Then suddenly in the 1970s we almost lost the automobile industry to the Japanese because they built cars that customers really wanted and that used less gasoline. They were making cars in Japan, shipping them to the United States, and selling them cheaper than we could make them.

The good part about this was that it helped wake up American industry to the fact that we are in a new economic age and that listening to the customer is perhaps the most vital part of it. We no longer had the comfort of competing with one another with a poor product. We are now competing with the Japanese who have excellent products. Since the 1970s, the automobile industry has come a long way in understanding this and doing something about it. Having one division of a major American automobile company win the Baldrige award is a step in the right direction. If, in time, other automobile companies can establish the same level of perfection, we will beat the Japanese. This is perhaps the best example of being in a new economic age.

Another point that Deming makes concerning the new philosophy is that we should recognize that higher quality costs less, not more. This is a new way of understanding things. In the past a product was shipped no matter what—meet the numbers, meet the schedules, bribe the inspectors, do whatever you needed to do to meet those production numbers and, therefore, in some cases, ship garbage to the customer. In some instances, some companies fix their product in front of the customer. This has become known in the world of quality as external failure, meaning when the external customer knows the company has failed because the customer has experienced that failure in some way.

Deming's formula is that as quality improves so does productivity. Lowering waste, restarts, and rework allows companies to produce higher quality goods and services at lower costs so those companies can stay in business and provide more jobs over the long haul.

These are all thoughts that come to mind when discussing the second point of adopting the new philosophy. Those companies that adopt it will be around a long time. Those that do not will die.

3. Cease dependence on inspection.

This is one of the more misunderstood of Deming's concepts. There is a story of a small company president going to a four-day Deming seminar and returning to his company announcing that all inspection would cease. In a matter of six months that company almost went out of business. Deming does not say to eliminate all inspection. What he says is do not try to get quality by inspecting it in. One must examine the process to find the origin of the defect or the mistake and fix it at that point. If you wait until the inspection takes place, very often it is impossible to find out what is causing the defect.

In his four-day seminar, Deming used the analogy of the tire manufacturer that had inspectors at the end of the line, very carefully examining tires, finding defects, and putting all the defective tires in a corner, then making a report and a log of those defects. What happened over time was that inspectors found bad tires and put them in a corner. They stayed there for a while, other inspectors came and looked at them more thoroughly and wrote up more detailed reports on the defects, but never got back to the source of the defect and to fixing the process. This is the point of this whole business of ceasing dependence on mass inspection.

4. Cease doing business based on price tag alone.

You must know what you are buying, not just the price. Another way of looking at this is to look at the concept of total cost rather than just initial cost. What this means is that purchasing people should be taught not just to buy the cheapest product. Very often the cheapest product introduces variation into the process and, therefore, introduces failure and defects which then become known to the customer. Deming suggests that the total cost of that way of doing business should be compared with the total cost of buying a more expensive product and benefitting from it being introduced into the process and into the system.

Another point that Deming makes is the idea of establishing long-term relationships that include loyalty and trust with sole suppliers rather than an array of suppliers. In the old days it was thought that the more suppliers you had the more protection you had. In the event that one supplier goes bankrupt or out of business, you always have a backup. Deming suggests establishing long-term, solid relationships with your suppliers so they can anticipate and help your company almost as a right arm. The point here is that once suppliers understand they are with you for the long haul they will try to do better. At StorageTek, we went from 2200 suppliers seven years ago to approximately 400 today, even though our revenue has tripled.

5. Improve constantly and forever the systems of production and service.

As Deming would put it, "We in America have worried about meeting specifications in contrast to the Japanese worrying about uniformity, working for less, and less variation." I wrote an article for *Quality Progress* magazine in which I discussed the process of variation with two viewpoints in mind. Masaki Imai, who wrote the book *Kaizen,* states one viewpoint very explicitly. There are two kinds of criteria: process criteria and results criteria. The process criteria is the kind of work that goes on daily to improve on processes and is stimulated actively by supervisors who want to hear about ways to improve the process. The process criteria that Imai discusses in his book include better communication, better morale, more participative management, and better time discipline. When these things are in order, Imai tells us that better results such as bottom-line results of return on investment, margins, and gross profits can occur. In the United States we concentrate on the result part first without paying adequate attention to the process criteria that Imai discusses.

The other viewpoint mentioned in the article was that of Dr. Walter Shewhart, who is often quoted by Deming. Shewhart gave us two reasons for variation: (1) common causes that are process problems and 100 percent owned by management; and (2) special causes that are usually in the area of defects or errors caused by people, machines, or tools. The point I made in the article was to stress that both Imai and Shewhart are saying that what is needed is emphasis on the process and that this is a major point for American managers to understand. Very often American managers manage the special causes very well but do not manage the common causes, and, therefore, we do not get to the source of the problem in the process and fix it once and for all. Defects keep occurring.

When you improve quality, you improve productivity and costs go down when you improve the process. This gets back to Deming's original formula about attacking waste in terms of restarts, rework, and workaround. What industry is beginning to discover is that savings begin to accrue the minute companies put forth serious effort to improve quality. Robert Galvin, former CEO of Motorola, has stated this succinctly. He indicates that Motorola, without knowing it, started saving in a major way when it embarked on its first quality improvement effort, even though quality needed to be improved and was improved over the years. He does say that this is very often unknown, and you can't put your finger on a dollar here or a dollar there, but it accumulates very rapidly in terms of real savings for any company.

Also implied in this discussion of improving the process on a constant basis is the idea of not blaming people for doing a bad job. It goes back to the discussion earlier about variation and its causes, that is, common causes and special causes. The experts tell us that common-cause situations happen about 85 percent of the time and special-cause situations happen about 15 percent of the time. In my work with over 100 small groups in several different companies, the data come out 82 percent and 18 percent. What this implies is that if we are constantly looking for the people area, we are in the 15 percent area and missed the boat of following the process problems 85 percent of the time. We definitely need to stop blaming people for doing a bad job.

Deming also urges to stop studying defects. He would say, "Do not manage defects, study the system that produced the defects." I hope this discussion helps clarify the reasons for this. Deming constantly points at the process and the need to improve it. We have discussed this previously in terms of common cause/special cause.

6. Institute training.

Deming suggests that training should start with management. This relates directly to the common-cause situation, to try to teach management how to recognize the fact that the process is the thing that needs to be fixed. Management needs intensive training because it is indeed a new way to manage, and we did not manage that way in the past. At first, training should make management aware of this fact but then help by explaining all of the tools that are available to help analyze and contribute to fixing the process. At StorageTek we have developed a three-day ETQ core training program that concentrates heavily on our nine-step quality improvement process. In order to emphasize the importance of management participating in this training, we use the cascade approach. A manager goes through the training first with his or her manager and then with his or her people. Each manager in the company has had two exposures, one as a true student with his or her boss present and then as a mentor, coach, and leader in the session with his or her people. When I went through the course with my people, I actually taught the sections of variation and and CE/FFA.

This kind of training needs reinforcement and follow-up with other courses. These kind of courses do not need to be aimed at the entire employee population, but rather focused on specific groups. Such courses could include subjects such as benchmarking, statistical analysis, and measurements.

At StorageTek, in addition to the kinds of courses that are directly related to quality improvement, we must consider the myriad of courses that we teach to management and professional employees. We analyzed this and found that many of the courses in this category do indeed complement our quality courses. This is a very positive situation. In the management curriculum we have courses such as The Experienced Leader, Managing Quality Improvement and Team Effectiveness, Managing the Business, The StorageTek Manager, The StorageTek Manager Refresher, Quality Improvement and Team Effectiveness, Quality Leadership, and Organizational Effectiveness. As far as elective courses are concerned, without listing them all, we have courses such as Basic Project Management Skills, Conflict Management, Customer Satisfaction Skills, Effective Meetings, Effective Presentations, Situational Leadership, Team Leadership Skills, and Time Management.

Deming also suggests not cutting long-term education programs—we need more education, not less. Every company should be encourage its employees to attend college courses, both for degrees and for self-improvement. When corporations build alliances with colleges it is a very positive and value-added activity.

As far as training managers by frequently transferring them from job to job, Deming suggests that we should keep managers in place long enough for them to make a contribution. This kind of job hopping, whether every six months or every year or two, has an unsettling effect on organizations because it doesn't give the kind of leadership that's necessary for constancy of purpose. In addition, job hopping is not favorable to the manager. That kind of framework really doesn't provide the true environment for learning the business. The manager who is dissatisfied because of a lack of a promotion every two years is one to watch out for.

Training should help each employee know and understand the requirements of the next stage of the process, Deming suggests. How often have we seen employees in manufacturing operations doing their one small part, but not knowing what happens in front of them and even worse, not knowing what that final product looks like? In some cases final products are produced in other work areas or even in other buildings or other geographic locations. It is extremely important that the employee know about the entire process from beginning to end, and training should be initiated to accomplish this. There is no better way, of course, than a hands-on look at the entire process, but where this is not possible, training programs could include slide presentations and/or videotape presentations of the entire process.

7. Institute leadership.

Deming has been talking about leadership for years, and suddenly people in the field are now beginning to talk about leadership. There are many books today concerning leadership and how to become a leader. People are generally beginning to understand that leadership is different from managership. A leader has a vision of where the organization or corporation is headed in the long term and can communicate that vision extremely well. He or she then observes behaviors and makes sure to keep people in the organization and moving in the right direction. Finally, a leader provides the feedback necessary for subordinates to react to and change their direction if needed. The manager, on the other hand, manages. He or she manages people, machines, and tools effectively. There is no question that most people are in a management role, but it is also vital for leadership to occur at many levels simultaneously.

Deming suggests eliminating the abuse of on-the-job training. How many times have we seen people who are about to move, asked to train someone else on their job, whether or not they know the job well or are good teachers? Training should be in the hands of people who know how to train and know the process well enough and/or are certified to do that training.

Deming discusses leadership in terms of managers learning how to lead people to help them do a better job. He states that in this new economic age it is better for supervisors to be coaches, teachers, and facilitators. Many supervisors feel more comfortable managing things than people. This is often a result of their backgrounds and education. Most managers, for one reason or another, have engineering and business-type orientation, and are interested in and more knowledgeable about how things work than how people work. This kind of situation demands attention. It is one of the reasons that many large corporations spend enormous amounts of money on training. In some companies this can be as much as 5 percent of the total payroll.

Training in people skills, in the education centers of corporations, needs to be endorsed and followed back on the job. How many times have we, as managers, greeted a person who has just come back from a one- or two-week training course and made the comment, "How did you enjoy your vacation?" or "Let's get back to work." I can recall one situation when a person in my group went to training for a week. When he returned I asked the question, "Well, now that you have had that training, what do you suggest we do differently?" This question flabbergasted the employee. He said, "Well, I haven't thought about that. Let me get back to you with some answers. I didn't realize anyone was going to ask that kind of question when I got back."

Deming suggests that focus on the outcome, that is, management by numbers alone using the MBO and/or zero-defects approach, must be abolished and replaced by leadership. Focus on the process is what is needed, as we have said many times in this particular chapter. It is important to identify with the process improvement that Imai talks about and put that in relationship to the results that must occur later on from placing emphasis on the process. Deming and Imai are very much together on this issue, although, they talk about it in entirely different ways.

In addition, Deming talks about the tremendous waste from the micro-management mentality that results in overcontrol of the system. Joe Muscari from Alcoa uses another term for this: laser-beam management. I think all of us in the world of business have experienced this kind of management at one time or another and have realized the costly waste that occurs. An example of this in the political arena was when a U.S. president micro-managed an attempt to free hostages in a foreign country. This resulted in total chaos, loss of lives, and loss of planes, and the mission was not accomplished. Our most recent experience with the crisis in the Middle East resulted in total victory because it was managed properly. The president gave the order but then backed away and allowed the generals to figure out how to get the job done. This is exactly what Deming is referring to when he talks about the devastating effects of micro-management.

Deming also states in his section on leadership that the system must be based on a deep regard for people and on recognition that people are the organization's most important resource. How often have we heard words like this, and yet how often have we watched the acts and deeds go a different way? It's important that management walk the talk in regard to this recognition that people are the organization's most important resource. There is no company or organization that can survive without the total dedicated effort of its work force, so we need to determine ways to recognize and reward people for their effort. At the same time we must provide the coaching and leadership that's necessary to achieve what Deming is talking about.

8. Drive out fear.

Deming states that "without an atmosphere of mutual respect, no statistically based management system will work." When discussing this subject he often says that the enormous waste due to fear is something that is really one of those invisible numbers that doesn't get management's immediate attention. Very often when discussing this subject, Deming talks about the word *secure* and its Latin derivative, *se,* meaning without, and *cure,* meaning fear. He believes that people should not be afraid to express ideas or to ask questions and should work in an atmosphere totally free of fear.

Scherkenbach, in his book *The Deming Route to Productivity,* talks about the fear aspect. At one point he states how many hours have been wasted because of the raised eyebrow of the CEO. He feels that this waste is based on fear.

The challenge for managers in all of this is to recognize that the fear syndrome truly does exist. We need to be aware of this and take action to alleviate and eliminate fear when and wherever possible. We could think of many more examples particular to each industry. The military would have one set of examples and a hospital another. Nevertheless, fear exists in American industry, and Deming suggests that we eliminate it totally to help increase productivity.

9. Break down barriers between departments.

Deming reminds us that corporate politics cannot only destroy quality but destroy a company. I use the phrase "If you can't look better, the next best thing is to make everyone else look worse." I wonder how many executives have played this game. In my experience I know that, especially in the early days, this was the regular way of operating. This was caused by objectives or MBOs that were totally oriented to the individual and, therefore, sometimes led to achieving those goals at the expense of counterparts. It is, perhaps, for this reason that Deming advises that the annual performance appraisal is the biggest inhibitor to continuing improvement.

Deming suggests that we should identify walls and tear them down. The reason walls exist in American industry is the way we are organized. We generally have a vertical structure, and communication often goes extremely well within that vertical structure. As we have come to learn, however, big things usually are done horizontally in organizations. In a cross-functional approach representatives of the various vertical organizations need to work together to help improve the processes that exist among those vertical organizations. Very often what happens, due to the walls being built, is that people in organizations don't talk to one another. They need to learn to participate well in a cross-functional team environment. This must be a high priority throughout the 1990s. We need to spend time and effort in learning how to work better in a cross-functional environment.

Another barrier that has come from the past is how bosses are viewed by employees. Some view them as the most important customer. When this happens the real customer suffers and teamwork is short-circuited. We are now teaching our managers how to coach, teach, and even nurture to change the perspective of the boss being the customer. In some cases it is advisable to work out definitive customer/supplier agreements. What we are moving toward in the decade of the 1990s, though, is a more participative style of manager.

Deming constantly reminds us that management does not understand the difference between common-cause and special-cause variability. Management usually treats everything as if it were a special cause. I first learned of this theory in October 1983 from Deming at one of his four-day conferences sponsored by the Western Electric Co., Merrimac Valley Works. I was astonished that this theory had been around since 1924. Deming is teaching a theory that was taught to him by Shewhart of Bell Telephone Laboratories. I often wonder how much better things could have been if we had understood that theory back in the 1920s or even 1930s, 1940s, or 1950s and practiced this for all those decades. This is really what Deming taught the Japanese in 1950, and it brought them to the financial success of their economic achievements.

In discussing this subject with various classes at StorageTek, I tell them that I learned the theory of special cause from Deming in 1983 and, at that time, realized that I had been managing incorrectly for about 25 years. At one time I helped manage one of the largest cable plants in the world. We worked seven days a week, three shifts a day, and I would come in on Monday and look at the reports, find something wrong, and ask, "Who did it?" instead of asking the question, "Is the process in need of fixing?" So, in asking the question, "Who did it?" I was in the 15 percent area of special causes. These are things that happen as a result of mistakes people make, machines that are not provided, or tools not provided or kept in good repair.

When we ask the question, "Is the process messed up?" we are in the 85 percent area of common causes. Management is 100 percent responsible for owning and fixing the process.

10. Eliminate slogans, exhortations, and targets from the work force.

There's a story of an automobile plant general manager who hired a fire engine. He asked his staff to assemble on the fire engine, and at a given time during the day he drove the fire engine down the largest aisle of the plant where workers were encouraged to assemble to watch the spectacle. The staff on the fire engine all waved flags at the workers, and on the flags was imprinted the slogan ZERO DEFECTS. The workers looked at the fire engine and the flag-waving exercise with dismay because they really were doing the best they could do and didn't know how to do any better to prevent defects from happening. This whole scenario represents the fact that what really needs to happen, as mentioned in point 9, is an all-out attack on fixing the processes so that defects don't occur. Very often we exhort workers to work harder, exhort them to make no errors, and hang flags and banners all over the place to remind them of this constantly. This actually has a very negative effect on the worker. If the theory of variability taught to us in 1924 by Shewhart is true, then we all need to spend more time, not less, examining the process-type problems and eliminating common-cause mistakes. Special-cause situations do not necessarily take care of themselves; they need attention, but we need to refocus the attention and meaning of the 85/15 percent relationship.

Excellence through quality is entirely different because it is void of exhortation and relies upon a step-by-step evolutionary approach of training internal consultation and implementation.

Deming states that the causes of low quality and low productivity belong to the system (the process) and thus lie beyond the power of the work force. This is at the heart, I believe, of the 14 points. Deming suggests that both the work force and management need a method to improve the process. Many companies are developing step programs— six steps, nine steps, 14 steps—all aimed at improving the process. Later in this book you will read about the StorageTek nine-step quality improvement process, which is aimed directly at improving the process we have been talking about.

Deming reminds us constantly that motivation and awareness may help limit variability, but there are no substitutes for training, for knowledge of the process, and for tools and methods to help manage that process.

In his four-day seminar, Deming demonstrates the idea that exhortation doesn't work by use of what he calls the red bead experiment. It took me quite a while to fully understand this. Although somewhat simple, there is a lot involved in it. Deming asks for volunteers from the audience and calls them willing workers. Some of the workers are assigned to production tasks of taking white beads out of a tray with a ladle. There are indentations in the ladle, and the beads can fall back into the tray when taking it out of the tray, which also contains red beads. When Deming starts this exercise, he states that there are specifications. The specifications read that the ladle shall contain only white beads, and he then trains the workers on how to hold the box of beads, what angle to place the ladle, and the manner in which the excess beads can be shaken off. All of this is special training. Then there are other people assigned to inspecting the ladle and counting the number of red beads. Although the specification may call for zero red beads per ladle, what normally happens is that there are from five to 17 red beads on the ladle. When there are more than three red beads, Deming himself, acting as supervisor, actually scolds the person. I can recall vividly, he said, "Now Mary, you know you got a merit raise yesterday. You are one of our best employees and yet you have 10 red beads. What horrible performance." When I reflect back on that, I can recall saying similar things to employees throughout my career without looking at what causes the red beads to appear on the ladle in the first place. This is a simple exercise, but one that really demonstrates that the exhortation and brow-beating of the past is certainly not the way of managing in the future.

If you do not have the luxury of seeing Deming perform the bead experiment, there is now a videotape available.

11. Eliminate work standards, MBO, and management by the numbers, substitute leadership.

Deming suggests that work standards tend to cap the amount of improvement that can be achieved. In my experience this is true. The work standard during the time of Frederick Taylor was based on the assumption that employees are lazy and try to get away with doing as little as possible. I believe the opposite is true. Employees come to work to do a good job. They will do as much as they can and don't need to be prodded by work standards.

In fact, on some occasions this could evolve into collusion between supervision and workers to reach work standards or just beyond them so that bonus money could be paid. I recall a situation when a supervisor in charge of making packing material had his employees work on the night shift to build packaging entirely differ- ent than the specifications. By using staples instead of nails, he could produce more. Each week, when a certain number of boxes had to be made, but less than the required amount was produced, he always added to that amount from the stock he had stashed away that the night shift had built. That particular section had been paid a bonus over a three-year period because it used this method which obviously cheated the company. The management and workers were part of the whole scheme. This is only one example. I worry about how many millions of examples one could come up with over a period of the last 20 years.

Another point that Deming makes in regard to point 11 is that objectives are often understated so they can be met or exceeded easily. That should not come as a shock to anyone who has been in the busi- ness for more than five years. This occurs repeatedly, and again it con- tributes to enormous waste and endless debate. So what Deming suggests is that standards maintain a level lower than it should be. Instead of telling the employee how much to make, Deming believes the supervisor should help the employee make more.

We touched on the devastating effect of erroneous use of MBOs. In the old days, and perhaps even today in some industries, when MBOs are based on an individual contributor's contribution, the effects can be devastating in the way the individual contributor reaches those objectives. One alternative that we have found success- ful is to have executives share MBOs. In StorageTek, for instance, the top executives share four MBOs, one of which is implementing the ETQ effort. That represents 25 percent of the entire MBO for every executive in the company.

12. Remove barriers that hinder all employees and rob them of pride in workmanship.

Deming suggests that the annual performance appraisal is a barrier that robs employees of pride of workmanship. A suggestion here is to somehow separate performance appraisal from merit review. I think the fact that these two elements are combined is at the source and the reason for the barrier and misuse of appraisals that exist in American industry today. We do not perform appraisals to help people improve, to point out weaknesses, to develop a career plan. We do appraisals to pay people. This is why there is confusion and why people get erroneous appraisals. Every organization is faced with a bracket to reach in terms of the amount of money that can be given out, whether this is 3 percent, 5 percent, or 10 percent. There is always some kind of a limit, and that limit forces an erroneous distribution of people who can earn the amount within that particular bracket.

If we sever the method of payment from the appraisal process, then we can give fair appraisals. We need to stop categorization of people in separate slots. I have seen managers pretend they know the difference between a person rated at 2.3 and a person rated at 2.4. I would suggest that this argument is merely to get a person more money and no other reason, because there is no real difference between a 2.3, a 2.4, or a 2.5. So what we should do is have two buckets for appraisal: one meets requirements, and the other does not meet requirements. Then pay people based on a scale in relation to the market value of their job. This, I understand, can be readily found out by our human resource experts. The person who is at 20 percent of market value obviously should earn less merit raise than the person who is between 80 percent and 100 percent of market value.

It is important that this area be addressed realistically because, as Deming reminds us, the barriers against pride of workmanship may well be one of the most important obstacles to the reduction of cost and improvement of quality in the United States today. One of the main sources of lack of pride is the appraisal system. It is a demoralizing kind of system. As Deming said, "No one knows who did it, but somebody decided that everyone should be appraised once a year." In 36 years of work experience, I cannot recall one appraisal session where I enjoyed being appraised or one session where I enjoyed appraising others. It was just a task that had to be done. Very often what happens is that the loud, boisterous people—the squeeky-wheel syndrome, if you will—are the ones who get the raises. Those who are quiet and hard working very often end up with what is left over.

There are groups out there that learn to posture through various experiences in different kinds of companies. I call them the pretenders. These people are perhaps the most devastating because they know how to play politics and how to network to the hilt, but when you look for a record of accomplishments, it is just not there. The pretenders very often are the ones who get the highest ratings. (It's far more realistic to sift these kinds of people out and appraise them as they should be.) Very often these particular types either manage to bargain a higher rating by escalation or, when they are not able to face the truth, end up with a transfer or resignation. This brings to mind Deming's observation that the small percent that fall in this category, actually through peer pressure or pressure caused by themselves, tend to take care of the problem themselves by deciding on different career paths.

The whole idea is to emphasize that the excessive maneuvering and thrashing that occurs because of the current appraisal system, point to the need for change. It would be interesting to see if different companies could use Deming's approach and reintroduce pride of workmanship back to the work force.

13. Institute a vigorous program of education and self-improvement.

Deming suggests that this kind of education differs from training on job skills. He is talking about the more broadening type of training, learning new skills constantly. He suggests that people need more than money in their careers; people need opportunities to add something to society—materially and otherwise.

14. Put everybody to work to accomplish the transformation.

Deming suggests use of the Shewhart cycle as a guide for constant improvement. The Shewhart cycle includes planning the work, doing it, checking to see if we did what we said we were going to do, and then finding the flaws and acting to improve the full cycle. This has become known throughout the world as the plan/do/check/act cycle.

I recently spoke to a group of Chinese industrialists who were touring the United States. When I got to the Shewhart cycle of plan/do/check/act, the entire group of 100 Chinese industrialists started talking to one another. I looked at the interpreter and asked, "Am I in trouble or what?" She said "No, they really like this because they have heard of it before." I was amazed.

Steps to consider in implementing the 14 points are as follows:

- Management should decide on the direction to carry out the 14 points.

- The entire team should take pride in the new direction.

- The direction should be explained to critical masses of people throughout the company.

- Consider every activity and job as part of a process.

- Initiate an organization to guide continual improvement of quality.

- Everyone should take part in a team.

- Organize so that quality improvement projects occur throughout all departments in the entire company.

Summary

These are the 14 points that Deming talks about in his four-day seminar and that are described in his book *Out of the Crisis*. Many companies are now addressing these points very seriously. There are many Deming groups forming throughout the world that meet periodically to share their experiences in implementing the 14 points. I participated in one of these.

At StorageTek many of our top executives carry in their wallet or in their shirt pocket two things: the ETQ principles and Deming's 14 points. I recently visited one of our corporate officers, and as I walked into his office he was putting the little card with Deming's 14 points back into his wallet. He was relieved that he had been able to use the card beneficially to discuss problems with an employee who was upset about something.

The 14 points are not something that you can unleash on a group and say, "Okay, let's concentrate on number nine today." Or, "Let's implement three, four, and six." It just doesn't work that way. Many times you'll be working on three, four, or more issues based on the situation involved. It is not easy. It is not something you can dissect, and it is not something you can delegate (that is, three points to one group and four points to another). It just doesn't work that way. This is a holistic approach to Deming's idea that the American style of management needs to be transformed and these are the guidelines by which that transformation can take place.

Are we at StorageTek there yet? Absolutely not! We are in our fourth year and to implement and understand all Deming is trying to do with his 14 points could take a decade. When looking forward a decade seems like a long time; when looking back it's a very short time. Transformation of the American style of management takes time. Success can be achieved from the very beginning.

Chapter 4
Implementing Excellence Through
Quality—The Early Stages

The implementation strategy for any quality improvement effort needs to consider an evolutionary approach rather than a revolutionary approach. In organizations that have not even begun to take the first step toward quality improvement, I usually start with a three-phase process. Phase I is a discussion with, at minimum, the top management team, but when possible the entire management team, about the basics of quality improvement. During phase II I work hands-on with a small group of six to 10 people over a six- to 10-hour period to analyze a specific problem or analyze why a specific organization is not as efficient as it should be. Phase III is the report by the phase II group back to the management team on what needs to be done to help things improve. In this three-phase process, we use CE/FFA, which is discussed in the phase II section of this chapter.

Phase I

The phase I discussion is broken down into five parts: (1) educating yourself, (2) finding a friend, (3) implementing quality improvement in that friend's organization, (4) recording and telling about successes, and (5) waiting for the phone to ring. In the first part, educating yourself, I usually discuss the participation that our company has had in the annual National Quality Forum. This started back in 1985 when James Olson, who was then president and CEO of AT&T, was chair of National Quality Month. The start that year included presentations in New York to about 300 people but then grew from that with Olson's leadership to include satellite broadcasts throughout the United States. I have participated as a listener in each of these forums since that date.

Distinguished people such as Jamie Houghton of Corning Glass, David Kearns of Xerox, Colby Chandler of Kodak, Fred Smith of Federal Express, and John Akers of IBM have served as chairs of the National Quality Month Forum. This is usually a three-hour broadcast in which major companies and executives participate to share with the entire audience what their companies are doing in the area of quality improvement and the progress that is being made.

In 1988, 42 StorageTek executives participated in the conference. This grew to 200 in 1989, 250 in 1990, and 300 in 1991. The bottom-line benefit is for the entire management team to hear the progress that other companies are making and to gather momentum and ideas on how to proceed down the path to quality improvement. An important part of this session includes discussion of the two major thrusts that I believe are important in quality improvement today. One of these is to capture the energy, skill, and knowledge of those closest to the work.

In my years of work with various teams in various companies, I have found that those people who are closest to the work processes understand best how to improve them. The idea is to use their knowledge, skill, and energy, and continue to improve the process on a daily basis. It is management's job to support and encourage this kind of activity. This notion is one of the basic elements in the work that I have been able to accomplish so far in working with small groups in using the powerful tool CE/FFA.

The second major thrust is knowledge of the theory of variability that we touched on in earlier chapters. The basis of the theory is well known to all quality practitioners but now must be understood by every manager, every director, every vice-president, and every CEO in every U.S. company. The more readily this theory is accepted and understood, the more readily improvements can be made.

The basis of the theory is the common-cause/special-cause theory we discussed earlier. Deming used to say that common-cause situations occurred 85 percent of the time and special-cause situations 15 percent of the time. In his book, *Out of the Crisis,* he has changed this to 96 percent common causes and 4 percent special causes. I think he is trying to get management's attention. In my work with 75 groups at AT&T and about 20 or 30 groups in several other companies, and in my latest work with StorageTek in working with 42 groups, I've tracked the data. The data show that 82 percent of the time we are dealing with common-cause situations and 18 percent of the time we are dealing with special-cause situations. As I've said, my data show that it is still closer to 85/15.

Common-cause situations involve problems with the process. Deming stresses the notion that is most important—examining the process first and eliminating the root cause of problems at the source rather than trying to manage improvement by counting or inspecting the number of defects. Defect detection alone will not improve the process because very often the defect occurs or is found long after the incident occurs. It is this incident that needs to be tracked back to its source. We also know that the people closest to the process and who work in it every day have an enormous contribution to make.

Special causes are attributed to people, machines, and tools. People make mistakes. Machines are provided and not tuned, and the same goes for tools. In some cases, machines and tools are not provided. At any rate the major point is that the common-cause situation happens about 85 percent of the time and, therefore, that's where the attention should be placed.

During the phase I session we recognize the contributions made by people such as Don Peterson, former CEO of Ford; David Kearns, former CEO of Xerox; authors John Nesbitt, Tom Peters, and Frank Price; and also the quality experts such as Deming, Philip Crosby, Armand Feigenbaum, and Juran. We discuss Deming's 14 points.

The writings of Imai are also discussed. In his book, *Kaizen,* he presents a diagram that I have referred to many times in writings and in speeches whereby the Japanese work daily to improve the process and use encouragement techniques to ensure that this happens. Then results occur after examination of the processes. The difference between the Eastern and Western forms of management is that the West very often starts with the results part and does not spend the time and attention to improving the process as does the Eastern management. This is now beginning to change because of the enormous emphasis on quality in the West during the 1980s. We also discuss in this section the Shewhart cycle which Deming teaches regularly. This consists of four categories: plan, do, check, and act.

The next major section, finding a friend, means to work in a non-hostile environment. Often when the environment is hostile, no matter how much the people might try to cooperate, the hostile environment precludes any real long-term effort toward quality improvement. People who want to make a change know there will be hard work involved, in terms of making time for people to participate in teams, and sacrifice, in terms of shedding the old ways of management. These people are a joy to work with and make progress without any great degree of handholding. Their desire, willingness, and sincere interest to approach management from a different viewpoint and to embrace the basic ideas of total quality management are the reason for their vast improvement over time. I could list friends in many different companies and many different countries who have embraced the basic principles and have reached different levels of improvement.

The next major section in the phase I discussion is implementing quality improvement in the friend's organization. In this section I discuss the history and strategy of StorageTek and how strategy was formed and the ETQ effort was developed. I discuss in detail, which we will touch on later in this chapter, the five basic change mechanisms that are important in the implementation of the quality improvement strategy.

The next major section is recording and telling about successes. StorageTek has success stories from many different internal organizations using the basic quality tenets. We share those regularly in a monthly printed news bulletin and also by word of mouth at various staff meetings. The idea of sharing successes is twofold: (1) to give credit to those who have reached new levels of improvement, and (2) to get those who have not yet embarked on the improvement mission to consider doing so.

The next major section is waiting for the phone to ring. This implies that when successes are shared, people and organizations find out about them and want to embark on quality improvement, and they literally volunteer to do so. My phone has been ringing off the hook for the last decade from folks that have begun to understand that quality improvement is a way of life and the enlightened way to manage in the 1990s.

Phase II

Cause and Effect/Force Field Analysis

I first became familiar with the discipline of force field analysis in 1970 as a result of managing a complex project at AT&T. The project objective was to examine and analyze, and then recommend better ways to provide engineering, installation, and service center services throughout the United States. The task force contained experts from each of these major divisions as well as experts in information systems, accounting, engineering, and legal.

We started the project off by meeting together for a period of one week at the corporate education center in Princeton, New Jersey. The objectives were identified, a roadmap was developed, and all 18 members of the team seemed to reach a point of understanding during the week of training.

At about the second month, the project appeared to be in grave jeopardy, and it was obvious that many problems needed major attention. I called for advice at our corporate education center management training group, and I spent three days learning about the discipline of force field analysis. As a result, I had an understanding of the forces that were impeding the project. I was able to define specific actions that could be taken to alleviate those negative forces. This is the essence of the technique of force field analysis. Without it, the project objective would not have been met. This entire effort is documented in Part 6 of the latest edition (1991) of my book, *An Approach to Quality Improvement That Works*.

A decade later, in an entirely different organization and environment, I had been exposed to the discipline of cause and effect that was developed by Ishikawa. We developed the cause-and-effect analysis due to the fact that we needed to make major recommendations to the highest level of management in that particular area of the company within three days. While doing the cause-and-effect analysis, it dawned on me that each cause was ripe for a force field analysis. It was at this time, during 1980, that these two disciplines were combined.

Force field analysis was developed by Dr. Kurt Lewin and has been around since the 1930s; cause and effect has been around since the 1950s. Both have been taught and are even listed together in various training programs throughout the world. The two disciplines have not been directly connected. In this section the power that exists when the two disciplines are used in concert will be explained.

How Cause and Effect/Force Field Analysis Works

CE/FFA can be used in two different ways: (1) on specific defect or problem areas, and (2) on more generic situations where an entire organization may need to improve or become more efficient.

When using CE/FFA on a specific problem area or defect area, the problem or defect is usually known. For example, years ago I worked on a problem with a group of installers in Alabama. That particular area of the country had been plagued by lightning storms resulting in outages in local telephone offices. Upon examination of this, it was determined that poor grounding by the installation forces was the cause. The manager of that particular area asked me to conduct a CE/FFA on grounding. The manager put together a group of about 13 people, including himself, that knew the subject of grounding extremely well.

I started by asking the group members for a list of problem areas that they felt were in need of attention. Although the list contained about five items, they all concurred that grounding was the number one problem to be solved at that time. Grounding defects became the effect and the major causes ranked in order as follows: too many sources of information, engineering problems, tools, inadequate training, pressure, and installer errors. This could be illustrated in a cause-and-effect diagram as shown in Figure 4.1.

I believe that ranking causes is a necessary step because during the rank ordering process the list is refined almost 100 percent of the time. Causes become combined, other causes become more clearly defined, and the rank ordering process helps do this. I stress to groups that it is important to address all of the causes and not just focus on the top two or just take care of one at a time. If there are six causes and number six would take 24 hours to solve, I encourage groups to take care of those first, then get into the more difficult problems with more analysis and more data to make sure that those problems are as highly weighted as the group originally believed.

The next step is to do a force field analysis on each of the causes. This particular group performed the force field analysis on "too much information" as the number one problem. They tackled the problem as follows. First the facilitator drew a line across the middle of the easel paper. He described that line as *the level of* line. Usually it is very good to try to use the words *the level of* as the first three words of defining that particular force field. In this case we changed the words *too many sources of information* to *the level of information is too high*. Then I asked the group members to envision the line across the middle of the page as being too high and asked them what was causing

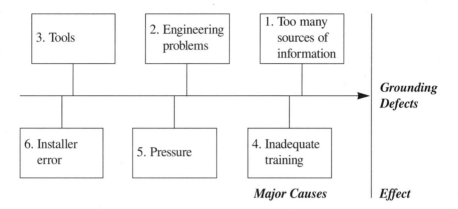

Figure 4.1.   Cause-and-effect diagram.

the line to be that high. We usually call these *restraining forces,* to go along with the classic Lewin technique.

I have had other groups that have named these to suit their needs such as *negative and positive aspects.* It doesn't matter really what we call these, although my desire is to stay with Lewin's words. The idea is that there is something causing that line to be as high as it is.

This particular group came up with these kinds of ideas: different requirements on each type of equipment, changes in requirements, different interpretations, too many sources, and can't keep up with all the sources (see Figure 4.2).

The next step is to determine what can be done about each restraining force. Lewin calls these *driving forces.* The group came up with an array of driving forces as follows: standardize, get notices out on time, clarify information, make it simple, have one source, everybody use the same source, and put it in the spec (see Figure 4.3).

This discipline does not apply only in production-type situations. It is also valuable in white-collar areas. I have used it in accounting, billing, marketing, sales, legal, research and development, engineering, and information systems. In fact, I can think of no discipline in which CE/FFA could not be used. Some people have called me and indicated they have used this to help improve even real estate and travel agency operations. One person used it in a church environment and another in a school environment.

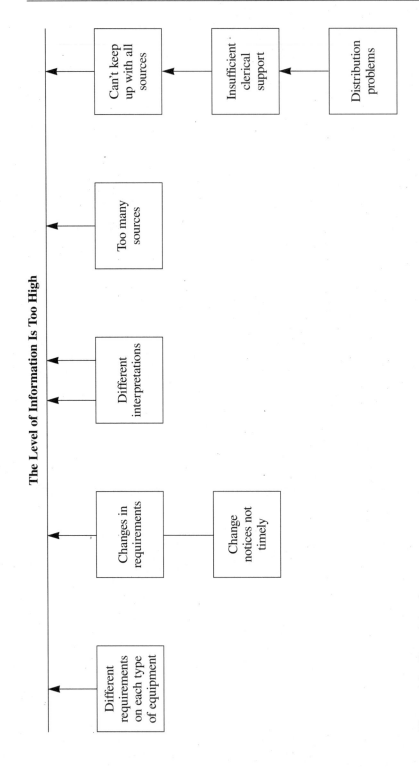

Figure 4.2. Restraining forces.

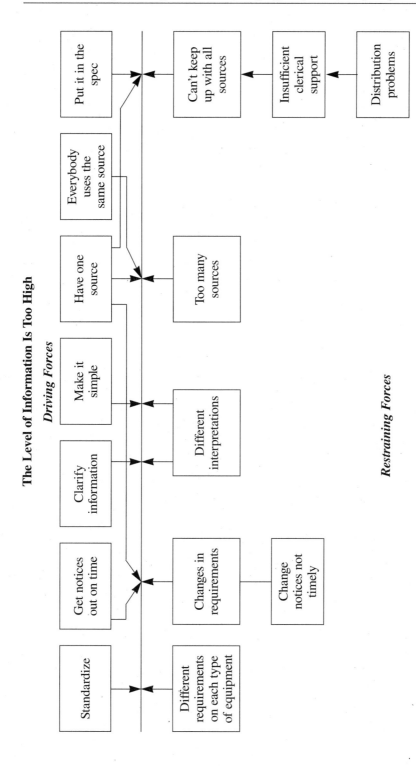

Figure 4.3. Another example of restraining forces.

An example of white-collar use is shown in Figure 4.4. In this particular situation, an accounting director was having difficulty dealing with late payments. She put together a group of 10 people who were experts in the accounting and late-payment discipline, and within 12 hours the group had developed the following analysis.

Figure 4.5 shows force field analysis done on one of the causes of late payments. A force field is done on each cause; the figure shows an example of one.

After the CE/FFA is complete, I ask the group to tell me whether the driving forces can be implemented by management, or worker, or both. Usually when a driving force includes any kind of management action at all, it is a common-cause situation, and when a driving force includes only worker action, it is a special-cause situation.

This has been an eye-opener to hundreds of managers and executives across the world in helping them understand this theory. I have used this technique in StorageTek subsidiaries in Japan, Australia, England, France, Germany, Switzerland, and Italy. Perhaps my biggest

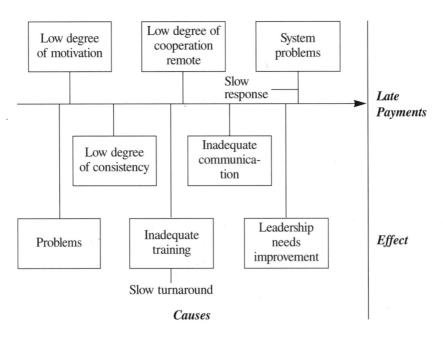

Figure 4.4. Cause-and-effect diagram.

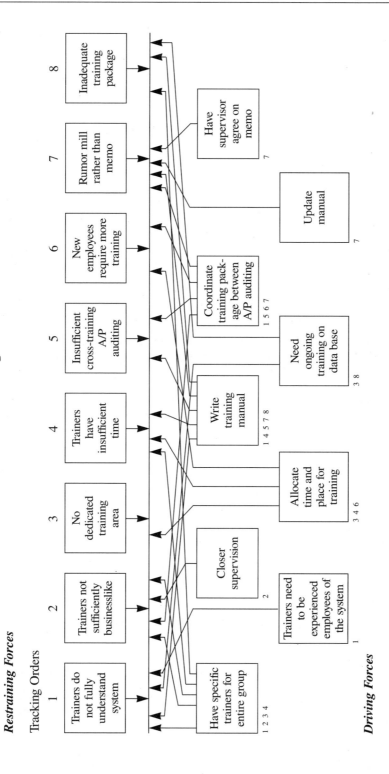

Figure 4.5. Force field analysis diagram.

challenge in terms of being a true facilitator was holding the debate in the language of the country. Sometimes it is best that a facilitator does not understand the detail of the debate but does understand the process thoroughly.

How to Position Use of Cause and Effect/ Force Field Analysis Properly

Over the years a three-phase process has evolved in introducing organizations to the use of CE/FFA. This three-phase process includes phase I which is a general discussion of the quality improvement movement, where it has been, where it is today, and what it includes. This session also includes a detailed definition of use of CE/FFA. Phase II is actually working, hands on, with a group of 6–10 people on a given problem or on a more generic problem using the CE/FFA technique. Phase III is having the small group make a report back to management on the details of the CE/FFA study.

Phase I is usually aimed at the management team to help team members understand the nature of the analysis and the need to move rapidly into the quality improvement area. The new economic age does not allow years and years of effort to reach a plateau of satisfactory quality improvement. We must learn to maximize and reduce the cycle time of introducing quality improvement throughout all industry. This new technique answers this need.

I have found that during phase II, in working with vice-presidents to workers at all levels, the groups appreciate the technique and actually enjoy the time together in using it. It illustrates that small groups with in-depth knowledge of various processes do have enormous amounts of energy, knowledge, and skill that need to be tapped.

The technique has a self-correcting mechanism that is worthy of note. Groups can actually forget a major cause in hour one and yet in hour three, four, or five realize this and make the correction in the middle of the course. Another part of the self-correcting nature of the technique is something that I mentioned earlier: the rank ordering of the causes. Very often the refinement is made that is needed in those array of causes. A definite advantage to the technique is that when groups cannot meet for an entire 10 to 20 hours, which is usually the case, the diagram that they have used brings back the memory of the group discussion. This is called a *group memory technique.* Each individual could remember something different, but with the use of the CE/FFA diagrams, everyone can get to the point of understanding in the second, third, or fourth meeting.

Phase III

Presentation to Management

The phase III sessions are interesting to observe. In most cases members of the phase II group are reluctant to speak in front of multiple levels of management. But these sessions are structured in such a way that management understands that its role is to listen and not to challenge. Questions for clarification are fine, but negative comments are not allowed. What usually happens is that the reluctant phase II participant, when standing in front of the entire group with the strength of the CE/FFA diagrams, actually does a magnificent job in presenting the situation clearly.

I remember many who thought they couldn't do it and at the end of 20 or 25 minutes of very detailed conversation received applause by the entire group. One manager whispered in my ear during a presentation by an accountant, "How did we teach this person to speak so eloquently?" She said that it took her six months of charm school to learn how to get up in front of a group and make that kind of an impression. My answer was that we didn't spend one minute on speaking techniques. A person speaking about a subject with which he or she is totally familiar doesn't need to worry about the techniques of delivering a speech. He or she always comes across positive, refreshing, and knowledgeable.

At the end of the phase III session, I ask for a quality resolution team to be formed and for a manager-level person to chair that group and to organize and implement all of the driving forces that were discussed in the meeting. Then I ask for that particular manager to name his or her group and invariably, because of the knowledge and skill that was demonstrated by the quality action team (QAT) members, some of this group usually participates on the quality resolution team (QRT). The QAT develops the CE/FFA. The QRT is headed by a manager and implements the driving forces (action items) developed by the QAT.

Example of a Quality Action Team and Quality Resolution Team at Work

StorageTek recently acquired a small company in Fremley, England, that primarily manufactures tape drives. It experienced a performance deficiency on an open reel tape drive that resulted in delayed shipments and considerable engineering time in dealing with the problem. Skew performance was outside the specification limits in about 10 percent of the cases. (Skew is a measure of the squareness of tape to the head stacks. It is measured by loading a calibrated *skew tape* into the drives.) Using the CE/FFA technique, the QAT and QRT reduced the failure rate to less than 0.5 percent.

A QAT was formed and the cause-and-effect analysis is shown in Figure 4.6.

The QAT from Fremley, England, did a force field analysis on each of the causes (see Figures 4.7–4.14).

A QAT was formed to address each driving force and put it in place through implementation, or change it appropriately. Table 4.1 shows a list of actions taken and gives the status of the implementation and completion dates.

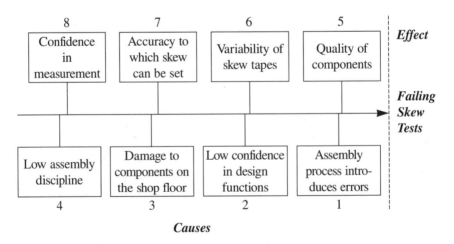

Figure 4.6. Cause-and-effect diagram.

The Possibility That the Assembly Process Introduces Errors Is Too High

Driving Forces

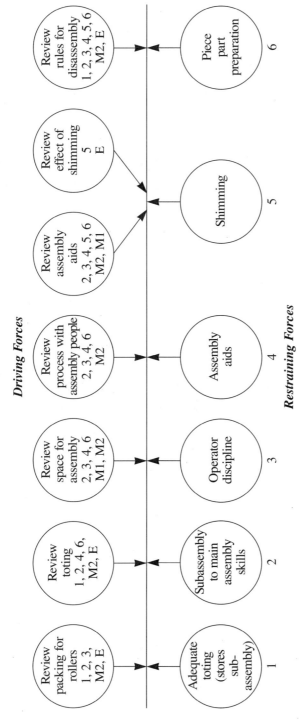

Restraining Forces

Note: The M refers to management levels; E refers to engineer.

Figure 4.7. Force field analysis performed by quality action team.

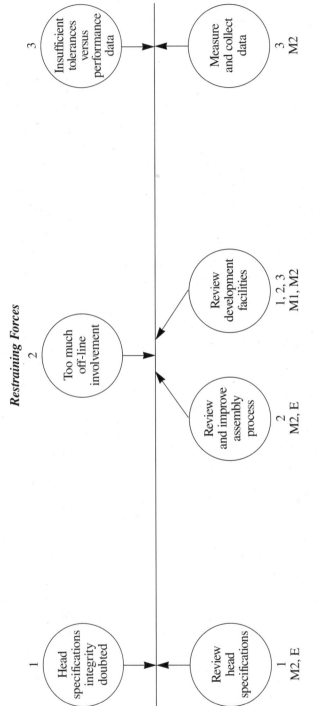

Confidence That the Design Functions Well in All Tolerated Conditions Is Too Low

Restraining Forces

Driving Forces

Note: The M refers to management levels; E refers to engineer.

Figure 4.8. QAT force field analysis, continued.

The Possibility of Damage to Components on the Shop Floor Is Too High

Driving Forces

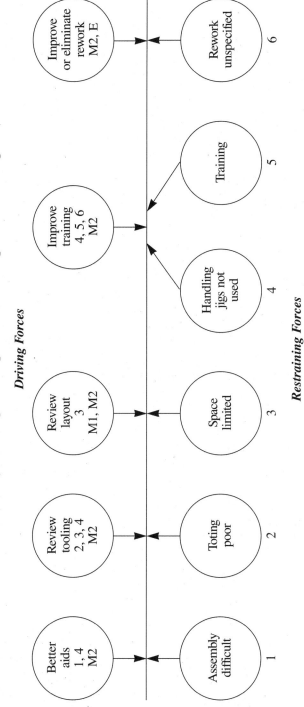

Restraining Forces

Figure 4.9. QAT force field analysis, continued.

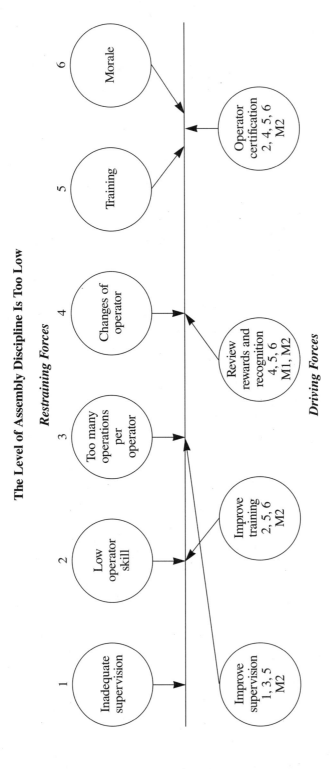

The Level of Assembly Discipline Is Too Low

Restraining Forces

1 — Inadequate supervision
2 — Low operator skill
3 — Too many operations per operator
4 — Changes of operator
5 — Training
6 — Morale

Driving Forces

Improve supervision 1, 3, 5 M2

Improve training 2, 5, 6 M2

Review rewards and recognition 4, 5, 6 M1, M2

Operator certification 2, 4, 5, 6 M2

Figure 4.10. QAT force field analysis, continued.

The Level of Assembly Discipline Is Too Low

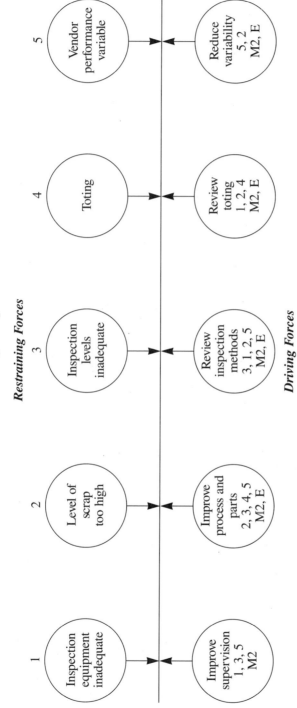

Figure 4.11. QAT force field analysis, continued.

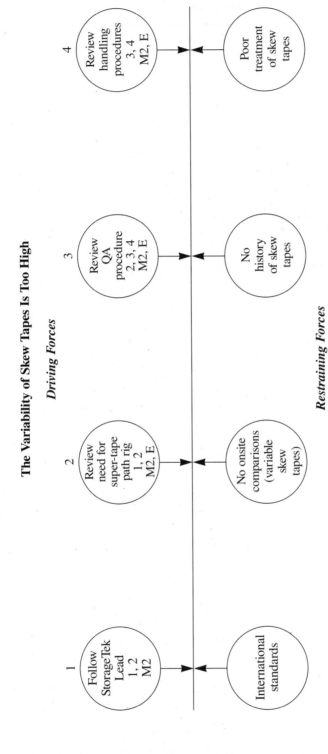

Figure 4.12.   QAT force field analysis, continued.

The Accuracy to Which Skew Can Be Set at Level 4 Is Too Low

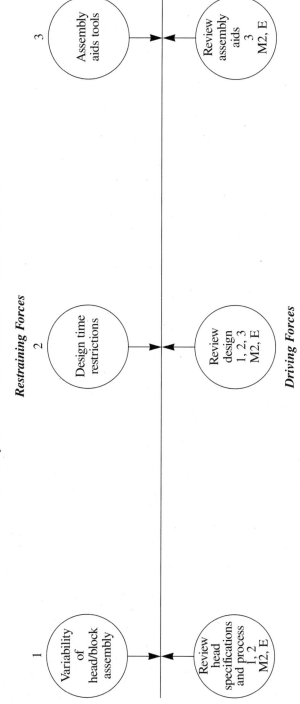

Figure 4.13. QAT force field analysis, continued.

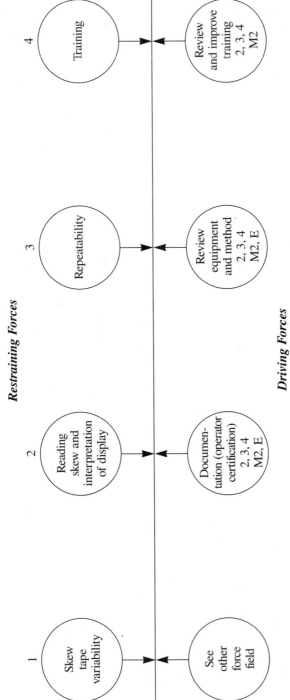

Figure 4.14. QAT force field analysis, continued.

Table 4.1. Action item register.

No.	Action	Grade	QRT control	Action on	Status	Report received	Implemented yet	Open/closed	Completion date
The Possibility That the Assembly Process Introduces Errors Is Too High									
1.1	Review packing for rollers	Maj	RF		No longer considered a problem	No	No	Closed	10 Oct 90
1.2	Review toting of head plate assemblies	Crit	RF	B Coles	Toting implemented Satisfactory	Yes	Yes	Closed	17 Sept 90
1.3	Review space for assembly of head plates into base casting	Crit	RF	M Branch	Replaced by action 1.8 (introduction of pinned castings)	No	No	Closed	17 Sept 90
1.4	**Review assembly process with operator**	**Maj**	**PV**		**Meeting held Results to be monitored**	**No**	**Yes**	**Ongoing**	**Ongoing**
1.5	Review assembly aids	Maj	PV/GP		Tools reviewed Most important action is 1.8 (introduction of pins)	No	Yes	Closed	
1.6	Review effect of shimming	Min	JB		Work done. Shims have little effect	Yes	No	Closed	31 Aug 90
1.7	Product guidelines for correcting tape paths	Maj	CD	J Baithwaite	Guidelines received NWR roller fixes retro-fit problem	Yes	Yes	Closed	6 Jan 91
1.8	Accelerate the introduction of the pinned head plate casting	Crit	CD	A Davison H Roberts D Fray	Pins now in use	No	Yes	Closed	11 March 91

Table 4.1. (continued)

No.	Action	Grade	QRT control	Action on	Status	Report received	Implemented yet	Open/closed	Completion date
Confidence That the Design Functions Well In All Tolerated Conditions Is Too Low									
2.1	*Review the head specification, particularly the gap scatter allowance*	*Maj*	*GP*		*Report issued suggesting larger tolerances are acceptable Under review*	*Yes*	*No*	*Closed*	
2.2	**Review development facilities**	**Min**	**JB/GP/CD**		**Taguchi program started**	**No**	**Yes**	**Open**	**Ongoing**
2.3	**Collect data to quantify problem**	**Maj**	**GM**		**A less intensive data collection system has been approved**	**No**	**No**	**Open**	**Ongoing**
2.4	*Analysis of tape path operation*	*Maj*	*JB/CD/RF*		*Taguchi program Refer to action 2.2*	*No*	*Yes*	*Open*	*Closed*
2.5	*Implement narrow width roller*	*Crit*	*GM/CD/RF*		*Roller issued to production*	*Yes*	*Yes*	*Closed*	*End Jan 91*
2.6	*Anneal head block moulding*	*Maj*	*CD*		*Test results from Talana show no problem*	*No*	*No*	*Closed*	*21 Dec 90*
2.7	**Use captive screws to fix head plate to base casting**	**Min**	**CD**	**E Farr**	**Prototype tried To be implemented with the die-cast head plate Machining drawing to be up-issued**	**Yes**	**No**	**Open**	**30 Jun 91**
2.9	*Increase clearance around rollers*	*Crit*	*CD*		*Now targeting new castings See action 1.8*	*No*	*No*	*Open*	*Next batch*

Table 4.1. (continued)

No.	Action	Grade	QRT control	Action on	Status	Report received	Implemented yet	Open/closed	Completion date
The Possibility of Damage to Components On the Shop Floor Is Too High									
3.1	**Improve training of operatives** **Certification of operatives**	**Min**	**GP**	**R Baker**	**Operatives not certified** **Not a critical issue at present**	**Yes**	**Yes**	**Open**	**Ongoing**
The Level of Discipline Within Assembly Is Too Low									
4.1	*Review methods of improving supervision*	*Min*	*GP*	*R Baker*	*Recognized issue* *Beyond scope of team*	*Yes*	*No*	*Closed*	*TB stated*
4.2	*Review methods of rewards and recognition*	*Min*	*GP*	*R Baker*	*Recognized issue* *Beyond scope of team*	*Yes*	*Yes*	*Closed*	*TB stated*
Confidence in the Quality of Components Arriving On the Shop Floor Is Too Low									
5.1	*Review inspection equipment* *Ensure facilities are available to fully inspect all tape path piece-parts*	*Crit*	*AD*		*Done*	*Yes*	*Yes*	*Closed*	*28 Sept 90*
5.2	*Ask vendors to supply inspection data*	*Crit*	*AD*		*Chester Hall complying* *The cost is not felt to be justified at IEC*	*Yes*	*Yes*	*Closed*	*28 Sept 90*
5.3	*Ensure vendor processes are capable of easily meeting specified tolerances*	*Maj*	*AD*		*Established* *The squareness of the tacho and tension arm bores are tight*	*Yes*	*Yes*	*Closed*	*28 Sept 90*

Table 4.1. (continued)

The Variability of Skew Tapes Is Too High

No.	Action	Grade	QRT control	Action on	Status	Report received	Implemented yet	Open/closed	Completion date
6.1	Review the procedure StorageTek uses to certify and handle skew tapes	Maj	GM	P Jacobsen	Had response: generally practice similar to STML	Yes	No	Closed	31 Aug 90
6.2	Review adequacy of 8900 used for comparison of skew tapes Consider issues of servicing, repair, and disturbance of reference deck	Maj	GM	P Martin	Second 8900 provided	No	No	Closed	31 March 91
6.3	Review procedure for tracking skew tape history	Maj	GM	P Martin	Scheme implemented	Yes	Yes	Closed	6 Sept 90
6.4	Review handling procedure for skew tape	Maj	GM	P Martin	Scheme implemented	Yes	Yes	Closed	6 Sept 90
6.5	**Review need for STML to generate their own skew tapes**	**Min**	**GM**	**P Martin**	**Until better correlation with StorageTek skew tapes, this will not progress Although desirable, this is not seen as essential**	**No**	**No**	**Open**	**31 March 91**

Table 4.1. (continued)

No.	Action	Grade	QRT control	Action on	Status	Report received	Implemented yet	Open/closed	Completion date
The Accuracy With Which Skew Can Be Set At Level 4 Is Too Low									
7.1	Review the procedure for assembling head azimuth assemblies onto the head plate	Maj	RF		Not seen as problem	Yes	No	Closed	18 Sept 90
Confidence in Measurements of Skew Is Too Low									
8.1	Review the documented procedure for skew measurement Ensure it is being followed	Maj	CD	J Bourne	Spec checked out okay Some questions regarding design of test box	No	No	Closed	30 Nov 90
8.2	**Suggest improvements and/or alternative equipment to the method of measuring skew**	**Maj**	**CD**	**J Bourne P Nicholls**	**Meeting to be held**	**No**	**No**	**Open**	**30 April 91**

Chapter 5
Announcing the Strategy

On January 19, 1990, StorageTek CEO, Ryal Poppa, formally announced the Excellence Through Quality (ETQ) strategy to his corporate staff. Each of the executive vice-presidents participated in the meeting by enumerating how they would support ETQ and also the specific steps that each of the organizations they controlled would take to implement the effort. Poppa presented the final signed version of the plan to the officers and asked for their commitment in implementing the plan. He asked each of the QAG members to outline the advantages and concerns they had in implementing the ETQ strategy in each organization. The chair also presented the new quality policy to the officers and indicated he would give the status of the progress of ETQ at the quarterly all-manager meetings held at headquarters, which would be videotaped for distribution worldwide. The following are excerpts from the quality manual.

Foreword to the Excellence Through Quality Manual

In December 1988, the corporate management committee formally recognized the need for a total quality process at StorageTek. Don Stratton, vice president of corporate quality and education, was appointed to lead a quality improvement team composed of senior managers from the major operating functions. This team was given the responsibility for developing a five-year corporate strategy and implementation guidelines assuring continuous quality improvement at StorageTek. This strategy, named *Excellence Through Quality,* is based on the premise that customer satisfaction is StorageTek's number one business priority.

The work of the five-year quality improvement team was reviewed by the corporate officers on July 21, 1989, and again on January 19, 1990. Their suggestions and recommendations have been incorporated into the strategy document which contains the implementation guidelines for ETQ. It is a working document from which operating functional strategies and plans were developed and implemented.

ETQ may be the most significant strategy that StorageTek embarks on in the 1990s. Active support by all employees is required to continually improve its processes and ensure that StorageTek will be a preferred supplier of high-end data storage and retrieval products and services.

The Significance of Excellence Through Quality

In the 1990s, StorageTek will confront an increasingly complex array of consumer and market issues. Global competitors will place increased pressure on the company to produce quality products, services, and solutions more quickly, at lower cost, and in wider variety. Proud as we are of our accomplishments, we must be mindful of the environment in which we compete. Sophisticated customers are doing business only with companies that recognize that their continuous improvements in quality are the best source of competitive advantage. Our competition, particularly the Japanese, learned well the techniques of building quality and reduced cycle times into systems. It is clear that we must face squarely these issues of improved quality and reduced cycle times as key determinants in StorageTek's ability to survive and grow in the information storage and retrieval industry.

The Meaning of Excellence Through Quality

ETQ is a comprehensive process involving all StorageTek employees. It focuses on the continuous pursuit of quality improvement. ETQ is based on the principle that by establishing quality as our basic business priority, we will ensure StorageTek's competitiveness and our customers' satisfaction. The StorageTek Quality Policy is the foundation of ETQ.

StorageTek Quality Policy

The common goal of ETQ is to provide internal and external customers with error-free products and services that satisfy their needs.

Customer satisfaction is our number one priority. Achieving this priority occurs from involving each employee in a prevention-based approach to continuous quality improvement.

Implementing Excellence Through Quality

The primary vehicle for implementing ETQ is the quality improvement process known as quality improvement process (QIP). By implementing the QIP we focus individuals and work groups on customer requirements and on the continuous evaluation and improvement of our work processes.

- The QIP promotes evaluation of our work processes
- Strong customer/supplier communication
- Effective measures of process performance
- Cross-functional teams
- Decision making based on facts
- Identification of the root causes of problems
- Prevention-based management

The QIP consists of the following nine steps:

1. Document process flows and identify process ownership.
2. Identify customer requirements and establish effective measurements.
3. Identify the cost of quality.
4. Identify and prioritize improvement opportunities.
5. Organize a team(s) and develop improvement plans.
6. Present improvement plans to management.
7. Implement plans and monitor results.
8. Maintain the solutions.
9. Reward and recognize.

Each of these steps will be covered in the following paragraphs. The examples are from StorageTek experiences with the quality improvement process.

Step 1: Document Process Flows and Identify Process Ownership

Overview

The first step in the QIP is to document the sequence of tasks involved in a process as it currently exists. It is critical that the current operation of the process is accurately represented so that improvement opportunities can be identified in step 4.

Documenting the current process with a flowchart helps everyone who works in the process understand how the process actually operates, including the interactions with customers and suppliers. A flowchart is a sequential description of the movement of people, material, documents, and information. The flowchart includes the beginning and end of the process, the inputs, the outputs, the customers, the suppliers, the major tasks, and any relevant subprocesses.

Processes can be flowcharted at different levels. A high-level process flow generally looks at various functions, departments, or organizations. High-level flowcharts usually do not contain fine detail because their major purpose is to help tighten cross-functional interfaces. The card assembly/test process flow that follows is an example of a high-level flowchart. The card assembly/test process includes subprocesses such as component prep, auto insertion, PWA assembly, wave solder, incircuit test, functional test, ESS thermal, ISP test, and machine test. To highlight process improvement opportunities you may need to depict subprocesses at a more detailed level. Once the process is described, identify the owner of the process. The owner is the manager who has responsibility and authority for the results of the process. By assigning process accountability, we can focus on resolving problems in the process rather than ascribing blame.

Procedure

1. Identify all major processes in which you take part.

2. Document the processes as they currently operate.

   • Define the purpose of the process.
     The purpose of the process should be clearly identified so that those not working within the process can clearly

understand it. A purpose statement should be concise and to the point. Let's look at the example of component prep.

> **Purpose of the Component Prep Process**
>
> The purpose of the component prep process is to deliver ready-to-insert components to the assembly load lines.

- Define where the process begins and where it ends.

> The process begins when production control delivers the components.
>
> The process ends when the prepped components are delivered to the load line.

- Identify the process outputs and customers.
  Outputs are defined as the materials, information, and/or services provided to others as a result of your work. A customer is the recipient of the outputs of your process.

Output	Customers
Prepped components	Assembly load lines

- Identify the process inputs and suppliers.
  Inputs are the materials or information required to complete activities to produce a desired result. Suppliers are those, either internal or external to the company, who supply your process inputs.

Inputs	Supplier
Components	Production control

• Document the process flow using the appropriate flowchart symbols.
Process flowcharts are constructed with easily recognizable symbols to represent the type of processing performed. With no more than four symbols, you can graphically depict any process.

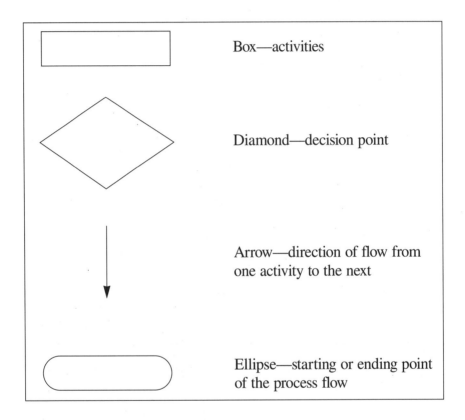

Box—activities

Diamond—decision point

Arrow—direction of flow from one activity to the next

Ellipse—starting or ending point of the process flow

Start with the receipt of the initial input and ask the question, "What happens next?" Continue to ask that question until you have documented all activities that occur between the beginning and end process. Be sure to include any rework loops, ad hoc procedures, and workarounds that may occur. Do not document the process the way you would like it to operate. Remember the purpose of the flowchart is to identify improvement opportunities. This requires that your flow represents what really happens, as opposed to how you think things should happen or how they were originally designed. After completing the flowchart, verify that the process boundaries are still appropriate and the lists of inputs, suppliers, outputs, and customers are complete.

3. Identify an owner for each major process.
   The process owner is a manager who will take responsibility for the performance of the process. A process owner may be assigned by executive decision or defined by existing job responsibilities. A process owner must have the authority and resources to resolve process problems.
   The process owner should do the following:

   - Document the process.

   - Assign ownership for subprocesses, if applicable.

   - Communicate with customers to understand their requirements.

   - Ensure that the QIP is applied to the process.

   - Establish measurements to track the process and continuously improve it.

   - Initiate regular process reviews.

   - Allocate resources and resolve or escalate cross-functional issues.

Step 2: Identify Customer Requirements and Establish Effective Measurements

Overview

Step 2 of the QIP is essential to achieving true quality improvement. Quality means providing customers with products and services that fully satisfy their requirements. Requirements are customer needs or expectations that your output must satisfy. Customer requirements generally fall into the following categories:

Category	Example
Timeliness	"I need your activity report by 8 A.M. Monday."
Accuracy	"The document will be rejected if it contains any errors."

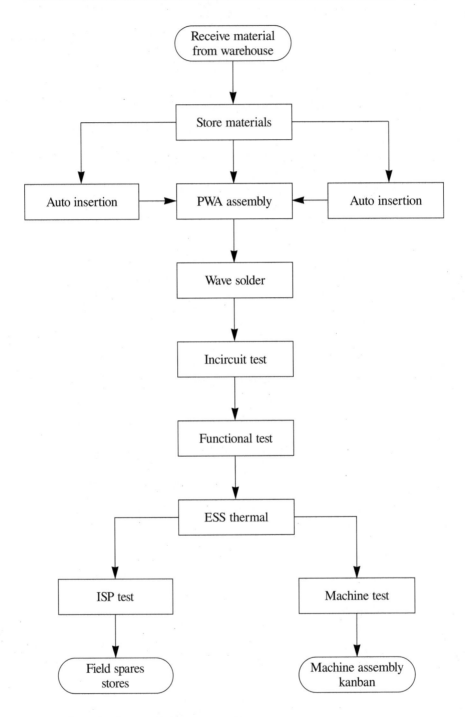

Figure 5.1. Card assembly/test process flow.

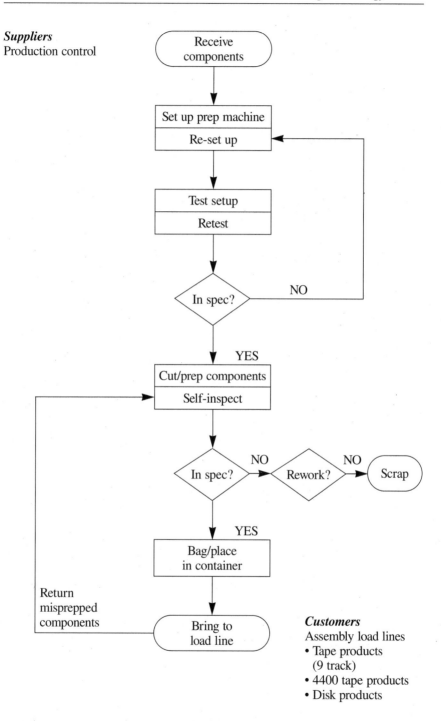

Figure 5.2. Component prep process flowchart.

Category	Example
Completeness	"All fields must be completed before the document will be processed."
Cost	"The total cost of the assembly cannot exceed $50."
Quantity	"I'll need 30 gallons of the solution each month."
Dimension	"The completed unit must be less than 30 inches in length."
Reliability	"I need to rely on 99.5 percent uptime from your equipment."
Serviceability	"I need to be able to repair your equipment within 30 minutes should it fail."

Knowledge of the customer's needs and expectations is a prerequisite to satisfying them. It is critical that these requirements be understood and reflected accurately in specifications for products, services, and processes. Identifying customer needs enables you to establish specific and measurable requirements which, together with business objectives, are the primary driving forces directing process improvement. To be able to continually assess conformance to your customer requirements and monitor process performance, an effective measurement system must be established. Effective measurements provide information to recognize when improvement is required and to support decisions to improve the process. If you cannot measure your results, then you cannot control your process and improve your performance.

Procedure

1. Meet with your customers to identify their needs and requirements.

   • Determine the customer's objective. As a supplier, you are more knowledgeable than the customer is about your product or service, and you may have a different and sometimes better way of achieving that objective.

   • Work with your customer to identify the quality characteristics of your output that are most critical such as timeliness, accuracy, completeness, and dimension.

• Define specific and measurable requirements. Requirements should be stated in specific terms so that there is no question about their meaning. Requirements should be defined in measurable terms so they can be tracked and assessed over time. Target values that represent satisfaction should be defined for each measurable requirement.

2. Meet with suppliers to communicate and define your requirements.

• Often the ability to meet the requirements of your customers depends on the quality of inputs received from your suppliers. Therefore, you should define specific and measurable requirements with your suppliers.

3. Document customer/supplier agreements.

• Now that you understand your customer requirements, you must negotiate with your customers the expected levels of conformance to those requirements. For example, in printed wire board assembly, a customer of component prep has a requirement that components are cut within ±.030 inch of specification. Is 100 percent conformance to this requirement a reasonable expectation for today? It is critical to come to a clear understanding of the expected levels of conformance. You may need additional time to determine the level of performance your process is capable of producing.

Do not agree to conformance levels that your process is incapable of meeting. If the customer has conformance requirements that are beyond your process capabilities, explain the situation to your customer so that other options can be explored. You should negotiate expected levels of conformance to your requirements with your suppliers as well.

• Document customer/supplier agreements between you and your customers and you and your suppliers. A customer/supplier agreement is the documentation of the customer requirements and the expected levels of conformance. The agreements should also state the priority of each requirement.

4. Establish effective process measurements.

- Evaluate the effectiveness of the measurements that you currently have in place. Effective measurements help to assess the performance of the process as it relates to supplier and customer requirements. Effective measurements should also provide early identification of potential problems and actions required to improve the probability of meeting customer requirements. Keep current measurements that reflect these requirements and consider eliminating those you don't find useful.

- Implement new measurements as appropriate. Three types of measurements should be considered within a process.

    (1) Measurements for evaluating inputs to the process. The information derived from these measurements helps you assess whether or not your supplier is meeting your requirements.

    (2) In-process measurements. These tell you how well you're doing at a given point in the process. In-process measurements focus on internal efficiency and respond to business objectives as well as customer requirements. To select in-process measurements, ask yourself where the few critical areas of activity are in which favorable results are absolutely necessary to achieve success. If something were to go wrong, where and how would you be able to get the earliest indication of the problem? Then place a measurement at each critical point in the process.

    (3) Measurements for evaluating process outputs. These measurements gauge whether your output conformed to the requirements defined by your customer. Concentrate on the "vital few" measurements that provide essential information about the quality of your output.

5. Establish a feedback system with customers and suppliers to objectively monitor performance and foster improvement.

    Periodically meet with your customers and review their requirements and satisfaction levels. Monitoring process performance with respect to customer requirements provides the basis for improving the process.

Another Tool for Customer/Supplier Agreements

Warren Nickel, formerly of IBM, shared with me an extremely effective tool to help describe and measure customer/supplier agreements on an 8½-by-11-inch sheet of paper. This can be done by organizations and customers, and it can be internal or external.

The process starts by determining the mission of the organization. Key people, or everyone, if possible, should take part in this. It continues to surprise me how this single task gets so complex because most people really do not understand the mission of their organization. You will know you are there when everyone agrees. This will take some time and effort.

The next step is to determine the responsibilities of the organization to accomplish the agreed-upon mission.

Then you determine suppliers, primary and secondary, on the input side of the chart. It is good to also determine requirements you place on each supplier, and the issues and inhibitors at this stage. Ask what the issues and inhibitors are that help or hinder the supplier in meeting or exceeding these requirements.

Now determine outputs to your customers. Also consider requirements of the customer and issues and inhibitors to meet or exceed customer requirements. Divide the customer into primary and secondary, if possible. (I say "if possible" because it is easy to trap yourself by categorizing any customer as secondary.) The best example here may be classifying a customer with whom you have been doing business for 10 years as primary versus a customer who may be on your potential list. Once customers begin doing business, they gain primary status.

The next step is determining, with the customer, how the customer will measure your output. In some cases the customer may want you to do this. I believe this will be a common way of doing business by the year 2000. Barriers are still up and customers feel they must measure outputs from suppliers. As long-term relationships are established and the barriers go down, it will be commonplace for suppliers to provide these data.

The last step is establishing a solid feedback link between the customer and your organization. Analyze the feedback and determine what action needs to happen to satisfy or *delight* the customer.

The diagram shown in Figure 5.3 describes the process we have discussed here. The requirements, issues, and inhibitors were discussed in depth and then documented. The chart shows the mission, customers, and measurements. This particular chart was first developed in 1988 and has been revised and updated many times. It is used regularly by our supplier quality assistance group to focus on how to accomplish the mission of that particular group.

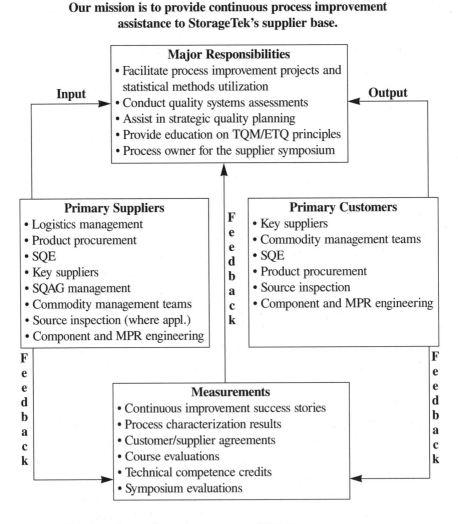

Figure 5.3. Supplier quality assistance group (SQAG).

Step 3: Identify Cost of Quality

Overview

In any corporation, the total cost of doing business is composed of two distinct categories of costs. Basic costs are those associated with performing the activities that add value to and are essential for producing the required outputs. Quality costs are the costs specifically associated with the achievement and maintenance of product or service quality. Quality costs are the total of the following:

- The investment cost of preventing failures

- The cost of appraising the product or service for conformance to requirements.

- The costs incurred by failure to meet requirements.

At StorageTek we categorize quality costs as follows:

- Prevention. The costs of trying to ensure that the right things are done right the first time.

- Appraisal. The costs of checking to see if the right things were done right the first time.

- Internal failure. The costs incurred when we discover the right things weren't done right the first time.

- External failure. The costs incurred when the external customer discovers we didn't do the right things right the first time.

The strategy for reducing quality costs is to do the following:

1. Take direct action on failure costs and try to drive them to zero.

2. As you gain confidence in the reduction of failures, reduce appraisal costs accordingly.

3. Invest in prevention activities to maintain improvements and keep unsatisfactory products from being produced in the first place.

Cost of Quality Reporting

Cost of quality reporting is a valuable management tool to prioritize and initiate improvements and measure the progress of quality improvement on a corporatewide basis. Cost of quality is a common measurement that can be understood and used across functional process boundaries to enable StorageTek to focus the appropriate resources on the most important improvement or problem areas.

Excessive effort and expense should not be incurred to capture every incidental cost when collecting cost of quality information. Precision in the figures is not nearly as important as consistency. Data, however, should be collected at enough detail for each process to ensure that opportunities for improvement are not missed.

Procedure

1. Identify the categories of costs for each activity in the process flow (Figure 5.4), that is, basic (B), prevention (P), appraisal (A), internal failure (IF), and external failure (EF), using the decision tree (Figure 5.5).

2. Determine the percentage of people-time for each activity on the process flows and summarize by cost category.

3. If there is more than one work process in the department, weight the percentage of all processes to get the percentage of P, A, IF, EF, and B for the total department.

4. Use these percentages to calculate the cost of quality from the actual expenses account summary, except for those accounts such as scrap, rework, education, and so on, that can be allocated directly to quality cost categories. Subtract the allocation accounts such as charge-ins, MIS, telecom, and occupancy from the total actual cost to get the subtotal of actual cost less allocation. Use this subtotal to calculate the cost of quality and the percentage of total cost less allocation. This allows department managers to count only those expenses incurred in their departments and excludes the charges coming from other departments such as charge-ins as mentioned previously.

Step 4: Identify and Prioritize Improvement Opportunities

Overview

The first three steps of the QIP enable you to understand the process and its ability to satisfy customer requirements. Investigating the

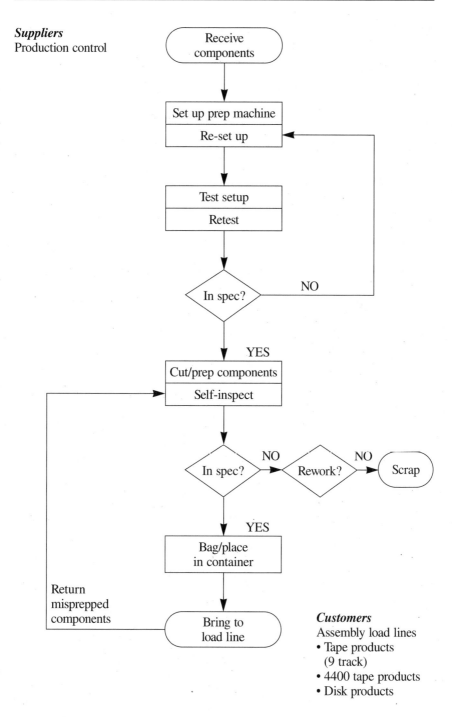

Figure 5.4. Flowchart component prep process.

Asking the following questions can help identify
the major categories of quality costs.

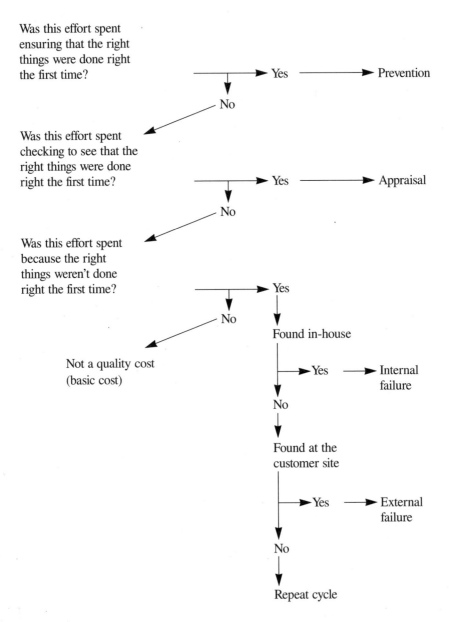

Was this effort spent
ensuring that the right
things were done right
the first time?

Yes ➤ Prevention

No

Was this effort spent
checking to see that the
right things were done
right the first time?

Yes ➤ Appraisal

No

Was this effort spent
because the right
things weren't done
right the first time?

No

Not a quality cost
(basic cost)

Yes

Found in-house

Yes ➤ Internal failure

No

Found at the
customer site

Yes ➤ External failure

No

Repeat cycle

Figure 5.5. Decision tree.

process to identify and better understand the sources of difficulties is essential to eliminating problems that affect output quality. Step 4 requires you to identify improvement opportunities and prioritize those opportunities.

Significant improvement opportunities can be revealed by analyzing process flowcharts (step 1), customer satisfaction and in-process measurement (step 2), and quality cost data (step 3). Prioritization allows you to decide which opportunities are most likely to improve customer satisfaction and/or meet internal business objectives.

Procedure

1. Analyze process flowcharts for sources of error and opportunities for simplification.

    Investigate improvement opportunities by asking questions such as:

    • Is the activity needed (does it add value)?

    • Is the activity performed to correct errors (rework)?

    • Is the activity performed to undo the work of someone else?

    • What are the obvious redundancies?

    • Are there undue delays?

    • Is there a more efficient means of transmitting information or materials?

    • Are there activities that could be performed better if they were placed elsewhere in the process?

    • Should someone else perform any of the activities?

2. Identify critical problems with the process output based on your assessment of conformance to customer requirements.

3. Evaluate data from your in-process measurements, such as error rates and throughput time, to identify internal process problems.

4. Identify the process activities significantly contributing to the cost of quality. Review the major quality cost elements and determine in which part of the process these costs occur. Gather measurable data, such as scrap and rework costs, to quantify the potential impact of specific process improvements.

5. List all the activities or opportunities for improvement.

6. Rank improvement opportunities and select improvement projects based on the following priorities:

    • Customer needs

    • Internal business objectives

    • Cost/benefit ratio

    • Potential for improvement

    • Resources required to implement improvement

    • Available resources

Step 5: Organize a Team and Develop Improvement Plans

Overview

In step 4 of the QIP, you identified and prioritized improvement opportunities. Step 5 requires that you organize a quality improvement team and develop an action plan to address selected opportunities. Generally, steps 1–4 of the QIP need to be completed to identify opportunities for bringing your process to a new level of performance. However, opportunities for immediate improvement may become obvious at any point. Whenever these opportunities arise, the StorageTek problem-solving process can be used to identify root causes of problems and find the appropriate solutions. Figure 5.6 shows the relationship between the quality improvement and problem-solving processes. Completion of steps 1–5 of the problem-solving process will help determine the necessary actions for process improvement.

Procedure

1. Organize a QIT. The team should be made up of people who work closely with some aspect of the process under study. Because a problem may have its root cause in another functional area, members of the team may be drawn from several functional organizations. Team members should consider their participation as a priority responsibility, not an intrusion on their real jobs. The project is now part of the members' real jobs.

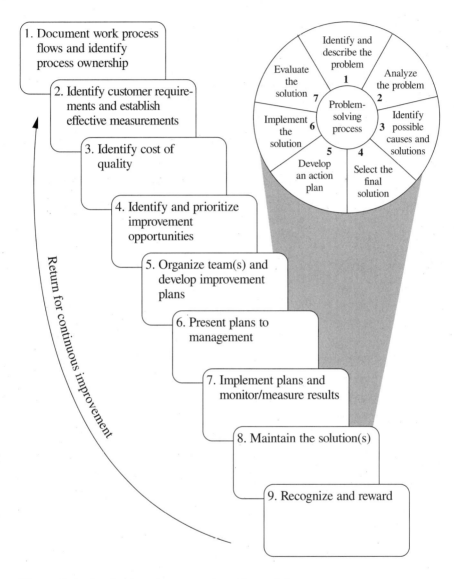

Figure 5.6. Quality improvement and problem-solving processes.

Once the team membership has been established, a team leader should be selected. The team leader is the person who manages the team: calls and facilitates meetings, handles or assigns administrative details, assigns team member roles and responsibilities, and orchestrates all team activities.

The team leader should have a view of the process and understand the impact of any changes to the process on higher level processes. Additionally the team leader should be skilled in the techniques of quality improvement and be reasonably good at working with individuals and groups.

2. Use steps 1–5 of the problem-solving process to identify root causes of process problems and develop an action plan for implementing an appropriate solution(s).

Once the team is organized, the next step is to develop the improvement plan. Effective, permanent solutions and improvements result only from careful forethought and planning.

StorageTek Problem-Solving Process

1. Identify and describe the problem. Improvement opportunities were identified and prioritized in step 4 of the QIP. Once the specific process improvement opportunity has been identified, the team should complete these tasks:

   • Prepare a problem statement. Before your team can make improvements, each member must thoroughly understand the process. As a team, examine the following questions: How does the process currently work? What is it supposed to accomplish? Who are its customers and what do they expect? How is the process performing in relation to customer expectations? Use this information to develop a statement that clearly defines the process problem.

   • Identify the project goals. The team should specify a quantifiable goal that describes what changes are expected to result from this project. Specifying a quantifiable goal helps provide direction and also makes evaluating the effectiveness of the solution objective. Goals need not be stated in numerical terms, but can be described using words such as *increase* or *decrease*. If goals are stated numerically, make sure everyone knows they only indicate the magnitude of the desired improvement and must never be used as measures of a team's performance.

• Determine the resources. Discuss what resources you will need—training, budget, time, people, and so on. What expertise or technical abilities will you need that are not represented by team members? How much time must be allotted so team members will be able to complete the project?

Before moving on to the next step in the problem-solving process, the team should reach consensus on the answers to the following questions:

–Does everyone in the group have a common understanding of the problem?

–Is the problem within the group's control or influence?

–Is the problem worth solving?

Potential tools:

–Flowcharts

–Customer/supplier agreements

–Cost of quality data

–Pareto charts

–Check sheets

4. Select final solution(s). The key to quality improvement is to develop solutions that really solve process problems. Changes to the process should eliminate or negate the effect of the root causes of the problem. To identify optimal solutions that eliminate these causes, evaluate the alternatives developed in step 3 by examining the following questions:

• Which solutions deal directly with the root causes of the problem?

• Which solutions are the easiest to implement and maintain?

• What are possible disadvantages, negative consequences, or other weaknesses of each alternative?

• Which solutions are likely to result in achievement of the project goals?

Compare the proposed solutions and work toward reaching consensus on the best solution or set of solutions. If the team is unable to reach consensus, collect additional data on a variety of potential solutions. The use of advanced problem-solving techniques, such as design of experiments, may be required to determine the optimal solution(s).

Potential tools:

–Scatter diagrams

–Check sheets

–Ranking methods

–Screening experiments

–Taguchi factorial designs

–Solution selection matrix

5. Develop an action plan for implementing the solution. Divide the solution into sequential, easily managed steps to provide reference points that can be used to determine whether or not implementation is on target and is meeting the stated goals. Assign responsibilities and set measurable and unambiguous objectives for everyone who is going to be involved in imple-mentation. Communicate these clearly and ensure as much as possible that nothing is left open to misinterpretation or guess-work. Set up a monitoring system to track whether specific tasks are being performed or short-term targets are being achieved as planned. Ensure that measurements and data col-lection mechanisms are in place to evaluate the effectiveness of your solution.

Step 6: Present Improvement Plans to Management

Overview

Sometimes a group's recommendation must be approved by one or more levels of management before it can be implemented. This situa-tion can arise when the following occur:

• A senior manager has asked the group to address the problem and recommend a solution but reserves decision-making responsibility.

- The problem, and therefore its solution, involves other functions or departments.

- The cost associated with the recommended solution requires approval by the next level of management.

Procedure

Prepare and deliver a presentation to management to gain its approval for implementing your solutions. Present the following clearly and specifically:

- A concise definition of the problem

- The impact of the problem and why it's important

- The solution you are recommending and the benefits of implementing the solution

- What you want from the members of the group you are addressing

- A summary of the significant facts and recommendations

A negotiation process may be required to receive a final approval. Ensure that all necessary budgetary investments are addressed and approved.

Step 7: Implement Plans and Monitor/Measure Results

Overview

Once quality improvement plans are approved, the implementation process begins. The QIT should implement the solution according to the action plan developed in step 5 of the problem-solving process. Following implementation, the effectiveness of the solution should be evaluated to determine the extent of improvement in process performance.

Procedure

1. Use step 6 of the problem-solving process—implement the solution—to implement the approved quality improvement plan. Review the action plan for implementing the solution developed in step 5. Include everyone affected by the solution in the implementation process. Divide the implementation effort into manageable steps and monitor each step. Be prepared to modify plans as unexpected events occur.

2. Use step 7 of the problem-solving process—evaluate the solution—to evaluate the effectiveness of the solution. After implementing the solution, collect data to evaluate process performance. Compare these data with the stated goal from step 1 and with data collected to analyze the problem in step 2. Based on this information, repeat the process as necessary to ensure that the problem is completely resolved. Check for new problems that may have been created by implementing the solution.

Step 8: Maintain the Solution(s)

Overview

To achieve improvements in long-term process performance, formal procedures must be in place to maintain the solution(s) implemented in step 7 of the quality improvement process. Procedures should be established to control the process at a new level and to continually monitor performance to ensure lasting results.

Procedure

1. Follow through to maintain the process at the new performance level.

    • Establish, document and communicate revised procedures.

    • Standardize to ensure uniform application.

    • Train in the new procedures.

    • Implement ongoing data collection and reporting.

    • Establish a system for customer satisfaction feedback.

    • Ensure adaptability of the process.

2. Perform a periodic review to assess potential for long-term process results.

    • Determine the extent to which new methods and practices are being effectively applied.

    • Assess conformance to customer requirements.

    • Review and refine customer requirements as necessary.

    • Take corrective action as necessary.

    • Identify further opportunities for improvement.

Step 9: Give Recognition and Rewards

Overview

Recognizing and rewarding successful efforts are critical to sustaining motivation for continuous quality improvement. In step 9 of the quality improvement process, successful quality improvement efforts are recognized by management and others at StorageTek.

Procedure

Management should provide appropriate recognition and reward for improvement efforts. In addition to the regular merit increases employees receive for achieving their quality improvement goals, there are both formal and informal approaches available to reward and recognize outstanding contributions.

Options include:

- Cash rewards
- Plaques
- Dinner
- Ceremonies
- Pen and pencil sets
- Articles in corporate internal publications for employees
- A verbal "thank you"

Five Change Mechanisms

An important part of the ETQ strategy is concentration and implementation of five change mechanisms. These five change mechanisms are education, implementing a management network, implementing the quality improvement process (already discussed), and emphasizing recognition and reward. The five change mechanisms are discussed here in detail.

Communication

First of the five change mechanisms is to communicate the ETQ strategy to all employees and stress the importance of quality improvement. The QAG develops communication plans that are implemented annually throughout the corporation. This includes material that will be shared in written form as well as in meetings with employees throughout the year.

Each quarter the chairman meets with all managers at headquarters and discusses various subjects. ETQ has been the first item on his agenda since May 1989. In addition, managers throughout the corporation have regular employee communication meetings where employees are updated on the progress of ETQ in their organizations. In a worldwide corporation, communication across several languages can be a major problem. Therefore, our basic quality policy and strategy is published and available in many languages.

Concerning external communication, we encourage our key people to participate in conferences such as the ASQC Annual Quality Congress, the annual Juran IMPRO program, and local ASQC meetings throughout the nation. We also promote the idea of communicating quality improvement to focus groups of key customers and suppliers.

Education

The second change mechanism is to give all employees the skill and knowledge needed to continuously improve quality and customer satisfaction. A three-day ETQ core curriculum has been delivered in six languages to our 10,000 employees worldwide. Through a cascade approach, management goes through first with their superiors and then again with their employees. The idea is that the first time managers participate in the core they are in a learning mode; when they go through the second time with their employees, they are in a teaching, coaching, and facilitating mode, working with the quality education staff. It is vital for managers to learn various tools, techniques, and processes, and to be able to teach them to their employees. We are training key people throughout the corporation to act as facilitators to aid in the coaching necessary after core training takes place. We will back up the initial three-day core curriculum with what we refer to as phase II courses that address specific areas such as statistics, facilitating, process understanding, measurement, and leadership.

Our research shows that benchmarking against best-in-class is far better than comparing against past practices within our own company. Benchmarking was initially used by Xerox, and we continue learning from that company about this technique.

We also have plans to integrate the education process outside of StorageTek. Our diligent work with suppliers over the years has led us to recognize their specific achievements at our annual Supplier Symposium. Throughout the year we keep close tabs on what suppliers are doing in the area of quality improvement and then recognize those that have excelled. We are also planning to share with our customers, at their request, our experiences in successful implementation of the quality improvement processes.

For the last three years, StorageTek has taken part in the National Quality Forum in October. The first year 42 managers attended, the second year 250 managers, and the third year over 300 managers attended the three-hour conference. At the end of the conference CEO Poppa announces the winners of the StorageTek Annual Chairman's Quality Award.

Management Network

The third change mechanism is implementing the management network necessary to drive the implementation of ETQ throughout the corporation. At the highest level, we have our Corporate Management Committee Process Improvement Council (CMCPIC). This is the very highest council in the corporation and its main job is to steer the effort. Next we have process improvement councils at the vice president, director, and higher manager levels throughout the corporation.

We have also appointed quality officers worldwide. Each major organization in the corporation has a quality officer who reports directly to the top person in that organization. As mentioned earlier, in our headquarters location we have quality officers and quality advisory group, that meet weekly to help steer the effort. Throughout the world we have quality officers in our U.S. regions and our international subsidiaries who have direct contact with the corporate quality organization at headquarters and meet regularly to discuss implementation efforts.

Each quality officer has implemented the use of workbooks that feature identical indices to help document implementation of the processes throughout the corporation. The workbooks follow the Baldrige award criteria very closely.

Quality Improvement Process

The fourth change mechanism is implementation of our nine-step QIP. The three-day ETQ core training concentrates heavily on helping our employees understand each step of this process. As detailed in the previous section, step 1 develops process flows; step 2 identifies customer requirements. Each person in each organization in the corporation has been asked first to identify inputs from suppliers and the requirements associated with those inputs, outputs to customers, and specific customer requirements. It is important to think of this step in reference to both internal and external customer/supplier relationships. Measurements based on customer expectations are developed in this step.

Step 3 is to identify quality costs. We have adopted the classic cost of quality definition and used the flowcharts mentioned in step 1 to help identify waste, restarts, and rework, as well as basic costs. We use the classic categories of basic, prevention, appraisal, and failure.

Step 4 is to prioritize improvement opportunities using the data from flowcharts, customer requirements, and quality costs. It is important to prioritize the opportunity for improvement before launching into any meaningful improvement activity. Once the areas for improvement are prioritized, we organize teams that develop plans to tackle these improvement opportunities. This is step 5. We use all the known approaches in team effort including quality action teams, quality circles, and design for manufacturability teams to help reach solutions. Once the teams develop their plans for improvement they use step 6 and present plans to management to garner management support. At this phase management approval is sought to proceed to the quality resolution stage where the plan is implemented. This is step 7.

Step 8 maintains the solutions. Once the plans have been implemented, it is necessary to monitor the process to assure that improvements are ongoing. Step 9 rewards and recognizes, which is the next change mechanism we will discuss.

Recognition

As mentioned earlier, an annual chairman's award is presented to departmental and cross-functional teams. We have also set up a rewards and recognition group that meets weekly to benchmark with other companies and formulate recommendations for improvement for the QAG and the CMCPIC. At this time the group is leaning toward ways to reward teams versus individuals only.

As a corporation, we have been leaning in this direction for some time. For instance, our top officers equally share 80 percent of their management objectives as a team. Only 20 percent is individually based. Of the 80 percent, 20 percent is directly related to implementing ETQ. We are also piloting a gainsharing program, and we are using sociotechnology approaches in manufacturing units with an eye toward expanding this if successful.

Summary

These are the five change mechanisms that our corporation is now concentrating on in order to fully implement our ETQ strategy. We are finding that these five areas serve as extremely good agenda items for quality council meetings. Through careful tracking of these five change mechanisms, one can immediately diagnose strong and weak areas, concentrating on those weak areas and bolstering them wherever and however necessary.

We are beginning to hear quality success stories from across the world. Our major quality measures have improved dramatically and have been verified by outside agencies. Over the last several years we won the Xerox Award of Excellence, a result of our long-time supplier relationship with Xerox. We won the Shell Partnership in Quality Award due to Shell's active involvement in the design of one of our primary products known as the 4400 automated cartridge system library. We won the Convex Computer Corp. award, the Avis "We Try Harder" award, and the United States Postal Service award for high quality and on-time delivery of products. We were honored by the Juran Institute and selected by them as the keynote company at the Juran IMPRO '92, and we earned ISO 9001 certification from the British Standards Institute. Perhaps the most complimentary event thus far is that some of our key customers are beginning to ask us to help them with their quality improvement effort and most feel our quality initiative is better than or on a par with theirs.

The Roadmap Concept

Specific items to be accomplished each year are determined by the QAG to implement the entire strategy. These specific roadmap items are approved by the CMCPIC. The implementation of these items is followed closely by the QAG and each process improvement council, starting at the very top. The following is an example of the roadmap items that have been accomplished for 1993.

1993 Excellence Through Quality Roadmap

Quality Improvement Process

Item 1:   *30 pts.*   *Integrate the QIP into day-to-day activities to support the achievement of key business goals and objectives.*

Deliverable

(5)   A. January. Gain agreement on the key corporate business processes and select process steering committees, leaders, and teams.
Measurement: CMC approval and communication of StorageTek's key business processes and identification of a steering committee, process team, and team leader for each identified key process. Owner: QAG.

(10)   B. March. Process teams document (model) key business processes and define process metrics. Measurement: Documentation of each key process and definition of process performance metrics. Owner: key process steering committees.

(10)   C. June. Plans for process improvement that support the four key strategic goals approved by CMCPIC and communicated to all employees. Measurement: Improvement plans formally presented to and approved by the CMCPIC and communication to employees through the *StorageTek News* or other vehicles summarizing plans to improve the performance of the

corporation's key business processes. Owner: key process steering committees.

(5)   D. September. Key process steering committees review process improvement progress with the CMCPIC.
Measurement: Presentations by each key process steering committee to the CMCPIC outlining progress against improvement plans. Owner: functional PICs/key process steering committees.

Communication

Item 2: *10 pts.* *Provide consistent communication to StorageTek employees, customers and suppliers about ETQ progress and activities.*

Deliverable

(3)   A. September. Develop a CMCPIC-approved 1994 plan for communicating ETQ to StorageTek employees, customers, suppliers, and community. Measurement: Documented plan approved by the CMCPIC. Owner: QAG.

(4)   B. December. Complete the execution of the 1993 corporate ETQ communication plan. Measurement: Assessment by the QAG that the activities outlined in the plan have been accomplished. Owner: QAG.

(3)   C. February. Quarterly update on ETQ by the chairman at all-managers meetings. Measurement: Update presented at each all-managers meeting. Owner: vice president of corporate quality and education.

Education

Item 3: *10 pts.* *Provide ongoing education to StorageTek employees in the skills, knowledge, and practices needed to continuously improve quality and customer satisfaction.*

Deliverable

(5) A. May. Implement the training/education requirements defined in the Employee Development
and Educational Assistance Corporate Practice.
Measurement: Memo from FPICs stating compliance and successful BSI audit of ISO 9001 element 4.18. Owner: FPICs.

(5) B. July. Develop and pilot *Managing ETQ* course
for StorageTek managers.
Measurement: Pilot course completed. Owner:
corporate quality and education.

Management Network

Item 4:   *20 pts.*   *Obtain and maintain registration of the quality
management system to the ISO 9001 quality
standard.*

Deliverable

(4) A. March. CMCPIC reviews the effectiveness of
the quality system on a quarterly basis.
Measurement: Minutes of management review of
the quality system with a focus on corrective
action. Owner: CMCPIC.

(2) B. May. Publish and distribute an approved revision of the StorageTek corporate quality manual.
Measurement: Corporate quality manual
approved, published, and distributed. Owner: corporate quality.

(10) C. September. Obtain registration to the ISO
9001 quality standard.
Measurement: Certificate of registration to ISO
9001. Owner: CMCPIC.

(4) D. December. Maintain compliance to the
requirements of ISO 9001.
Measurement: Successful completion of any ISO
9001 maintenance audits by BSI. Owner:
CMCPIC.

Item 5:   *5 pts.*   *Assess StorageTek's quality system against the criteria of the Baldrige award and develop a plan for application in 1995.*

Deliverable

(1)   A. July. Establish assessment/application teams. Measurement: Definition of assessment teams and team leaders to assess StorageTek's quality system against the Baldrige award criteria. Owner: QAG.

(2)   B. October. Publish an assessment of StorageTek's strengths and weaknesses against the Baldrige award criteria.
Measurement: Present an assessment of the StorageTek quality system's strengths and weaknesses against the Baldrige award criteria to the CMCPIC. Owner: QAG.

(2)   C. December. Develop a plan for applying for the Baldrige award in 1995.
Measurement: Develop a CMCPIC-approved plan for applying for the Baldrige award in 1995 which includes activities to improve the weaknesses identified in the assessment. Owner: QAG.

Item 6:   *10 pts.*   *Continue to drive continuous quality improvement through the implementation of functional ETQ roadmaps.*

Deliverable

(5)   A. February. Develop FPIC-approved functional roadmaps to ensure the five change mechanisms effectively drive continuous improvement.
Measurement: Louisville/Longmont FPICs, regions and subsidiaries define functional roadmaps for implementing ETQ in 1993. Owner: FPICs, regional and subsidiary quality officers.

(5)   B. June. Initiate formal biannual assessments of progress against the functional ETQ roadmaps.
Measurement: Documentation of a formal review

of progress against items outlined in the functional roadmap and plan revision if appropriate. Owner: functional, regional, and subsidiary management.

Reward and Recognition

Item 7:   10 pts.   Ensure alignment of compensation/recognition systems with the principles of ETQ.

Deliverable

(2)   A. February. Pilot the key initiatives survey in the worldwide field operations and controllers functions.
Measurement: Survey conducted in the pilot areas. Owner: human resources, functional pilot groups.

(3)   B. May. Expand recognition systems to better interface between discretionary and variable pay.
Measurement: Proposal approved by CMCPIC. Owner: functional PICs.

(2)   C. September. Recommend a direction and program for variable pay based on corporate success.
Measurement: CMCPIC approval. Owner: human resources.

(3)   D. October. Develop and deliver a new performance management system in conjunction with base pay recommendations.
Measurement: Deployment begun. Owner: human resources.

Item 8:   5 pts.   Review Chairman's Quality Award criteria in support of ETQ and CEO present awards during national quality month.

Deliverable

(3)   A. March. Distribute 1993 application guidelines.
Measurement: Application guidelines mailed to all StorageTek managers. Owner: corporate quality.

(2)   B. October. Award presentations.
Measurement: Award recipients announced by CEO. Owner: corporate quality.

Chapter 6
Implementation—Later Stages

Excellence Through Quality Core

ETQ Core Training is a course that has been provided to over 10,000 people in StorageTek worldwide in six languages. We completed the training of over 10,000 people in less than two years.

One of the major points that made the entire training effort successful was a decision early on to select dedicated trainers who would be trained by the people who developed the initial course. The training was very stringent, although it took just over three intensive weeks during which the candidates actually did stand-up presentations on portions of the course and were rated on their efficiency by their peers and by the trainers. Not all trainers attained certification. Some found during the training that they were not cut out to be trainers. The point is that the training was very stringent and the trainers who delivered the course delivered it consistently throughout StorageTek.

At one point a tentative decision was made to train hundreds of trainers with the main objective being to complete the training very quickly. This was a bad decision because each trainer would only deliver two or three courses. When we evaluated this and discovered the enormous variation that could exist in doing it this way, we backed off.

Approximately 15 trainers delivered the three-day ETQ core course to our 10,000 employees. At headquarters four classrooms were built next to each other. Each class held 30 students at four tables. Each table contained a process team headed by a manager. These classes ran simultaneously for about 20 months.

Because of geography, the field classes contained less than 30 students most of the time. This made the task difficult, but it was completed in two years as planned.

Five Modules of ETQ Core

The ETQ core training consists of five basic modules. Module I talks about the quality direction and the main objectives are as follows:

Module I—Direction and Objectives

- Compare/contrast StorageTek's past quality efforts and identify lessons learned.
- Describe the foundations of the ETQ strategy.
- Define quality and basic ETQ concepts and definitions.
- Describe the importance of data-based decision making.
- Define the roles of StorageTek employees in ETQ.
- Identify elements necessary to create an environment that will facilitate successful implementation of ETQ.

Included in module I is a discussion of the Deming philosophy and a general reference to his 14 points. There is a brief discussion of understanding variation and also the basic elements of ETQ.

The elements of ETQ were based on the Baldrige award criteria, with some minor variations. These elements are leadership, quality planning, information and analysis, human resource utilization, education, quality assurance, quality results, and customer satisfaction. Module I also includes a definition of StorageTek's quality policy and specific discussion on the five major elements of that policy, including focus on the customer, focus on the process, total employee involvement, continuous improvement, the quality improvement process itself, and a brief reference to benchmarking.

Module II—Team Effectiveness I

- Participate in icebreaker activity
- Describe the purpose of an icebreaker
- Describe and utilize consensus

At various times throughout the course, the instructors use an ice-breaker in the beginning of a session or just after lunch. The icebreaker in this case is to ask each employee to write on a card three things about themselves—two true and one false. The instructor reads the three items aloud, and the group tries to guess who wrote the card and then which of the three things is not true. This brings about some pretty lively discussion, and the group has a lot of fun doing this. The purpose of this is to do just what the title infers—to break the ice, to break the barriers, to open up conversation, and to use humor in a positive way.

The next segment of module II is to discuss, define, and ensure that everyone understands what consensus is. In the training manual there is very bold print that says "Consensus is not voting." Then the instructor gets into the critical questions of consensus such as, "Can I live with this decision?" "Can I support this decision?" "Can I agree not to sabotage this decision?"

Module III—Process Identification

- Define a process
- Identify various process levels
- Explain cross-functional focus
- Select process upon which to apply the QIP

A process is defined as the organization of people, equipment, energy, procedures, and material into the work activities needed to produce a specified result or work product. Examples of a process are accounts payable, card assembly, cash management, collections, component preparation, customer billing, customer service, distribution, inventory control, manufacturing, order entry, payroll, product development, and purchasing.

Module III addresses the difference between the traditional organizational approach, with a definition and example of a vertical organization, and a process-oriented approach that flows across many organizations. The cross-functional is stressed very heavily in this particular section.

StorageTek has divided its major activities into eight key business processes. These processes are explained and the owners identified to each of the groups. Some of these processes include things such as planning, integration and reporting, strategic planning, market selection, development in manufacturing, delivery of products and services, market information, cash management, and human resource utilization.

Module IV—QIP

The QIP is a nine-step process that will assist in the continuous process improvement. It was developed to give StorageTek a common process throughout the company. It facilitates communication among department functions and organizations, and focuses on customer needs. The QIP promotes the following:

- Strong customer/supplier relationships
- Cross-functional teams
- Data base decision making
- Identification of root causes and problems
- Prevention base management

In steps 1–3, we become familiar with our current process.

Step 1:

- Document process flows.
- Identify process ownership.

Step 2:

- Specify customer requirements.
- Institute effective measurements.
- Assess conformance to customer requirements.

Step 3:

- Identify cost of quality.

Upon completion of step 3, we have a great deal of information which we can use to proceed with the QIP. In step 4, we use that information and more, if necessary, to complete the following:

- Identify improvement opportunities.
- Prioritize improvement opportunities.

We then proceed to step 5 where we complete the following:

- Develop improvement plans.
- Form a team to address the plans if necessary.

In step 6 we may need to get management approval to complete these tasks.

- Allocate resources.

- Implement solutions.

When management approval has been obtained, in step 7 we oversee these tasks:

- Implement solutions.

- Monitor process performance.

When solutions are proven effective over time, step 8 requires that we continue the following:

- Monitor the gains in performance.

- Maintain the gains in performance.

- Standardize the improved process.

Conclude with step 9: recognize and reward both team and individual contributions to quality improvement, as appropriate.

As you can see, the QIP gives us a common process and language for continuous quality improvement. It is a structure that guides us toward more effective, efficient, and adaptable processes.

Module V—Team Effectiveness II
This section concentrates on how members of teams can learn to be team players. It discusses the kinds of problem behaviors that are encountered in meetings and has the objective of trying to get team members to handle the meeting more efficiently. The objectives of module V are as follows:

- Identify a problem behavior exhibited at a team meeting and develop two strategies that could be effective in dealing with it.

- Identify meeting effectiveness techniques to apply for future quality improvement team meetings.

- Demonstrate the ability to be a productive quality team member by sharing information, using common language and tools, suggesting procedures, and facilitating team effectiveness.

Excellence Through Quality Closing

The closing includes discussion of the Shewhart cycle. The cycle involves plan, do, check, and act. *Plan* is usually done by engineers who plan what is to be done. *Do* is usually done by production that produces the product. *Check* is performed by inspectors and/or management to see if we've done what we said we would do. *Act* implies acting to improve based on the checking data to go full cycle. The session ends with an exercise in which the conferees actually do a project with time limits on the planning of the project, actually doing it, checking to see if it was done right, and then acting to improve it. They end up in this project with a display that portrays what they have learned in the ETQ core, and we see many of these displays throughout StorageTek.

Results

In our discussion with customers we often talk about our dramatic improvements in financial performance and product quality. Over the last five years total revenue is up 38 percent, and revenue for employee is up 27 percent; debt-to-equity ratio is down 66 percent.

Then we talk about the improvement in our product life in terms of field replaceable units, which we refer to as *FruLife*. In terms of our library subsystem we've had a threefold improvement since the start of our QIP effort over the last eight quarters. For our DASD subsystem, we've had another fourfold improvement over the past 11 quarters. In our 18-track subsystems there has been a sevenfold improvement over the last eight quarters. Our head disk assembly life improvement is up sevenfold over the past eight quarters. Our head disk assembly failures by build month is down almost to zero. Inventory as a percent of assets is down 46 percent; inventory turnover is up 288 percent. We attribute the entire improvement to our ETQ effort.

The chapter 11 legacy also resulted in significant change. We went from 10 levels of management to five; the outstanding rating for managers went from 75 percent to 20 percent; debt-to-equity went from 1.50 to .40 and external cost of quality went from 31 percent of revenue to 5 percent. There was also a dramatic improvement in our customer satisfaction index for product and service since the start of ETQ. This is the ultimate metric.

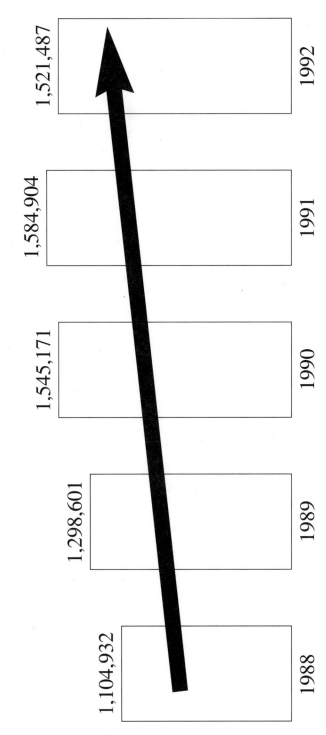

Total Revenue
In Thousands of Dollars

38% Increase

1,104,932	1,298,601	1,545,171	1,584,904	1,521,487	
1988	1989	1990	1991	1992	

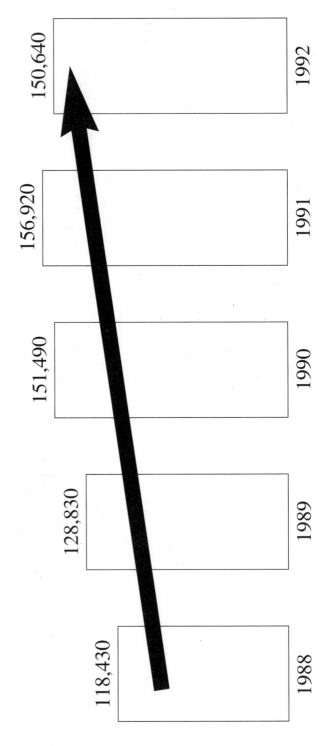

Revenue Per Employee
In Dollars

27% Increase

118,430	128,830	151,490	156,920	150,640	
1988	1989	1990	1991	1992	

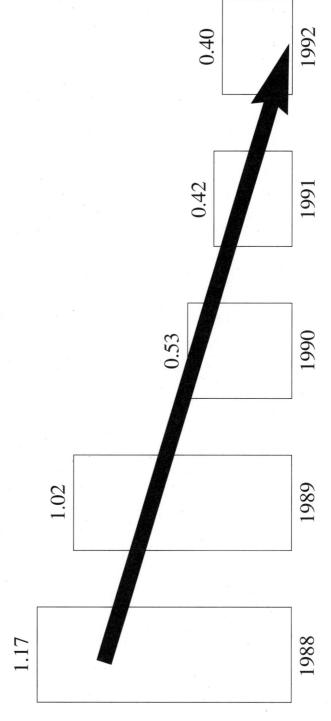

Long-Term Debt-To-Equity Ratio

66% Reduction

Year	Ratio
1988	1.17
1989	1.02
1990	0.53
1991	0.42
1992	0.40

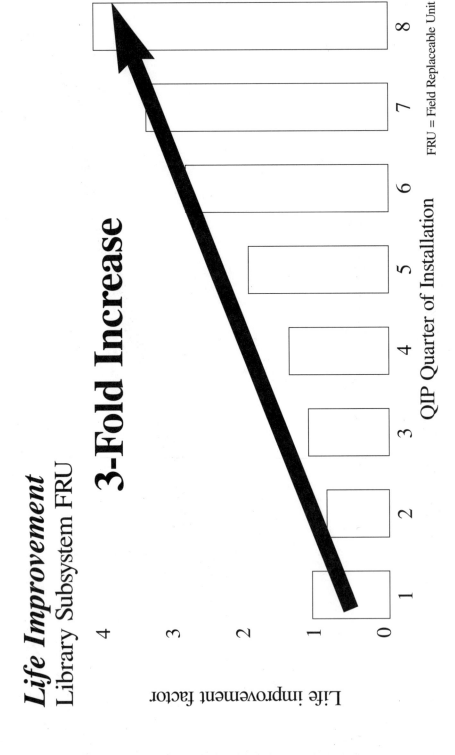

Life Improvement
Library Subsystem FRU

3-Fold Increase

Life improvement factor

QIP Quarter of Installation

FRU = Field Replaceable Unit

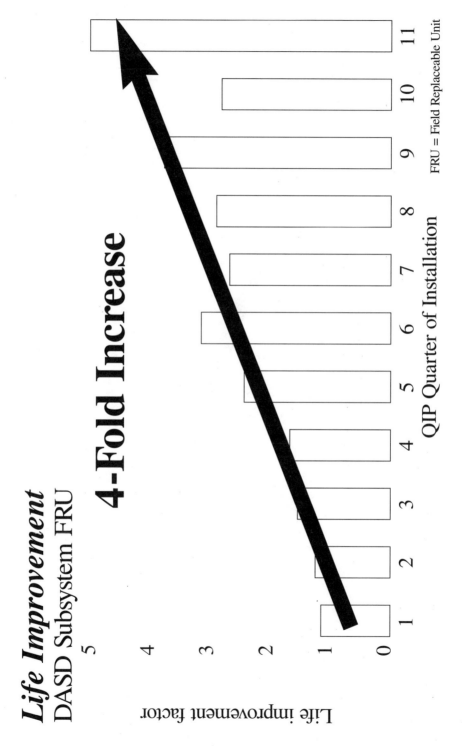

Life Improvement
DASD Subsystem FRU

4-Fold Increase

Life improvement factor

QIP Quarter of Installation

FRU = Field Replaceable Unit

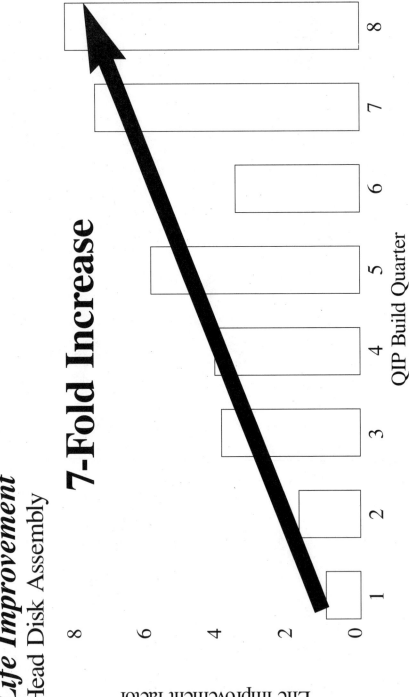

Life Improvement
Head Disk Assembly

7-Fold Increase

Life improvement factor

QIP Build Quarter

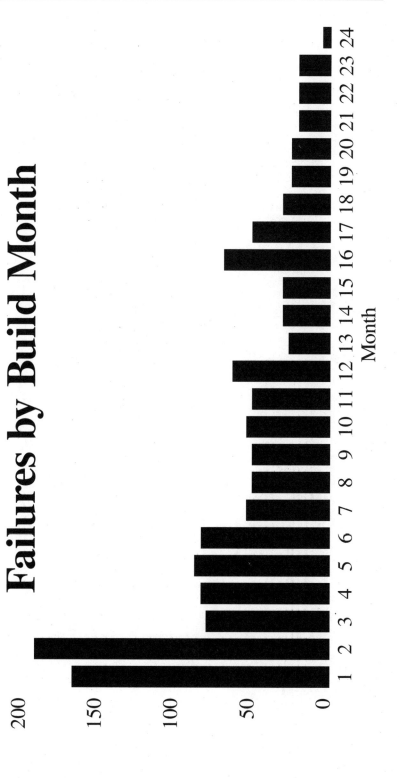

Head Disk Assembly
Failures by Build Month

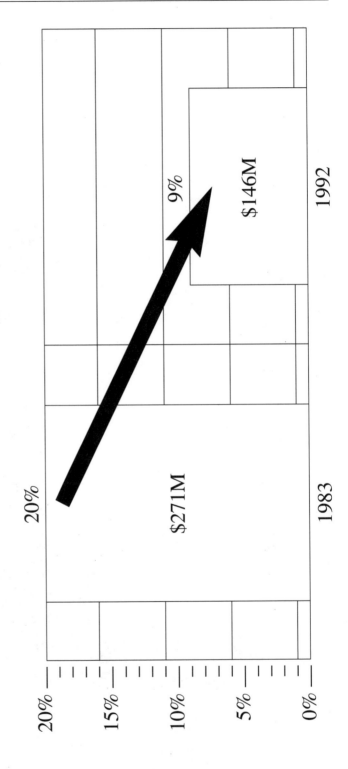

Inventory Percent of Assets
46% Reduction

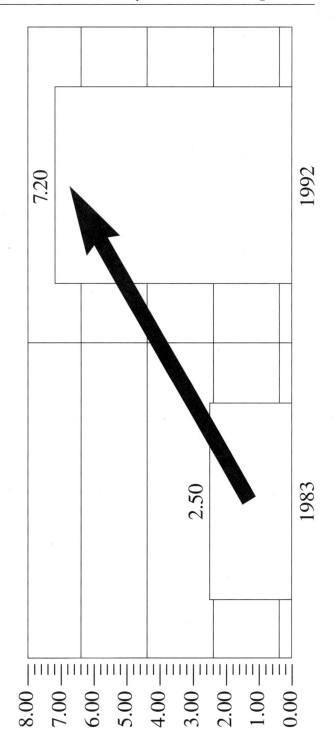

Chapter 11 Legacy

Then and Now

	Before Chapter 11	Today
Management levels	10	5
Outstanding managers	75%	20%
Debt-to-equity ratio	1.5	.40
External cost-of-quality	31%	5%

Reward and Recognition

The QAG commissioned the Reward and Recognition Task Force. This consisted of about 10 people carefully picked from various organizations to make up a cross-functional team. The group decided to benchmark with about 20 other companies about reward and recognition.

Charter and Mission

The charter and mission of the Reward and Recognition Task Force is to determine the most effective methods for rewarding and recognizing employees for their involvement and contributions to StorageTek success and to revise the performance appraisal process to reinforce the values of quality, teamwork, and participative management. The reward and recognition process must support the principles identified elsewhere in the ETQ program.

Role of the Reward and Recognition Task Force

The Reward and Recognition Task Force is responsible for the following:

- Definition of the reward and recognition philosophy to support strategic goals and ETQ at StorageTek

- Identification of system process improvements to support StorageTek cultural changes

- Development of the reward and recognition proposal and product line

- Development of roadmap and communication plan

- Sponsorship of pilots to evaluate progress against the rewards and recognition plan

- Ongoing review of the implementation plan

Philosophy

Reward and recognition can be powerful motivators of behavior. A solid direction for all locations worldwide and a corporate set of values tied to proper motivation are critical in developing the full potential of the work force and in achieving ultimate success for StorageTek. The rewards and recognition system emphasizes teamwork, process improvement, corporate profitability, and individual contribution.

Reward and Recognition Strategy

To support the foregoing mission, the overall strategy in the reward and recognition system includes three process and cultural changes.

Move from	*Move toward*
1. Focusing on individual events	1. Focusing on process improvement
2. Rewarding individuals only	2. Rewarding team and individuals
3. Using management judgment only	3. Utilizing customer/supplier/team/ peer feedback for assessment

The Plan

Reward and Recognition System

A system of reward and recognition products gives StorageTek management the flexibility to support behaviors and results in different scenarios, matching proper reward or recognition to the specific challenge.

The system being proposed for StorageTek is composed of both current and additional products. Many of the current products have been in use in limited areas of the corporation. By adding a few very significant products, and expanding judiciously those that are already in use, StorageTek can support the cultural moves toward teamwork and continuous process improvement. The phase-in or expansion of products correlates with the development of new behaviors, and the time required to tailor designs and to budget costs.

The programs will be under a corporate umbrella. Each function will develop detailed plans to support its specific objectives. Plans will operate at the functional, team, and individual level. In addition, there is a movement toward corporatewide recognition and reward.

Performance Management: Shift from Performance Appraisal to Personal Development Plan

The recommended revisions to the performance appraisal process will foster integration of this process with the evolving cultural changes. The mechanism for the employee's performance appraisal will shift from the manager's individual judgment of employee performance to a customer peer satisfaction indicator and progress toward a personal development plan.

Performance appraisal forms were redesigned to add quality and shared team goals. Every employee will have a process improvement goal with a weighting of at least 20 percent. In addition, management will place more emphasis on employee development and training.

Four management performance appraisal factors were added to the form to emphasize the importance of leadership skills and management style in the accomplishment of objectives. These factors reinforce the content and encourage application of the management development and ETQ training being given to all managers.

The process should require that goals be tied directly to customer/supplier agreements. The evaluation will consist of a customer satisfaction rating with the input coming from customers, internal and external. Because the goals will be based upon customer/supplier agreements, the evaluations could occur on a schedule tied to the conclusion of major projects rather than on a strictly annual basis.

Performance appraisals will be replaced by a personal development plan to emphasize personal growth and the future, rather than focusing on personnel deficiencies and the past. Individual ratings will be replaced by an indicator of personal growth and development. This indicator will be decoupled from directly driving merit increases. The concept of annual reviews will be eliminated. Progress indicators could occur at a frequency of 9–15 months based on project completion and the rate of an individual's personal growth. Team member/peer reviews will be implemented. Acquired skills, knowledge, specific competency measures, and market movement will determine a greater part of base pay, while customer satisfaction ratings and individual team results will determine performance pay (variable pay rewards that do not go forward with base pay).

These changes are intended to enhance ETQ implementation. As the corporation works its way through the quality improvement process, StorageTek will evaluate additional changes in the performance management system incorporating the broader spectrum of career planning, succession, and skills forecasting. The important point for now is that performance appraisal is a process and, as such, it will be undergoing continuous improvement as we strive toward excellence.

Shift from Cash Compensation to Total Renumeration
The compensation practice at StorageTek has been to pay employees a biweekly salary that represents or is approaching a market value of a job and is adjustable based on the individual's performance in that job.

To effect the cultural changes required by ETQ, StorageTek should move from cash compensation to total renumeration. This approach includes both capital accumulation programs and welfare benefit programs and creates measures of present and future value.

Base Pay Becomes Competency Pay

Current salary tools have the characteristic of being a fixed cost: slow to change in either direction, in spite of the dynamics of the business around it. Current salary tools do not motivate or reinforce behavior because the pay distribution is routine, and any increase is generally not tied directly, or in time, to the performance that created good results. The changes to the compensation system being proposed by the Reward and Recognition Task Force respond to the fixed cost and nonmotivating character of the current plan. The proposal is to tie some of the cash compensation for all employees directly to performance results, in the same time frame as the behavior that created the results.

Base pay is a platform that enables the corporation to attract and retain employees. It is important to keep focus on base pay because dissatisfaction with this component of total compensation will weaken any recognition program from being a strong positive motivator. Base pay should be targeted at the fiftieth percentile of select competitors. Change to base pay will be driven by acquired skills and demonstrated competencies, using steps based on specific competencies rather than salary ranges. In the proposed compensation system, base pay is not at risk, nor is it intended to be the sole method for meeting or exceeding competitive pay. A new method, performance pay, becomes the component that responds to both individual and team performance.

Variable Pay Becomes Performance Pay

The importance of the role that performance pay will assume in this system must be determined by the corporation and/or the functions. The sales function has established a pay plan with significant variable pay with a high degree of control vested in the employee. Other functions may choose a pay plan with less performance pay (variable component) as their employees will exercise their control more as team members than as individuals.

When the relationship is understood by employees, that (1) they have some control of their cash compensation, and (2) they are accountable and compensated for business success, then behaviors will adjust to support and drive business success. The compensation system will then support ETQ.

The products proposed by the Reward and Recognition Task Force are intended to help employees see their contributions, acknowledge their accountability, and be motivated by controlling their level of cash compensation (base pay plus performance pay) and recognition. Performance pay will be distributed based on a level of participation, process ownership, and overall functional and corporate performance. Its primary purpose will be to reward and pay for performance.

Addition of Recognition Programs

Based on employee feedback and benchmarking results, the Reward and Recognition Task Force has identified the need for increased recognition for individuals and teams to support the ETQ strategy. Recognition becomes an unlimited resource when it is spontaneous, flexible, and adapted to individual and team performance on tasks and process improvements.

To promote ETQ, recognition programs should meet the following guidelines.

- Corporate guidelines on appropriate recognition programs
- Programs developed and funded at the functional level to reinforce strategic process and behavioral goals of the function
- Acknowledgment of individual and team improvements and reinforced behaviors by:
  –Peer
  –Manager
  –Team

Review of functional recognition programs at this time indicates positive reaction in the 50 percent to 70 percent range and neutral reaction in the 25 percent to 45 percent range. The key is that recognition programs can be viewed as positive motivational tools rather than negative.

StorageTek and World-Class Quality

Juran wrote an article in *Quality Progress* magazine (March 1991) that outlined eight lessons from world-class quality companies. Juran isolates reasons for companies approaching world-class quality. I would like to discuss the eight criteria and indicate how StorageTek sizes up in regard to each.

The first criterion is that stretch goals can be met; however, they cannot be met using the pedestrian pace of the ordinary learning curve. Something extraordinary is needed and benchmarking can help. StorageTek has a very comprehensive strategic plan. The ETQ effort is referred to as the enabler of meeting the plan. Some of the goals are as follows:

- Develop some of our software capabilities to produce 8 percent of corporate revenues by the end of 1996.

- Increase the support and emphasis on non-U.S. business to achieve 50 percent international revenue attained by the end of 1993.

- Apply for and be granted an *A* bond rating by the end of 1995.

- Decrease worldwide cash conversion cycle time to meet corporate goal of 120 days by 1997.

- Improve FruLife to 2200 months in 1995 from 1000 months in 1990.

These are some of the StorageTek strategic goals; meeting them will be accomplished by implementing the ETQ strategy throughout the corporation.

The second characteristic that Juran talks about in his article is adopting the big Q concept. We have been preaching the big Q in StorageTek since late 1988. It goes back to an article published by the ODI Corp. that talks about product applying to services as well as goods. In other words, the entire company must be involved with the quality improvement effort, not just production. The article discusses the process as it applies to business processes throughout the company, not only to production processes. It also talks about the word *customer* applying to all who are affected, both internally and externally, and building customer/supplier relationships. Little q, on the other hand, is use of statistics only in the production areas, not looking at business processes in their entirety and not using the cross-functional approach that is so vital to success in the 1990s. StorageTek is practicing big Q all the way.

The third characteristic that Juran talks about is ownership of multifunctional processes and assigning executive leadership. As mentioned earlier in this chapter, StorageTek has defined five key business processes and has assigned executive leadership to each of these processes. They cut across the organization horizontally and are multifunctional. A list of subprocesses has been established, and management ownership of these processes is known.

The fourth characteristic in the article is to create an infrastructure for improvement. We have an infrastructure that starts at the very top with the corporate management committee process improvement council chaired by our CEO, vice-chaired by me, and made up of the CEO's direct reports. This group meets monthly to steer the entire effort. We also have process improvement councils at the executive vice-president, vice-president, and director levels throughout the entire company. I chair the QAG which meets weekly, represents the company, and steers the entire ETQ effort to advise the highest level councils and to advise the process improvement councils at the executive vice-president, vice-president, and director levels. We also have quality officers appointed at various levels in every major division and in every major region and subsidiary throughout the world. The job of the quality officer is to ensure that ETQ is implemented, that training is being pursued and accomplished, and that results are being achieved. The quality officers network on a regular basis with the corporate quality organization, the corporate quality and education vice-president, and other quality officers throughout the world.

The fifth characteristic is that a lot of work is required. There is no question of this, and our chair spends at least 25 percent of his time on the quality improvement effort. Some of our vice-presidents and directors spend as much as 40 percent of their time on quality improvement effort. The culture in the corporation has changed over the last three-and-a-half years in terms of the amount of time spent listening to quality action teams and quality circles, participating on quality resolution teams to make sure that action is taken to implement the recommendations, and ensuring that quality improvement is taking place in the organization. This doesn't take into consideration the enormous amount of time that is also spent in reading the books, going to the lectures, participating on the councils, and doing the hard work of continuing to learn about the quality improvement effort.

The sixth characteristic is that upper managers must personally lead the effort. As I have mentioned, all of our top-level people participate in the process improvement council chaired by our CEO, and the executive vice-presidents, vice-presidents, and directors chair their own process improvement councils. They are leading the effort, and it is becoming a very heavy part of their responsibility. I think, on average, each executive spends at least 25 percent of his or her time on the quality improvement effort.

The seventh characteristic is that the Taylor system must be replaced. We have been discussing this since day one of our ETQ effort. We have used Shewhart's plan/do/check/act cycle to explain it better. What happened in the past with the Taylor system is that we departmentalized. We put people in different buildings in different departments to do planning work. For example, the engineers did the planning work but didn't talk to the doers who were going to make the product the engineers were planning. The engineers would do the planning, throw the prints over the wall to the doers in manufacturing, and manufacturing wouldn't have any idea of how to make the product.

I'm talking in general now about American industry practices, not specifically to StorageTek, although there is some evidence that this was happening here also. The practices at StorageTek have changed. What we do now is put planners and doers together in the early design of a product. In addition, StorageTek brings customers into what we call customer advisory boards. The customers, at the design stage, actually give firm definitions of what they want in a product in terms of its life cycle, fault tolerance, cost, and so on. Shell Oil Company was so pleased with the product that they had helped develop, known as our 4400 Automated Cartridge System library, that they awarded StorageTek the Shell Partnership Quality Award.

The eighth and last characteristic is that quality goals must be incorporated into the business plan. As I mentioned earlier, each year StorageTek takes a very serious look at its strategic plans based on market forces, worldwide economic conditions, research and development, and expert personnel available, and makes revisions accordingly.

Summary

In this chapter we've talked about the latter stages of the implementation process of ETQ. We've talked about the three-day ETQ core course aimed at StorageTek's 10,000 people worldwide and the various modules that make up the course. The heart of the entire course is a very vivid discussion of hands-on activity relating to the nine-step quality improvement process.

We also discussed the macro results and product-related results of implementing ETQ, our strategy for reward and recognition, and then finally the eight characteristics Juran talks about that exemplify world-class quality companies. I believe that StorageTek exemplifies these eight characteristics absolutely. We are establishing stretch goals, utilizing the big Q concept, establishing ownership of multifunctional processes, and assigning executive leadership. We are creating an infrastructure for improvement and are prepared to do a tremendous amount of hard work. We have positioned upper managers to personally lead the effort and have replaced the Taylor system by breaking down barriers and ensuring that quality goals are incorporated into the business plan. You will notice that these eight characteristics fit very closely into the five change mechanisms we discussed earlier.

Chapter 7
Lessons Learned

Management Network a Must

Establishment of a management network to push the entire process throughout the company is an absolute must. Our management network starts at the very top with the CMCPIC. This council is chaired by the CEO and vice-chaired by me. In the first year we met once a week to help steer the whole effort. There were five people originally—the chair, the executive vice-president of operations, marketing, and sales, customer satisfaction, and me. This expanded to include others as the organization grew and responsibilities were delegated. The major thrust and responsibility, however, hasn't changed: that is, to keep on top of all the major issues and provide insight and direction to the various organizations, the quality advisory group, and the entire company. We use the five change mechanisms, reported on throughout this book, as the agenda for those meetings. At times we may talk about only one item, at other times we may talk about all five, and sometimes we talk about other than the five change mechanisms. The five change mechanisms do provide a solid agenda to help incorporate the transformation that we have been talking about throughout this book.

The management network also consists of the QAG, which is a very important catalyst to drive ETQ throughout the organization, and also to provide advice and counsel to the CMCPIC. This group has been meeting for four-and-a-half years, once a week from 10 A.M. to 1 P.M. every Monday. The agenda varies in that it covers the five change mechanisms but also includes input from other companies and experts in the field, as well as a major input from the members on how their organizations are implementing various aspects of the quality effort. Formal minutes are maintained for the QAG and published each Tuesday, with distribution to CMCPIC, QAG, and quality officers worldwide. There are those who anxiously await hearing about the various subjects discussed and relate them to their own policies and procedures in their own organizations.

Another important part of the management network is the fact that we have quality officers in every division and in every subsidiary throughout the world. This is an important part of our ability to drive ETQ throughout the entire organization. Many people ask if these people are full-time. The answer is no, most are not. The places where it has been decided to go full-time have been for very good business reasons. As the ETQ effort expands to using the effort as a secondary marketing strategy, it becomes necessary to have full-time quality officers. This is not true throughout the entire organization.

One aspect of the management network that is disruptive is the mobility of management. This phrase comes from Deming, as one of his seven deadly diseases. It may not be quite as bad as that phrase connotes, however, when one has to work with a top executive for six months to get him or her on the right side of the tracks and within a year that executive leaves and another comes in with zero knowledge and little concern about the quality effort. Then we have a problem. This is my problem to solve and usually a one-on-one with these people seems to be the best way to get results.

Report to the CEO

It is important that the top quality officer report to the top-level person in the company. In our case, that top-level person is the CEO, chair, and president. I'm not sure how it will work in a company where three people hold those jobs. It could be effective at the president level if the chairman and CEO were figurehead types. Where the chairman and/or CEO have hands-on management control of the entire organization, then it would be necessary for the quality officer to report to that particular person. Much would depend on the personalities involved, how well the two or three top people get along, and so on. The major point I want to make is that you can avoid a false start by ensuring that the quality officer reports to the person who is truly running the organization. The problem is that other people at the same level, especially in American companies, do not want to cooperate to make that person look good. This is exactly what would happen if an effort, such as quality improvement, which involves the entire company, would preclude cooperation by some. When reporting direct to the top person this cooperation evolves much faster, for obvious reasons.

Implement, Implement, Implement

I used these three words in my first book because of my belief that quality professionals, at all levels, need to know how to implement quality improvement. In my experience, many quality professionals know how to make a terrific presentation. In fact, some of the quality gurus fall into this category. What needs to be done is not only to be able to make presentations, but to be able to work with people throughout the company at all levels, especially the very lowest levels.

After implementing quality improvement in about 75 small groups in three or four different companies, I became convinced that CE/FFA was a powerful problem-solving tool. It went beyond problem solving, however. It did what Deming and other quality gurus have been saying needs to be done and that is get management involved. The third phase of that process, as many will remember, is having a small group make a presentation to management. At the end of the presentation we get management to buy into doing something. This is the dramatic change in terms of what we had been doing in the past. I can't tell you how many presentations I've attended where small groups make a presentation and management walks out and nothing happens. The CE/FFA process does not allow this. This mainly came from the learning experience of listening to Deming and then documenting in my own way the 85/15 rule.

Another thought that comes to mind regarding this is about getting instant results. I disagree with this. Although we can't prove it with numbers, we started to see results the minute we started down the quality path—in other words, you don't have to wait a decade to get results; immediate results can be likened to "plucking low-lying fruit." In most places I have been, employees have just gotten used to the idea that rework, scrap, waste, and workaround are a way of life. When they get the idea that management is not in favor of this kind of nonsense, they get turned on to eliminating it. In working with well over 100 small groups, we have attacked the old ways vigorously, and we've gotten rid of them over a period of weeks and/or months. What I think the gurus are saying when they say there are no instant results or instant pudding, as Deming would say, is that you can't stop after plucking the low-lying fruit. You must continue to achieve the major objective of continual improvement. You achieve those improvements rapidly but then go on to do what Juran would call breakthrough improvements.

The word breakthrough has been on the books for some time. There are so-called experts talking about reengineering or redesign. This is nothing new, and these experts are saying, "Oh, quality improvement is something you do gradually over long periods of time with very small improvements." What they don't recognize is the breakthrough idea. Breakthrough means dramatic improvement. It means doing the job entirely differently. It means changing the process in a dramatic way. It means eliminating major functions and doing things entirely differently. This is what the reengineering experts are preaching, but I strongly suggest that when one goes on the complete route of TQM or strategic quality management, you do get dramatic breakthrough improvement. One obvious clue: the tools of reengineering are not different from the tools of quality improvement.

Education

Education for quality improvement must be pervasive. It must include the entire company, and I recommend that the top quality officer be in charge of the entire education process. Culture change requires constant education and reeducation in all areas, not just in quality improvement. I am in charge of the education for marketing and sales for product delivery, for management and leadership education, as well as the quality education. All these have some common threads. As far as the quality portion, initially it is vital to develop a short course of three to five days that would give every employee a common language, basic knowledge of the quality improvement tools and some notion of why teaming is so important. We developed a three-day quality core course aimed at all 10,000 people in the company. The difficult part was delivering it in six different languages throughout the world. We did this and are proud of the accomplishment. Now that it is over, as mentioned in other parts of the book, we are busily working on other subjects that back up the core course and are handling this on an elective basis.

Communication

Communication is a never-ending process that needs to be addressed by the top-level quality officer in the company. Major success stories need to be shared. This can be done in a monthly newspaper; it can be done by individual organizations recognizing teams at staff meetings; it can be done, as we do it, with the chair's award, recognizing major accomplishments of teams each year; it can be done as annual team day affairs and, sorry to say, we have not yet implemented that at StorageTek. We build a communication plan each fall for the coming year. This is usually done by a group of communication experts who leave no stone unturned. The monthly news is important, but it is only one method.

Reward and Recognition

Just do it! Each company has its own culture and way of rewarding and recognizing. The main point is that we need to throw away the stuff of the 1950s and start doing this as if we were alive and well in the 1990s. We have had a 10-person group busily talking to other companies about their reward and recognition. We carefully pick companies that are serious about quality improvement. What we got out of this was a four-year plan, as mentioned under the reward and recognition section of this book, that we are implementing for the second year. We are experimenting with skill base pay, gainsharing, and self-managed work teams. We also have changed the MBO program considerably for the top people in the company. Five years ago each of the officers of the company had individual objectives and more than often they met those. Now the top officers of the company share four objectives, one of which is implementing the quality effort. This means that 25 percent of each executive's bonus goes toward specific activities that have helped implement the quality thrust throughout the company.

One of the major issues that I'm excited about (because it has been bothering me for about 35 years) is changing the appraisal system. I believe appraising people is one thing and paying people is another. We appraise people in order to find out what to pay them. This has resulted in an appraisal system that has 12 different categories for people in the same job skill. This is wrong. The main reason we need to appraise people is to figure out how to help them be better employees, not to figure out how to pay them differently. We are experimenting with this and appraising people for development purposes and paying them based on market value, job skill, and tenure. Our human resources department is working on this, and I'm sure that within the next year or so we will have more definitive answers on how to do this.

External Customers
Must Be the Number One Priority

We very often hear these words, but when you analyze why we do things and how people are paid we find that the external customer really isn't the number one priority. In the earlier history of this company, schedules and shipping became the priority. One neighboring company actually shipped bricks to meet shipping schedules. The question all companies have to ask is, although you may not be shipping bricks, are you close to it? At this point in our company, any employee can stop the line and they do this with a great deal of pride. We know that shipping and fixing in the field is no longer an appropriate strategy.

We keep track of how our customers feel about our products and service through a quarterly survey. Admittedly this survey is in need of revision, and we constantly are on the alert for better and different ways to do this. If I had to give one guideline about how to do customer surveys, it would be do it with simplicity. We recently learned from one of our customers, Grumman Data Systems, that it does a thorough daily survey—with simplicity. According to Grumman, its customers love the survey and are now paying executives based on the results of this particular survey.

Small Groups Are Powerful

In my work with many small groups over the past 10 years, I can say with a great deal of conviction that the small groups that have been working on processes for months and years know more about how to improve these processes than anyone. I can also say that Deming's previous 85/15 rule is true. This refers to the percent of the time that management is responsible for solving the particular problems. The more we listen to the small groups the better. They are eager, anxious, and willing to contribute and all management needs to do is listen and act. My data show that in 85 percent of the cases it takes management action to solve the problem.

CE/FFA in Perspective

My first book was primarily about using the CE/FFA technique in many different areas of AT&T and StorageTek. CE/FFA is a problem-solving technique, but it goes far beyond that. As some of you who read the original book may recall, the CE/FFA takes place in phase II. In phase III the small group gets the opportunity to make presentations to management on how to improve things. In phase IV we get management to take action by forming a quality resolution team, headed by a manager. We drive home Deming's theory about common cause/special cause; we identify these causes accordingly and insist that management get involved in solving the common-cause problems. This is the link to Deming's theory. This is the idea that has demanded action on the part of management, and this is what is happening in the many companies that are now using the CE/FFA approach.

Metrics, Metrics, Metrics—Not!

This is perhaps the most controversial area that you will hear from me. I know that the great majority says you can't get what you can't measure. There is a small minority who caution, "Watch out, you may only get what you measure." I happen to be in this latter category. Too often, during my 35 years in the business world, I have found that people measure what they can get rather than look at the entire picture and struggle with issues that are not as readily definable or measurable.

Let me be specific. In the case of StorageTek, we mentioned that the external cost of quality, prior to chapter 11, was 31 percent of revenue. This is not the total cost of quality. This is only the external portion of cost of quality. For a company of StorageTek's size, this is an enormous number. In those days no one worried or even knew about the number. All they knew about was how many products were being shipped per day, week, month, quarter, and year. The metric during those days was number of items shipped per whatever. The only unknown and unknowable numbers were the numbers of products that we shipped that failed in the field, and how much money were we spending in this process. We now know the number was in excess of 300 million per year. Would it have been better to concentrate on the processes to eliminate external cost of quality rather than the process of shipping? The answer is obvious.

I firmly believe Deming's observation of what you can measure is really only the tip of the iceberg. You can't measure the vast amount of things under the iceberg, and these are the things that can spell out success or failure for any company. I wave a big caution flag to those who advocate metrics, metrics, metrics, with the idea of using common sense and truly placing your customer as the number one priority in everything you do.

Malcolm Baldrige National Quality Award Criteria

As stated throughout the book, we have a great deal of support for the Baldrige award criteria. We have broken the original seven criteria into eight by separating education from human resources. Below are the eight categories broken up by subheadings and questions that may be helpful if you are on the Baldrige award path.

Leadership

Management's Personal Involvement

- Is management personally using the StorageTek quality improvement and problem-solving processes?

- Does management have clearly defined quality improvement objectives focused on corporate strategic goals and customer satisfaction?

- Has a plan been developed for ongoing management quality education?

Quality Values

- Is there a defined process for communicating to all employees the progress of ETQ?

- Is there a published mission statement that has been communicated to all employees?
- Are all employees aware of and knowledgeable about the StorageTek Quality Policy?

Quality Planning

Planning for Quality Improvement

- Are all employees aware of and knowledgeable about the key corporate strategic goals?
- Do all nonmanagement employees have measurable quality improvement goals focused on corporate strategic goals and customer satisfaction?
- Have action plans for achieving quality improvement goals been developed?
- Is there a defined process for management review of quality improvement plans?
- Are process improvement councils/department improvement teams in place throughout the organization and meeting regularly?
- Have plans been developed for the use of benchmarking?

Quality Improvement Process

- Has the use of the QIP been integrated into normal operational duties?
- Is there widespread use of the QIP throughout the organizations?
- Are quality improvement projects being tracked and documented?

Information and Analysis

Scope of Quality Data and Information

- Are data collected in conjunction with the QIP to assess the performance of key processes as they relate to supplier and customer requirements?

- Have in-process measurements been established to assess internal efficiency?
- Are data collected to monitor employee satisfaction?

Management of Quality Data and Information

- Are steps in place to ensure data are accurate and timely?
- Are data organized so that trend information can be generated?
- Are data made available to employees and easily accessed?

Analysis and Use of Data for Decision Making

- Are data analyzed in a timely manner to identify and prioritize improvement opportunities?
- Have data analysis techniques been reviewed by a qualified statistician?

Human Resource Utilization

Employee Involvement

- Is there a communicated recourse for employees in cases of potential quality deficiencies or compromises?
- Are there management practices and specific mechanisms, such as teams or suggestion system, to promote employee contributions to quality?

Employee Recognition

- Is there a defined recognition system in place that reinforces the principles of ETQ?

Quality of Work Life

- Is there a defined process for cross-training and/or job rotation?
- Are job responsibilities and expectations clearly defined for all employees?
- Are trends monitored in key indicators of well-being and morale such as absenteeism, turnover, and safety?

Education

Education and Training Needs

- Is an ongoing process in place to identify quality education and training requirements?
- Has a deployment plan been developed for ETQ core training?
- Has a plan been developed for quality training in addition to the core?
- Have local core trainers or application specialists been identified and their roles and activities defined and communicated?
- Is there a process in place to ensure new employees receive quality orientation?

Applications

- Have changes attributable to quality education and training taken place?
- Is there a process for measuring the effectiveness of training?

Quality Assurance of Products and Services

Process Development

- Are customers involved in the development/improvement of new processes?
- Are feedback mechanisms in place to ensure continuous conformance to customer requirements?
- For out-of-control occurrences, is there a defined process to ensure (1) root causes are determined; (2) corrections are made so that future occurrences are prevented; and (3) corrections are verified?

Supplier Quality

- Have specific, measurable requirements been defined and communicated to suppliers?
- Is there a system for providing timely feedback to suppliers?

Documentation

- Is there a defined process in place for recording quality-related procedures and practices and for retaining key records?

Quality Results

Improvement Results

- Are trends in quality improvement and current quality levels tracked for key product and service measures?
- Is there a process to ensure improvement results are standardized and maintained?

Relation to Strategic Goals

- Are quality improvement results tied to functional and corporate strategic goals?

Customer Satisfaction

Customer Needs and Expectations

- Have customer requirements and expectations been specifically defined and documented?
- Is there a process in place to measure and monitor indicators of customer satisfaction?

Customer Relationship Management

- Is customer feedback collected on an ongoing basis?
- Is there a process in place to ensure customer concerns are resolved promptly?
- Are customer complaints analyzed to determine underlying causes and prevent recurrence of problems?

Chapter 8
Review

The following comments are excerpted from each chapter for review purpose.

Introduction

- We should move from talking about tools to talking about our cause.

- This is indeed a very significant change, and one that will cause quality improvement to catapult into a top-priority goal in every American industry during the 1990s.

- Absolute and thorough understanding of the CEO Poppa of what quality improvement was about and his intention to use it helped move the company into the 1990s. He was not after a short-term fix.

- What is needed in the United States is an infrastructure of quality improvement that with guiding principles will work, as the giants of quality improvement have practiced throughout their lives.

- Let's discover what must be done to make the phrase "Made in the USA" one we can be proud of again.

- I propose that colleges and universities develop a graduate-level and undergraduate-level degree in quality improvement.

Chapter 1

- The dream of building a company that could compete with IBM in all areas, including mainframe computers, had ended.

- In just over two years Poppa was able to lead StorageTek out of chapter 11 and back into profitability. This is the fastest turnaround of any company in the high-tech industry.

- In 1988 Poppa decided to search for a person to lead the corporation in the area of quality improvement.

- In the days prior to chapter 11, StorageTek had always been a gunslinger, meaning the rewards went to rugged individualists who, for one reason or another, climbed the ladder by putting out fires. I was at least the seventh person to serve as quality vice-president over the last decade.

- The major mistakes were overextension and lack of attention to quality.

- In late 1988 highest level management decided that a group with a cross-functional mix should be put together to analyze the situation and make recommendations that would aid the organization in creating an integrated approach and an improvement plan for the entire company.

- We decided to develop a corporate strategy for achieving a total quality culture that defines and integrates the processes and systems necessary to continuously improve individual and organizational performance.

- People are the key to StorageTek's success. Individual recognition and advancement will be based upon performance that supports StorageTek's commitments to its customers and investors.

- We will act with integrity to ensure credibility in our relationships with our customers, investors, fellow employees, suppliers, and those communities in which we operate worldwide.

- Our standards of quality will ensure our competitiveness. We will sacrifice short-term gain for reliability and excellence in serving our customers' needs.

- Our business will be managed to achieve planned growth and long-term profitability. We will grow by building upon demonstrated strengths and meeting customers' needs.

- Each of us at StorageTek will participate in and contribute to the cost-effective, timely resolution of challenges and opportunities that continuously improve our customer commitment.

- Of the 89 driving forces, 90 percent fell in the management category and 10 percent in the worker category.

- Seventy-eight percent of the driving forces were aimed at director levels and above; at StorageTek, these are significantly high levels.

- There was no question that in due time the officers, after examining and evaluating the quality information, agreed that something needed to be done to move the corporation in the direction that the last task force had recommended.

Chapter 2

- A significant event in the history of StorageTek's quality improvement effort was a meeting that the chair scheduled at a retreat setting. He reminded the upper-level management attendees that all of the company's operations needed to be high quality, not just those directly related to the product line. The La Chaumière meeting could be characterized as the very beginning of serious movement toward quality improvement at StorageTek.

- A group that became known as the Five-Year Quality Improvement Team was formulated to examine practices in StorageTek and in other industries and to develop an overall quality improvement strategy for the corporation.

- During the norm stage, the group latched onto the Baldrige award criteria and really got to work, in terms of first understanding it and then applying it to the StorageTek culture.

- During the perform stage, most of the work took place by subgroups writing the different sections of the strategy, based on the elements of the Baldrige award criteria.

- All senior officers and executives will be role models through actions consistent with the principles of ETQ.

- Senior management will define and communicate the company's quality principles to all employees.

- Senior management will participate in and demonstrate leadership in the use of the quality improvement and problem-solving processes.

- Management will foster teamwork and obtain feedback from employees on the management style and behavior changes that are required to support ETQ.

- Senior management will use appropriate forms of recognition and reward to encourage employee practices in support of ETQ.

- A corporate officer process improvement council will be created to provide top-level leadership for achieving ETQ.

- Quality planning, establishing short-term and long-range goals, and allocating resources to attain these goals will be fully integrated with formal business-planning activities.

- The ETQ management network will drive the implementation of the process and ensure that the required resources are allocated.

- The Corporate Officer Process Improvement Council is formed. It is made up of the corporate management committee chaired by the CEO, and vice-chaired by the vice-president of corporate quality.

- Each corporate officer process improvement council member will appoint a quality officer(s) to support the execution of ETQ as a member of the Five-Year Quality Improvement Team.

- Chaired by the functional head and made up of all direct reports, the functional staff process improvement councils are responsible for managing the installation and operation of ETQ in their functional areas.

- All managers will act as leaders of their department process improvement teams.

- The corporate quality office, under the direction of the vice-president of corporate quality, will provide support to the management network in implementing ETQ.

- Benchmarking will be used as a key planning tool for meeting customer requirements.

- Information systems required to manage for quality improvement will be identified and prioritized.

- All data systems will meet specific criteria.

- All information systems will meet specific criteria.

- Methods will be defined for improving the integration of information systems.

- Balanced reward systems will be instituted to ensure that all employees are recognized on the basis of quality improvement, team accomplishment, individual contribution, and corporate profitability.

- A formal human resource utilization planning process will be integrated into the corporate business and quality plans.

- Continuous improvement in the quality of work life will be ensured through the implementation of programs in health, wellness, environmental concern, morale, and safety.

- Systems that value employees as the critical resource and asset of StorageTek will be instituted to attract and retain a high-quality work force.

- All StorageTek employees will be trained in the skills, knowledge, and practices required to achieve ETQ.

- A top-down implementation strategy will cascade the core training program throughout the organization using intact, project-focused work groups.

- The education capacity of the organization will be self-sustaining.

- Corporate processes will be developed and used to ensure that new products and services are designed to meet or exceed customer expectations.

- Systems will be developed to measure, evaluate, optimize, and maintain the capability of critical processes for new and existing products.

- Consistent process measurement philosophy and methodologies will be established.

- An audit process will be established to assess quality assurance systems and the quality of products and services.

- A standardized quality documentation system will be developed to define our systems and processes accurately.

- The current system for quality assurance of internal support functions will be upgraded.

- The current system for ensuring the quality of purchased materials, products, and services will be improved.

- Quality results will be based on the requirements and expectations of our customers.

- Trends in quality data will be used to identify improvement opportunities.

- The corporation will emphasize process rather than only results.

- Corporate measurements will be used to track quality improvement and not to provide goals for individual functions.

- Reducing cycle time within processes is a key strategic goal.

- New methods to understand customer needs and expectations will be developed and current methods will be improved.

- New guidelines for managing customer relationships will be created and existing guidelines improved.

- The systems and methods that StorageTek uses for determining customer satisfaction will be reviewed and documented, and new systems will be implemented where inadequate or no systems exist.

- Communication processes with customers, employees, and suppliers will be defined and improved so that all parties involved in any customer/supplier relationship become effective participants.

Chapter 3

- It is more important for a company to be in existence 10, 20, or 30 years from now than it is to reach the next quarterly dividend.

- The concept of delighting customers is that it's just not good enough to have only satisfied customers.

- Deming reminds us that only top management can establish the constancy of purpose necessary to know and exceed the customers' needs and expectations.

- Deming suggests that we are in a new economic age. This is the age of world competitors vying for producing products and providing services throughout the world.

- Deming's ideas have helped wake up American industry to the fact that we are in a new economic age and that listening to the customer is perhaps the most vital part. We no longer could experience the comfort of competing with one another with a poor product.

- Deming's formula is that as quality improves so does productivity by lowering waste, restarts, and rework. This allows companies to produce higher quality goods and services at lower costs so that those companies can stay in business and provide more jobs over the long haul.

- Deming does not say we must eliminate all inspection. He says we cannot get quality by inspecting it in.

- What happened over time was that inspectors found bad tires and put them in a corner. The tires stayed there for a while, other inspectors came and looked at them more thoroughly, then wrote up more detailed reports on the defects but never got back to the source of the defect to fix the process.

- What is being encouraged here is to go away from the old expensive way of doing business of trying to manage the outcomes by detecting defects.

- You must know *what* you are buying, not just the price.

- Very often the cheapest product introduces variation into the process and, therefore, introduces failure and defects which then become known to the customer.

- Another point that Deming makes is to establish long-term relationships that include loyalty and trust with sole suppliers rather than an array of suppliers. Connected with this is the notion that customers ought to help suppliers with their quality improvement effort.

- As Deming would say, "We in America have worried about meeting specifications in contrast to the Japanese who worry about uniformity, working for less, and less variation."

- Imai states that there are two kinds of criteria: process criteria and results criteria.

- Shewhart gave us the idea that there are two reasons for variation: (1) common causes are process problems and 100 percent owned by management, and (2) special causes that are usually in the area of defects or errors caused by people, machines, or tools.

- When you improve quality, you improve productivity. Costs go down when you improve the process.

- Motorola, without knowing it, started saving in a major way when it embarked on its first quality improvement effort, even though quality needed to be improved and was improved over the years.

- If we are constantly looking in the people area, we are in the 15 percent area and missed the boat of following the process problems 85 percent of the time.

- Do not manage defects; study the system that produced the defects. This requires intensive training because it is indeed a new way to manage and we did not manage that way in the past.

- Deming suggests not cutting long-term education programs. We need more education, not less.

- Deming suggests that training should help each employee know and understand the requirements of the next stage of the process.

- Deming has been talking about leadership for years, and suddenly people in the field are now beginning to talk about leadership.

- A leader has a vision of where the organization or corporation is headed in the long term and can communicate that vision extremely well. The manager, on the other hand, manages things.

- Deming suggests eliminating the abuse of on-the-job training.

- Deming suggests that training on the people skills, in the education centers of corporations, needs to be endorsed and followed on the job. This is exactly what Deming is referring to when he talks about the devastating effects of micro-management.

- It's important for management to walk the talk and recognize that people are the organization's most important resource.

- Deming states that "without an atmosphere of mutual respect, no statistically based management system will work."

- The challenge for managers is to recognize that fear exists. We need to be aware of this and take action to alleviate and eliminate the fear aspect whenever and wherever possible.

- Corporate politics will destroy quality and destroy a company. "If you can't look better, the next best thing is to make everyone else look worse."

- Deming suggests that we should identify walls and tear them down.

- We are now teaching our managers how to coach, teach, and nurture in order to change the perspective of the boss being the customer. (I was astonished that this theory had been around since 1924.)

- When we ask the question, "Is the process messed up?" we are in the 85 percent area of common causes.

- Causes of low quality and low productivity belong to the system; that is the process and thus beyond the power of the work force.

- We heard the bead story: "Now, Mary, you know you got a merit raise yesterday. You one of our best employees, and yet you have 10 red beads. What a horrible performance."

- Work standards tend to cap the amount of improvement that can be achieved.

- One alternative that we have found successful is to have executives share MBOs.

- A suggestion here would be to separate performance appraisal from merit review.

- Find a friend means to work in a nonhostile environment in implementing quality improvement.

- We gather success stories from many different organizations utilizing the basic quality tenets and share those regularly in the monthly printed employee bulletins and also by word of mouth in various staff meetings.

- The barriers against pride of workmanship may well be one of the most important obstacles to the reduction of cost and improvement of quality in the United States today.

- The Shewhart cycle includes planning the work, doing it, checking to see if we did what we said we were going to do, and then finding the flaws and acting to improve the full cycle.

- At StorageTek, many of our top executives carry in their wallet or shirt pocket two things: the ETQ principles and Deming's 14 points.

Chapter 4

- The implementation strategy for any quality improvement effort needs to consider an evolutionary approach rather than a revolutionary approach.

- This discussion is broken down into five parts: (1) educating yourself, (2) finding a friend, (3) implementing quality improvement in that friend's organization, (4) recording and telling about successes, and (5) waiting for the phone to ring.

- A primary thrust is to capture the energy, skill, and knowledge of those closest to the work. The second major thrust is knowledge of the theory of variability.

- Defect detection alone will not improve the process because very often the defect occurs or is found long after the incident occurs.

- Imai discusses a diagram that I have referred to many times in writings and speeches. The Japanese work daily to improve the process and use encouragement techniques to ensure that this happens; results occur after examination of the processes.

- I spent three days learning about the discipline of force field analysis and obtaining a better understanding of all the forces that were impeding the project, and then defining specific actions that could be taken to alleviate those negative forces.

- A decade later in an entirely different organization and environment, I was exposed to the discipline of cause and effect that was developed by Ishikawa.

- What I have not seen is the two disciplines directly connected. The power that exists when the two disciplines are used in concert is explained.

- Deming describes that line as *the level of line* and usually it is very good to try to use the words *the level of* as the first three words of defining that particular force field.

- One person even used CE/FFA in a church environment, another in a school environment, and another in real estate situation.

- Using cause-and-effect diagrams has been an eye-opener to hundreds of managers and executives across the world in helping them understand the theory of CE/FFA.

- The new economic age does not allow years and years of effort to reach a plateau of satisfactory quality improvement. We must learn to maximize on time and actually reduce the cycle time by introducing quality improvement throughout all industry.

- When a person is speaking about a subject with which he or she is familiar, he or she doesn't need to worry about the techniques of delivering a speech.

- Using CE/FFA, the QAT and QRT reduced the failure rate to less than 0.5 percent.

Chapter 5

- On January 19, 1990, the CEO Poppa formally announced the ETQ strategy to his corporate staff at StorageTek.

- This team was given the responsibility for developing a five-year corporate strategy and implementation guidelines to ensure continuous quality improvement at StorageTek.

- Proud as we are of our past accomplishments, we must be mindful of the environment in which we compete.

- It is clear that we must face squarely these issues of improved quality and reduced cycle times as key determinants in StorageTek's ability to survive and grow in the information storage and retrieval industry.

- Customer satisfaction is our number one priority.

- The primary vehicle for implementing ETQ is the quality improvement process known as QIP.

- Documenting the current process with a flowchart helps everyone who works in the process understand how the process actually operates, including the interactions with customers and suppliers.

- Processes can be flowcharted at different levels.

- Once the process is described, we must identify the owner of the process.

- Effective measurements help to assess the performance of the process as it relates to supplier and customer requirements.

- Establish a feedback system with customers and suppliers to monitor performance objectively and foster improvement.

- Quality costs are the costs specifically associated with the achievement and maintenance of product or service quality.

- Prevention costs are the costs of activities associated with planning, implementing, maintaining, and monitoring a quality system that will prevent the occurrence of failures. Do the right things right the first time!

- Appraisal costs are the costs of activities associated with determining the degree of conformance to quality specifications the first time through. How are we doing?

- Failure costs are the costs of the product and/or service found defective, plus the cost of effort associated with correcting or disposing of the failures.

- Step 5 requires that you organize a quality improvement team and develop an action plan to address selected opportunities.

- Prepare and deliver a presentation to management to gain its approval for implementing your solutions.

- Recognizing and rewarding successful efforts is critical to sustaining motivation for continuous quality improvement.

- A very important part of the ETQ strategy is concentration and implementation of five change mechanisms.

- The first of these five change mechanisms is to communicate the ETQ strategy to all employees and stress the importance of quality improvement.

- The second change mechanism is to give all employees the skill and knowledge needed to improve quality and customer satisfaction continuously.

- The third change mechanism is implementing the management network necessary to drive the implementation of ETQ throughout the corporation.

- The fourth change mechanism is implementation of our nine-step quality improvement process.

- We have also set up a rewards and recognition group that meets weekly to benchmark with other companies and formulate recommendations for improvement for the Quality Advisory Group and the Corporate Management Committee Process Improvement Council (CMCPIC).

- We recently won the Xerox Award of Excellence, a result of our long-time supplier relationship with Xerox. We won the Shell Partnership in Quality Award due to Shell's active involvement in the design of one of our primary products known as the 4400 ACS library. We won the Convex Computer Corp. award for high quality and on-time delivery of products, as well as the Avis "We Try Harder" total quality award and the United States Postal Service Quality Award. We have been honored by the Juran Institute when it selected StorageTek as the keynote company in 1992. We also earned ISO 9001 registration from the British Standards Institute.

Chapter 6

- ETQ core training is a course that has been provided to over 10,000 people at StorageTek worldwide.

- Included in module I is a discussion of the Deming philosophy and a general reference to his 14 points.

- Throughout the course, the instructors use an icebreaker at various times, such as just after lunch or at the beginning of a session.

- One segment of module II discusses, defines, and ensures that everyone understands the concept of consensus.

- A process is defined as the organization of people, equipment, energy, procedures, and material into the work activities needed to produce a specified result or work product.

- Module III addresses the difference between the traditional organizational approach, with a definition and example of a vertical organization, and a process-oriented approach that flows across many organizations.

- The quality improvement process is a nine-step process that will assist in the continuous process improvement.
- Module V concentrates on how members of teams can learn to be team players.
- In our discussion with customers, we often talk about the dramatic improvements in financials and in product quality.
- A discussion of the eight criteria indicates how StorageTek sizes up in regard to each.
- The first criterion is that stretch goals can be met; however, they cannot be met using the pedestrian pace of the ordinary learning curve.
- The second characteristic that Juran discusses is adopting the big Q concept.
- The third characteristic that Juran talks about is ownership of multifunctional processes and assigning executive leadership.
- The fourth characteristic is to create an infrastructure for improvement.
- The fifth characteristic is that a lot of work is required.
- The sixth characteristic is that upper managers must lead the effort personally.
- The seventh characteristic is that the Taylor system must be replaced.
- The eighth and last characteristic is that quality goals must be incorporated into the business plan.

Chapter 7

- Establishment of a management network to push the entire process throughout the company is an absolute must.
- The management network also consists of the QAG, which is a very important catalyst to drive ETQ throughout the organization.

- Another important part of the management network is the fact that we have quality officers in every division and in every subsidiary throughout the world.

- One aspect of the management network that is disruptive is the mobility of management.

- It is important that the top quality officer report to the top-level person in the company.

- What needs to be done is not only to be able to make presentations, but to be able to work with people throughout the company at all levels, especially the very lowest levels.

- Another thought that comes to mind is about getting instant results. I disagree with this. What I think the gurus are saying when they say there are no instant results or instant pudding is that you can't stop after plucking the low-lying fruit.

- What reengineering experts don't recognize is the breakthrough idea.

- Education for quality improvement must be pervasive.

- Communication is a never-ending process that needs to be addressed by the top-level quality officer in the company. Major success stories need to be shared.

- Each company has its own culture and way of rewarding and recognizing.

- Now the top officers of the company share four objectives, one of which is implementing the quality effort.

- One of the major issues that I'm excited about (because it has been bothering me for about 35 years) is changing the appraisal system.

- We know that shipping and fixing in the field is no longer an appropriate strategy.

- If I had to give one guideline about how to do customer surveys, it would be do it with simplicity.

- In my work with many small groups over the past 10 years, I can say with a great deal of conviction that the small groups who have been working on processes for months and years know more about how to improve these processes than anyone.

- CE/FFA is a problem-solving technique, but it goes far beyond that.

- I know that the great majority says you get what you measure. There is a small minority who caution, "Watch out, you may only get what you measure."

- I firmly believe Deming's observation that what you can measure is really only the tip of the iceberg.

Introduction
to Appendices

This appendix contains a series of examples of the work of teams in using the CE/FFA problem-solving method and the quality improvement process.

Appendix A was developed by the Division of Forestry in Florida. After experiencing the three-phase approach outlined in chapter 4, the DOF wrote this step-by-step procedure for all team members. This is a good addition to help managers understand how quality improvement can work in the service sector.

Appendix B is the work of an accounting group that worked to understand and develop means to level the amount of accounts receivable defects. The QAT made recommendations that resulted in setting accounts receivable targets and compensation plans, revising orders/invoicing process and policies as well as pricing policies.

Appendix C comes from an information systems team. They discovered why the help desk was not as effective as it could be. They brainstormed the issues/problems (page 213) then used this list to develop the major causes (page 215). The force field analysis on each cause is found on pages 216–221, with summary information on pages 222–223.

Appendix D describes an improvement in the media label process. Of particular importance in the team's work is the use of flow diagrams. The customer/supplier agreement on page 233 is also worthy of note.

Appendix E is the work of a software development group that worked to better meet its customer requirements. It also started with a brainstorming session found on page 237, the cause and effect on page 238, and the force field analysis on pages 239–243. Summary findings are on pages 244–245.

Appendix F is the work of an electrical development group. Its brainstorming session on page 247 evolved to a definition of causes on page 248 with the force field analysis following on pages 249–253. Summary findings are on page 254.

Appendix G is the work of a group on increasing inventory turns. Although the corporate strategy called for reaching 6.8 turns by 1994 this group's work helped the corporation reach 7.2 turns by year-end 1992, a 288 percent improvement since 1988. It used a modified force field analysis technique on page 256, flowchart on page 258, and customer/supplier agreements on page 259.

Appendix H is the work of an accounting group. It discovered a breakdown between two organizations (application systems and procedure review). It used the cause-and-effect method (page 262) and force field analysis (pages 263–267). Summary results are on page 268. Note that it reduced override errors by 80 percent and saved the company $3 million.

Appendix I is the work of an information systems team. The team tackled the problem of quality issues not being resolved. The five reasons for this are found in the cause and effect on page 271. The force field analysis follows on pages 272–275. The resolution and actions taken are described in the What's Next section.

Appendix J is the work of a cross-functional team from manufacturing and product procurement. It used the nine-step quality improvement process described in chapter 5. The use of two bin is now 100 percent. As a result, downtime is zero. Manual counting has been eliminated.

Appendix K is the quality action team that entered the national team competition sponsored by the Association for Quality and Productivity. The team won from the 18 teams selected throughout the United States, competing at a national conference held in New Orleans in spring 1993. It won the bronze award for third place.

The Customer Services Quality Invoicing (CSQI) Process Improvement Team was formed with the goal of addressing the problem of invalid special maintenance invoicing and with ensuring the integrity of approximately $11 million annually in maintenance revenues. All project objectives were completed due to StorageTek's strong commitment to quality improvement and the solid dedication of the CSQI team members.

Appendix A
Quality Action System
Facilitator Manual

Foreword

I fully endorse the Forestry Division (of Florida) Quality Action System Facilitator Manual. Much work went into adapting this process, which was described in the second edition of my book, *An Approach to Quality Improvement That Works.*

Advice to the Management Team

Listening to employees' ideas is not new; it's just something we need to learn how to do better in the 1990s. The CE/FFA problem-solving process is powerful in helping crystalize employees' ideas in a fairly short amount of time. Very often these ideas hit at the heart of better communication, better morale, better participation, and better use of time. When the problem being explored is technical in nature, more data may be required to verify direction. Use of the statistical tools may be necessary in these situations.

It is imperative that the appropriate levels of management attend the phase III presentation to management. The major role of the management team in phase III is to listen first and then agree to form a quality resolution team to pursue all cures and try to implement them.

It is very important that the appropriate manager chair the QRT. He or she should be supported with the kind of membership on the QRT that can get things done. It is not necessary that all members of the QRT come from management; some can be members of the original QAT.

Track progress on the implementation plan form and let the original QAT and the entire organization know about progress.

Advice to Facilitators

As noted in my book, always understand and believe that a small group of experts has an enormous amount of skill and knowledge that needs to be tapped and that your job is to tap that skill and knowledge. Use of CE/FFA as described in the handbook will help you do this.

Advice to QAT Members

You have been selected because you are highly thought of experts in the problem area being analyzed. The future of your organization may well depend on how well you succeed in using the CE/FFA tool. Be open, be honest, and do not fear to express your opinion. Your management team sincerely believes you can help improve operations, eliminate waste, and help provide lowest cost, highest quality services that will keep the division in business and provide more jobs.

A. Donald Stratton
Author, *An Approach to Quality
Improvement That Works*

Contents

Introduction

> *"I will not make decisions until I have considered the opinion of all who wish to speak; for I know that my power is only as great as their support."*
>
> tribal chief, Botswana Nation

Management at the Division of Forestry (DOF) believes that those doing the job are the experts, and the experts should be a part of the managerial decision-making process.

When employees contribute their ideas to improve operations or help solve problems, they become valued members of the team and not just workers. DOF managers know that by tapping the valuable employee resource, they will accomplish the DOF mission and provide a better service to customers, the people of the state of Florida; improve the quality of work life for employees; promote leadership; inspire teamwork; and improve communications.

This manual is a step-by-step process intended to enhance communications between employees and managers. The process is called the *quality action system,* and, simply put, it allows employees to break down a problem and make recommendations to managers that could lead to improved conditions.

This Quality Action System Facilitator Manual was developed for the Florida DOF by David Core, reforestation coordinator, and Jim Parry, organizational development coordinator. It represents a customized version of Don Stratton's published work, *An Approach to Quality Improvement That Works.* We wish to thank Mr. Stratton for reviewing this manual and providing us with his valuable editorial comments.

Phase I
Preparation (Before the QAT Session)

Step 1: Employees or Managers Identify the Problem
Anything that decreases the effectiveness of the DOF can be identified as a problem. Problems can be identified by anyone in the organization but should be approved for the quality action system process by the appropriate managers.

Step 2: Employees and Managers Select the Facilitator(s)

Once a problem is identified and approved for the quality action system process, the employees and managers involved with the problem should select a facilitator. The facilitator should be someone who has participated on a QAT and, by following the steps in this facilitator manual, could function as a QAT facilitator. To function as a QAT facilitator means the facilitator must do the following:

- Remain neutral.
- Allow free and open group discussions.
- Refrain from making speeches or censoring discussions.
- Keep the team on track without stifling contributions.
- Seek agreement when combining.
- Record true consensus on paper.

And, most important, the facilitator must sincerely believe and accept that the QAT knows more about the problem than he or she does.

Step 3: Employees, Managers, and the Facilitator Select the QAT Members

The QAT members may be selected by the employees, the managers associated with the problem, the facilitator, or all three. Selection criteria will vary with the issues, but members should always be employees who have direct and close association with the problem.

Each QAT member should have enough time to express his or her thoughts completely in the session. Normally, a team of from six to 10 people may need up to eight hours. (More members may require more time.)

The QAT may elect to define the problem (refer to phase II, step 1) at this time. A correctly defined problem statement at this point in the process may help the QAT members focus on the problem before the QAT session starts.

Step 4: Managers Select the QRT Leader

Managers should select a QRT leader during phase I because the leader will need time to select the other QRT members and schedule their participation at the management presentation. The QRT leader and members are required to attend the phase III management presentation.

The QRT leader should be the manager who is most closely associated with the QAT problem. QRT members should be primarily managers with the authority to implement recommendations from the QAT. One or two QAT members may serve on the QRT for the sake of continuity, clarification or recommendations, and so on.

Step 5: QAT Collects Relevant Information

Occasionally it may be necessary to collect information about a problem to analyze that problem effectively.

Before the QAT session, members and their facilitator should assign this information collection to QAT members or request it from other personnel in the organization.

Example

Problem statement: The number of fires caused by people in _____ County is too high. Collect information on the following.

• Statistics on types of fires caused by people

• Long-term fire frequency

• Statistics comparing the county with others

• History of the county's fire prevention program

• Pertinent weather information, and so on.

Another way to collect information is to invite experts in the field to participate as consultants in the QAT session.

Step 6: Facilitator Makes Logistic Arrangements

The QAT facilitator should be responsible for scheduling the QAT session time and place and notifying all QAT participants. He or she should also make the arrangements for the room and equipment.

The room should be free from distractions and large enough to seat QAT members in a semicircle around the facilitator with extra space for consultants. Consideration should also be given for space to accommodate managers during the phase III, step 3 management presentation.

The following equipment is suggested:

• Two flip chart pads

• Two flip chart easels

- Several differently colored markers
- Masking tape
- The Quality Action System Facilitator Manual

The QAT session is hard work and may require two facilitators. Frequent breaks, refreshments, and a proper lunch hour are recommended.

Step 7: Facilitator Organizes the Time Frame

The time table below is based on an average QAT session with six to 10 members. (Your time frame may vary.)

Phase	Step	Time Required
Preparation (Phase I)	Steps 1–7	Variable
Analyze the problem (Phase II)	Step 1	2 hours
	Step 2	4 hours
Presentation to management (Phase III)	Step 1	1 hour

Total = 7 hours (plus lunch and breaks)

Phase II
Analyze the Problem (During the QAT Session)

Step 1: QAT Defines the Problem and Determines its Causes

Defining the problem was first mentioned in phase I, step 1: The QAT may elect to accomplish this before the QAT session. Phase II, analyze the problem, is carried out during the QAT session. If it was not done before, the problem must be defined and stated correctly as a first step in the analysis. Defining the problem correctly may be the most important step in the quality action system process because an inaccurately defined problem could sidetrack or stagnate a QAT.

The problem must be stated in a way that will allow the QAT members to examine the various causes of the problem.

Examples of correctly defined and stated problems are as follows:

Example 1
The district volunteer program is not as effective as it could be.

Example 2
The number of fires caused by people in Suwannee County is too high.

The facilitator should use brainstorming and the problem/cause diagram shown in Figure A.1(a) to generate and record the team's work. The example in Figure A.1(b) shows how the problem/cause diagram is used for a specific problem.

There are three main points to remember when developing the problem/cause diagram.

1. Make general cause statements. They will be analyzed in detail in phase II, step 2.

2. Consolidate and combine cause statements as much as possible. There is no arbitrary limit to the number of causes to a problem, but too large a number to process (more than six) may exhaust the energy of the team.

3. Prioritize (or rank order) the causes and analyze them in your priority order.

Step 2: QAT Analyzes the Causes and Generates Recommendations
The disease/cure diagram shown in Figure A.2(a) should be used to analyze each cause revealed in the problem/cause diagram. (A creative DOF QAT suggested these specific reasons be called *diseases* for simplicity and understanding, and it stuck.) Each cause will have its own disease/cure diagram.

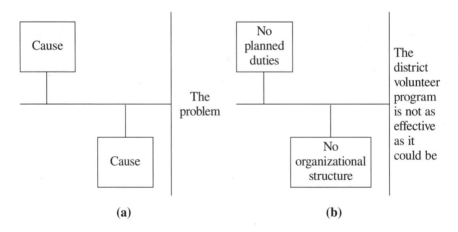

Figure A.1. Problem/cause diagrams.

Cause

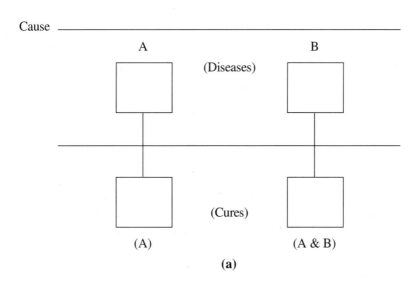

Figure A.2. Disease/cure diagrams.

This diagram helps the team to break down the general cause statement into specific reasons for the cause.

After the diseases are diagrammed, the team may then identify possible solutions for each disease. The same QAT suggested calling these solutions *cures.*

The important function of the QAT at this point is to identify the specific tasks that will accomplish each cure.

The specific tasks to accomplish each cure are important because they are the QAT's recommendations that will be categorized by the QRT on the implementation plan.

Each specific task must be described in detail to explain its intent to the QRT. For example, "conduct area meetings on a monthly basis," would be a specific task associated with the general cure "improve information sharing."

The example in the disease/cure diagram, Figure A.2(b), shows where these specific tasks are attached to each cure. Also shown are reference letters for each disease. This lettering system provides the basis for linking recommended positive action (cures) to disease by ultimately assigning its respective letter. Note in the illustration that a specific cure has been linked to more than one disease.

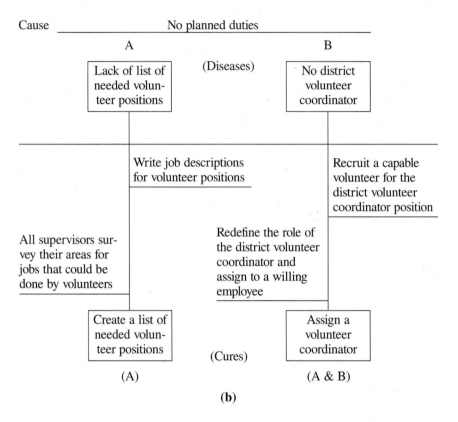

Cause _____ No planned duties _____

A   B

| Lack of list of needed volunteer positions | (Diseases) | No district volunteer coordinator |

| Write job descriptions for volunteer positions | | Recruit a capable volunteer for the district volunteer coordinator position |

| All supervisors survey their areas for jobs that could be done by volunteers | Redefine the role of the district volunteer coordinator and assign to a willing employee | |

| Create a list of needed volunteer positions | (Cures) | Assign a volunteer coordinator |

(A)   (A & B)

(b)

Figure A.2.   (continued)

Phase III
Presentation to Management (During the QAT Session)

The management presentation is the QAT members' opportunity to communicate their work to management. As mentioned in phase I, step 4, the QRT members consisting of managers associated with the problem are the management participants at this presentation. Remember, one or two QAT members may be needed to serve on the QRT to clarify recommendations made by the QAT. It has been assumed that the QAT members have an in-depth knowledge of the problem, and most are very willing to participate. This will also help provide communication back to the QAT in an informal way and provide a great opportunity to practice participative management.

Step 1: QAT Communicates the Problem/Cause and Disease/Cure Diagrams to the QRT
There is only one step in Phase III: present the problem/cause and disease/cure diagram material to the QRT. Participants should follow these specific guidelines to ensure successful communication between the QAT and QRT:

- The presentation to the QRT should occur during the last scheduled hour of the QAT session.

- Several QAT members should present the material from the flip charts.

- The QRT should not debate the merit of the QAT's recommendations during the presentation, but it may certainly ask questions to seek clarification on recommended actions.

- The QRT should ensure feedback to the QAT through the QRT implementation plan.

Phase IV
Implementation (After the QAT Session)
Step 1: QAT Develops and Distributes the QAT Report
Before the QAT session adjourns, the QAT should coordinate the transfer of the problem/cause and disease/cure flip chart diagrams to letter- or legal-size paper.

The QAT report includes these diagrams and a cover page consisting of (1) the problem statement, (2) QAT session location and date, and (3) names of facilitator(s) and QAT members.

The QAT report should be completed and distributed to all QAT participants within five working days after the QAT session. (The QRT cannot begin its work on the QRT Implementation Plan until it receives the QAT Report.)

Step 2: QRT Completes and Distributes the QRT Implementation Plan
After receiving the QAT report, the QRT should complete and distribute the QAT implementation plan within 10 working days.

The QRT should meet as a team and use the QAT report to complete the QRT implementation plan.

An illustration of the QRT implementation plan is included in this manual as Figure A.3.

Completion of the plan consists of filling in part 1 and part 2. The following is an explanation of the columns in part 2.

Recommended Tasks

Identify and list each specific task attached to its cure on the disease/cure diagram.

Implementation Categories

Place each specific task into one of the following implementation categories:

A = Accept recommendation and assign to
M = Accept modified recommendation and assign to
R = Reject recommendation because
O = Ongoing project (explain)
D = Directed to higher level of management (explain)

If the QRT members do not have the authority to assign or reject a task then that task is placed into the D category. The higher level manager has 10 working days to place the task into one of the implementation categories. This process continues until the task is placed into the A, M, R, or O category.

Explanation/Status

Give a brief explanation or status statement if needed.

Personnel Assigned

List the name and position of the person given an assignment or responsibility for an ongoing project or task.

Target Date

Note the anticipated date of completion for categories A and M.

Completion Date

Record the actual date of completion for categories A and M.

Copies of the completed QRT implementation plan should be distributed to QAT members and facilitator; personnel assigned in implementation categories A, M, and D; and the division organizational development coordinator.

QRT Implementation Plan

Problem statement: _____

Unit: _____ Date: _____ Facilitator(s): _____

QRT leader: _____

Name	Title
Name	Title
Name	Title
Name	Title
Name	Title

Implementation Categories

A = Accept recommendation and assign to

M = Accept modified recommendation and assign to

R = Reject recommendation because

O = Ongoing project (explain)

D = Directed to a higher level of management (explain)

Part 1

Recommended tasks	Implementation category	Explanation/ status	Personnel assigned	Target date	Completion date
Write job descriptions for volunteer positions	A	Determine jobs needing volunteers within each area; prepare job description	FASs	Sept. 2	Sept. 1
Redefine the role of the district volunteer coordinator and assign to a willing employee	M	Redefine the role and write a job description for volunteer	District manager	Sept. 15	Sept. 15
Recruit a capable volunteer for the district volunteer coordinator position	A	Check with other volunteer placement organizations	Duty officer supervisor	Sept. 20	Sept. 21

Part 2

Figure A.3. QRT implementation plan.

Phase V
Monitoring and Networking

Step 1: QRT Leader Responsibilities
The QRT leader is responsible for coordinating completion of the QRT implementation plan through the appropriate managers. This responsibility includes the following:

- Tracking each task to ensure its completion by the target date
- Updating the implementation plan when tasks are complete
- Providing feedback (implementation plan) to the QAT
- Submitting the implementation plan to the division organizational development coordinator when completed

Step 2: Networking
The division organizational development coordinator will network quality action system information to DOF personnel. The value of networking is that solutions to problems at one location may apply to other locations.

One method of communicating the status of QAT reports and QRT implementation plans is through DOF publications.

Quality Resolution Team Implementation Plan

Problem statement: _____

_____

_____

_____

_____

Unit: _____ Date: _____ Facilitator(s): _____

QRT leader: _____

QRT members:

Name	Title
Name	Title
Name	Title
Name	Title
Name	Title
Name	Title
Name	Title
Name	Title

Quality Resolution Team Implementation Plan

Recommended tasks	Implementation category	Explanation/ status	Personnel assigned	Target date	Completion date

Implementation Categories

A = Accept recommendation and assign to . . .

M = Accept modified recommendation and assign to . . .

R = Reject recommendation because . . .

O = Ongoing project (explain)

D = Directed to a higher level of management (explain)

Appendix B
Whipping Accounts Receivable
Quality Action Team

Task/Event

- Development of SPC charts

- Accounts receivable/SPC presentation to regional controllers

- Accounts receivable QAT meeting in Louisville
  –Accounts receivable process flows shared
  –Mission statement defined
  –Cause-effect diagram completed
  –First force field analysis tackled

- First draft of all eight force field analyses submitted

- Status review with top management

- Final input to force field analyses received

- QAT follow-up meeting in Atlanta
  –Force fields reviewed
  –Regional personnel interviewed

- Survey of accounts receivable representatives

- Presentation to management

Problem statement: Accounts receivable delinquency trends are up, indicating instability in the process.

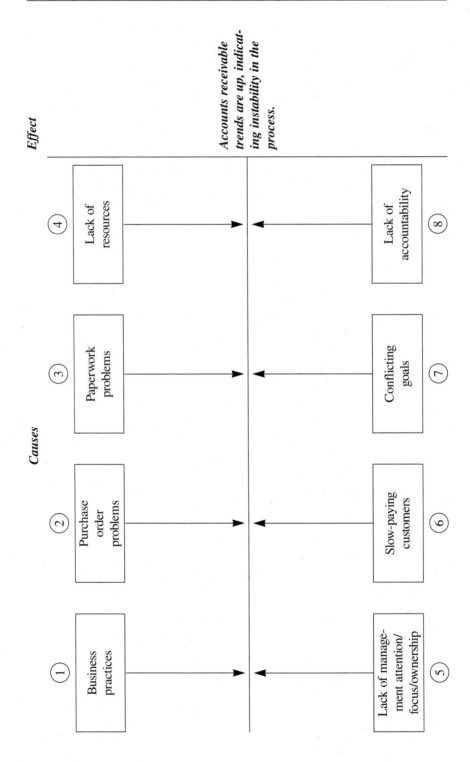

Effect

Accounts receivable trends are up, indicating instability in the process.

Causes

① Business practices

② Purchase order problems

③ Paperwork problems

④ Lack of resources

⑤ Lack of management attention/ focus/ownership

⑥ Slow-paying customers

⑦ Conflicting goals

⑧ Lack of accountability

1. The level of negative impact by business practices is too high.

Driving Forces

A, C, D, E, G, H	A	A, B, C, H	E, H	F	C		
Management focus [M]	Compensation plan changes—management incentive [M]	Awareness of accounting practices [M/W]	Hire regional contracts manager [M]	Evaluate invoicing policies/practices [M]	Review credit evaluation policy/procedures [M]		
–Address conflicting priorities –Evaluate practice of requiring purchase order –Implement credit watch	–50 percent commissions based on cash received for purchases –Address management bonus plans –Evaluate bonus plan for billing	–Reversing marketing-initiated third-party sales when appropriate –Invoicing –Early invoicing purchases –Payment terms	–Define responsibilities –Emphasis on up-front T and Cs and invoicing requirements	–Billing in arrears –Prompt pay discounts			
–Recognition of end-user sales –Measurement inconsistent	–Customers seek third-party financing after the fact	–Credit limitations	–Verbal orders –Large percent of business received at end of quarter –Distorts accounts receivable measurements—negative impact Over 60—positive impact		–Contributes to large volume of retroactive paperwork	–Dramatic effect of one invoice	
Revenue recognition modified	Fewer marketing-initiated third parties	Credit evaluations not completed on existing customers	Quarter end bunching of sales	Position not 100 percent defined or in place	Billing in advance	Larger business deals	Purchase orders not a requirement of invoicing
A	B	C	D	E	F	G	H

Restraining Forces

2. The level of negative impact on receivables as a result of delinquent/missing purchase orders is too high.

Driving Forces

A	B	B, D, E, C	B	E	B, C, D, E, F	B
Evaluate changing cycle billing to arrears [M]	Address conflicting goals [M]	Hire regional contracts manager [M]	Hold invoice requests pending purchase orders [M]	Standardize price changes [M]	Evaluate/analyze purchase order process [M/W]	Offer discount for timely issuance of purchase orders [M]
–Select active purchase order accounts –Evaluate change of payment terms	–Compensation	–Emphasis on invoicing requirements	–Develop regionalized listing of known purchase order customers –Address conflicting goals	–Field training –Rate increase QAT	–Understand bid process –Evaluate paperwork flow –Determine system requirements –Understand customer requirements	
–Shorter lead time to address changes	–Lack of clear responsibility –Commissions not impacted	–Nonpayment is first indication	–Modification to purchase order contract is required	–Business practices –Pricing committee –Increase notification problems	–Business practices –City, state, local governments/bids –Fiscal funded always late	
Cycle billing in advance	Purchase order not obtained before order submitted	Customer is not identified as purchase order oriented	Purchase order language is not in agreement with underlying contract	Purchase order does not allow for ongoing rate changes	Federal government schedule late	
A	B	C	D	E	F	

Restraining Forces

3. The number of paperwork problems is too high.

Driving Forces

A, B, C	A, B, C	A, B, C	A, B, C	A, B
Provide ongoing training [M]	Evaluate and improve the process [M, W]	Provide forum for communication [M]	Establish a rate administration QAT [M]	Complete system changes [M]

–Return on assets
–Advance requisition
–Billing
–Marketing representative
	–Define job responsibilities
	–Establish priorities
	–Address headcount/manpower issues
		–Administrative representation at the following:
		  territory reviews
		  district meetings
		  regional meetings
		  quarterly reviews
			–Address overall maintenance increase process
			–Address pricing guide updates	

–Correcting (rebilling, and so on) are low priority –Grooming of aging lowest priority –Increase discrepancies difficult to get reversed –Late submission of paperwork from the field	–Number of incorrect/insufficient paperwork received –Limited communication between groups –Unacceptable backlog levels –High turnover	–Lack of understanding with system or processes –Lack of resources and training –Retroactive paperwork –Little or no compensation for turning in paperwork on time –Untimely pricing guide updates		
Billing problems	Return on assets problems	Marketing representative problems		
A	B	C		

Restraining Forces

4. The level of negative impact by lack of resources is too high.

Driving Forces

A, B, C	B, C, E	B, C, D	B, C, E	B, C, E
Allocate budget dollars for a secretary for administration [M]	Evaluate and improve the process [M]	Complete index [M]	Provide training [M]	Optimize MIS support [M]
–Allocate –Share secretarial resources –Provide necessary support: statements, purchase order expiration reports, customer correspondence	–Address process changes made possible by transfer of cycle billing –Improve communication –Eliminate duplication	–Spartan system enhancements –System date recalculations –System download of all transactions	–Budget accounts receivable workshop 1991 –Share processes through QAT –Cross-train	–Relook MIS support structure

A	B	C	D	E
–Resources not available to send timely letters to customer –Clerical functions shifting from headquarters to regions	–End-user priorities –Change of philosophy from 60 to 30 –Preventative measures	–Headquarters accounts receivable support reduced from five to one over the last 12 months	–Incorrect sales orders –Untimely resolution of problems –Cumbersome reroute process	–Last U.S. accounts receivable workshop 1987 –Lack of cross-functional awareness
Lack of secretarial support	Lack of time to address all receivables	Reduction in headquarters accounts receivable support	Minimal completion	Lack of training
A	B	C	D	E

Restraining Forces

5. The lack of consistent management attention contributes to the increase in receivables.

Driving Forces

A, C, D	A, C, D	B	A, C, D, E
Monthly CMC focus [M]	**Focus on asset management** [M]	**WAR QAT** [M/W]	**Redefine measurements** [M]
–Develop list of key indicators –Establish ownership	–Possibility for improving corporate cash position	–Subsequent QRTs –Related QATs: rate ad, disputed special maintenance	–Regional controller initiated –Include accounts receivable representatives –Monthly targets –Regional management focus

–Focus on issue only when perceived as a problem –Focus on profit and loss, not balance sheet		–Accounts receivable not perceived as a sales issue	–One of many issues to deal with	–Quarterly measurements versus monthly –Field perceives goal (7 percent over 60) as arbitrary –Headquarters initiated; no field buy-in –Quarterly end volumes makes focus during quarter less meaningful

Management focus	Lack of consistent procedures	Ownership	Conflicting priorities	Many issues surrounding accounts receivable targets/measurements
A	B	C	D	E

Restraining Forces

6. The level of slow-paying customers is too high.

Driving Forces

E	I	D, H	A, G	B, C, F	B, C, F, J
Customer contact **[W]**	Offer customer incentives to pay **[M]**	Increase secretarial/accounts receivable/ROA headcount **[M]**	Motivate regional management/marketing representatives **[M]**	Enhance regional communication **[M]**	Understand customer requirements **[M]**
–Phone contact –Meetings –Timely proactive calls –Work load report –Send letters with statements	–Prompt pay discounts	–Evaluate processes of billing/accounts receivable/ROA for efficiency –Hire secretary or share secretarial resources	–Compensation plan –Management push/attention –Work reports for cleanup/potential business	–Awareness of accounts receivable function –Copies of customer correspondence –Meetings with regional personnel as appropriate –Participate in territory reviews/ regional/district meetings	–Marketing representative establish billing requirements on front end –Hire experts

Restraining Forces

B	B	C	D	E	F	G	H	I	J
		–Expired purchase orders –Customer approval hierarchy –Once received, do not match –No attention by MR	–Phone contact –Research/ audit/ follow-up	–Sporadic problem –Mailing address –Post office	–Conflicting terms; purchase orders versus contract –Pay when want –Corporate accounts payable cycle	–Erroneous invoices –Marketing representative does not process customer documentation –Month/quarterly end priorities –Advance billing –Lack of attention to notices	–New regional procedures	–Overall economy –Seeking financing –Mergers/ takeovers	–Cost service concessions –Free time, caps on increases, change of original information
Account representative disinterest in noncommission issues	Customized invoicing not requested prebilling	Purchase orders	Lack of personnel	Customers not receiving invoices	Disregard of StorageTek terms by customer	Late paperwork through system	Consistency in billing process/ follow-up	Customer cash flow	Communication account representatives (undisclosed agreements)

7. The level of negative impact as a result of conflicting goals of management is too high.

Driving Forces

A	B	C	D	C
Evaluate performance standards or reprioritize responsibilities [M]	Stronger support from district and regional management to encourage marketing representatives to submit noncommission documentation [M]	Management and accounts receivable targets be consistent [M]	Define accounts receivable targets to accommodate new direction [M]	Revenue recognition versus receivables [M]
–Define *aging grooming* responsibilities –Understand reasons –Evaluate process	–Receipt of purchase orders –Evaluate process	–More weight placed on accounts receivable results	–Address over 30 days	–Address conflicting objectives

A	B	C	D
–Emphasis is placed on processing rather than nonstandard paperwork	–Paid to sell; not compensated for total account management	–Goals are quarterly –Emphasis on revenue recognition	–1990 focus on over 30 –Over 60-day measurement discourages collection of current receivables
Document count	Marketing representatives quotas	District and regional goals	Collection of current revenue
A	B	C	D

Restraining Forces

8. The level of negative impact on receivables due to lack of accountability is too high.

Driving Forces

A	B	C	D
Publish guidelines memo [M]	Open lines of communication [M]	Educate all appropriate areas on their aging impact [M/W]	Reward for performance [M]
–Understand corporate direction/position –Revise the Mansfield/Douglas memo –Determine areas of responsibility –Define account handling timetables –Identify deadbeats earlier	–Regional team approach to address accounts receivable problems	–Consumables QAT –Miscellaneous invoicing –New billing administrator/regional order administrator (ROA)	–Relook accounts receivable emphasis on management bonus plans –Implement bonus plan for accounts receivable representatives (monthly achievement) –Evaluate bonus plans for ROA/billing
–No headquarters accounts receivable responsibility –Representatives too busy selling	–Marketing representatives (district managers) versus accounts receivables (ROA managers)	–Little combination –Follow-up slow/inaccurate –Different requirements for each department –Multiple problems with consumables	–+60 versus +30 –Perceived to be unrealistic/unachievable
Accounts receivable responsibility directive is outdated	Conflicting chains of command	Multiple headquarter areas impacting aging	No ownership or targets
A	B	C	D

Restraining Forces

Results Summary

- 37 driving forces (solutions)
- 98 percent common causes (management-owned process problems)
- 2 percent special causes (people, tools)

Of the 98 percent management-controlled problems:

- 25 percent can be implemented at lower levels of management
- 25 percent can be implemented by middle management
- 50 percent can be implemented by higher management

Opportunities for Improvement

- Communicate
- Management focus
- Bonus plans
- Analyze the process
- Provide training
- Hire regional contracts managers
- Complete system changes
- Evaluate staffing levels
- Evaluate StorageTek invoicing policies
- Evaluate StorageTek pricing policies

Recommendations for Immediate Improvement

- Communicate
- Focus
- Hire regional contracts managers
- Transfer responsibility to process owners

Recommendations for Quality Resolution Teams

Evaluation of:

- Accounts receivables targets/compensation plans
- Order/invoicing process
- StorageTek invoicing policies
- Pricing policies (maintenance increases)

Appendix C
Help Desk
Quality Action Team

Help Desk QAT Brainstorming Session (Issues/Problems)

- Help desk support lacking from suppliers (PCs)
- Communication
- Changes not communicated
- Help desk represents entire MIS—perception
- Resources (from five to one)
- Information available at help desk
- Customers'/suppliers' expectations of help desk
- No mission defined—expected to know everything (one phone number—3471)
- Importance of help desk
- No seven-to-24 coverage, no weekend coverage
- Users/MIS—problem communication
- No understanding of customer/user requirements (we don't understand what the other is doing)
- No training—all levels
- No MIS management support to help desk (operators and management do not listen)
- Customers/users in the dark
- No coordination of system downtime or maintenance with customer

- International users not part of planning
- No teamwork in system downtime planning
- No followthrough feedback
- Planned downtime versus actual downtime
- Customers'/users' perception of MIS is wrong
- Lack of networking
- Misleading messages
- Help desk employees blamed for all MIS problems
- Too many calls
- Help desk too manual—log
- Lack of tools/systems
- Lack of guidelines/procedures
- No training for help desk operators
- Lack of customer responsibility
- Vicki cannot say "%& &%$# %%$*" (job lacks authority)

Help Desk QAT—Cause-and-Effect Analysis

1A. Customer/help desk perception
- PC, LAN, WAN, etc.
- No mission/no authority defined
- Blamed for MIS problems
- Customer perception of MIS wrong
- No clear understanding of how help desk fits in MIS strategy

1B. Support to the help desk
- Management
- Suppliers
- Customers
- No clear understanding of how help desk fits in MIS strategy

2. Communication
- Changes not communicated
- No coordination
- Misleading messages
- Followthrough and feedback
- Networking
- No customer/suppliers information
- Involved planning
- Network
- Equipment
- Vendor equipment (terminals, controllers)
- Software (e-mail, Fixit Telnet)

3. Tools and resources/guidelines
- No guidelines
- No enforcement of procedures
- No seven-to-24 coverage
- Too many calls
- Too manual
- Misleading messages
- People
- Hardware/software

4. Training
- Help desk
- No understanding of customer requirements
- Lack of customer training

5. Unstable environment

Cause

Effect: The MIS help desk does not have the ability to effectively meet the customers' requirements.

Help Desk QAT—Force Field Analysis

1A. The customers' perception/expectations of the help desk's functionality is too high.

Driving Forces

A, B, C M1–M3	B M1, W	C, A, B M1–M3
Define help desk mission	**Communicate functional responsibility to customer**	**Establish the charter's responsibility**
–Make help desk strategic to MIS	–Publish additional help numbers (StorageTek directory)	–Address changes in a timely fashion
–Define help desk authority (problem priority)	–Educate the customer	–Customer and help desk training on existing systems

–Lack of priority	–Only one number (phone extension)	–New applications
–No clear understanding of how function fits in MIS strategy	–Blamed for all MIS problems	–Roadmap for existing systems
–Lack of authority	–No visibility of ownership (who should customer contact with problem)	–New hardware/software installations

A	B	C
No defined mission	**Focal point of all MIS communications problems**	**No charter for new applications**

Restraining Forces

1B. Support to the help desk is too low.

Help Desk QAT—Force Field Analysis

Restraining Forces

A	B	C	D
Management support is lacking	Supplier support is lacking	Customer support is lacking	Outside vendor support is lacking
–Virtual management –No backups –Can't make decision –Untimely response	–Can't find them –Limited availability –Hardware/software, applications vendors, operators, suppliers, data communications, Telecomm	–Impatient customer demands –Too dependent –Language barrier	–Service response (slow) –No status update

–Provide needed support –Management strategy –Establish key backups	–Make the supplier aware of the problems –Define key backups – Help desk process flow	–Evaluate performance –Establish measurement/feedback

Define help desk mission	Customer/ supplier agreement	Reestablish vendor/customer agreements
A, B, C, D M1–M3	B, C, A W, M1	D M1–M3

Driving Forces

Help Desk QAT—Force Field Analysis

2. Effective communication is too low.

Restraining Forces

A	B	C	D
No coordination	Lack of feedback and followthrough	Misleading messages	Unplanned outages
–Problem resolution –Too many cooks in the kitchen –Planned outages –All changes not communicated –No involved plan with customers –No customer/supplier agreement –No check for user utilization	–Vendor/customer/supplier results –Customer kept in the dark –No networking in customer/supplier areas –Restores not conveyed to customer	–Not customer-friendly –No commonality –A lightning bolt does not mean break time	–Inability to let the world know (any information) –No time frames communicated
–Customer/supplier agreement –Problem resolution networking –Customer involvement	–Notice to key customers –Determine and review key customer list –Promote customer networking –Track/monitor	–Time down and expected time up –Review and revise current messages –Customer involvement	–Stop them! –Parallel testing –Something like *Symon* –Time frames
Involved planning	Effective feedback and followthrough	Develop clear precise messages	Lessen impact
A, B, C, D M1, W	B, A, C, D M1, W	C, B, D, W	D M1, M2

Driving Forces

Help Desk QAT—Force Field Analysis

3. Tools and resources/guidelines are inadequate.

Restraining Forces

A — Insufficient resources/personnel
- No clone for Vicki
- No seven-to-24 coverage
- Not enough prime-time coverage
- Too many calls
- International impact
- No cross-functional training
- No trained prime time coverage backups

B — Lack of tools
- Phone log inadequate
- Access to systems
- Terminal access to multi systems inadequate
- Historical data unavailable
- Cannot communicate system status
- No vendor logging
- No turnover report
- No customer communication manual
- Not mechanized

C — Guidelines nonexistent
- No enforcement of procedures
- Responsibility of help desk
- No management support
- Too much/not enough responsibility

Driving Forces

A — Raise response efficiency (A, B, M1–M3)
- Add personnel
- Statistical analysis of call flow
- Automated process
- Higher level of training
- Consideration of seven-to-24 coverage (international)

B — Evaluate and supply tools (B, A W, M1–M2)
- Procure automatic phone log
- Develop customer manual
- Enhance terminal access
- *Symon*
- Require vendor logging and tracking
- Turnover standards and procedures

C — Develop guidelines (C, A, B W, M1–M3)
- Define help desk responsibility
- Publish those responsibilities
- Publish customer responsibility
- Define help desk authority

Help Desk QAT—Force Field Analysis

4. Level of training is too low.

Restraining Forces

A	B	C
Lack of help desk training	**Lack of customer awareness**	**Lack of supplier and vendor training**
–Better understanding of network	–No guidelines for relaying problems	–Uppity vendors
–Wrong people answering phones	–Insensitivity to help desk tears	–Lack of knowledge of customer impact
–Training on tools	–No knowledge of computer environments	–Impact on help desk tears
–Lack of phone etiquette	–Knowing who to call	
–Lack of understanding of customer requirements		
–Insensitivity to customer tears		
–Personality sensitivity		
–Knowledge of customer jargon		

A	B	C
–Cross-training and backups	–Develop guidelines for customer	–Train on StorageTek big picture
–Train in applications and StorageTek big picture	–Share help desk process	–Customer/supplier meetings
–Phone etiquette training	–Customer knowledge sharing (for example, customers talking to customers)	–Understanding impact of changes
–Managing the customer	–Customer tours of help desk	
–Common jargon		
–Knowledge of language differences		
–Training on tools		
–Touring customer environments		
Train help desk personnel	**Develop customer awareness**	**Improve relations and support**
A, B, C M1	B, A M1	C, A M1

Driving Forces

Help Desk QAT—Force Field Analysis

5. **The stability of the MIS environment is too low.**

Restraining Forces

A	B	C
Complexity of the network	Hardware	Software
–Too many types of networks –Too many changes to networks –Lack of coordination with network changes/additions –Lack of training and resources –Technology developed faster than StorageTek help desk training	–Unreliable –Too many different types –Too much movement –Lack of documentation –Lack of customer training on their equipment –Antiquated equipment	–Lack of thorough testing –Lack of capacity (MVS, VM, Telenet . . .) –Invisible changes impact customers –Support and ownership of old applications –Lack documentation

–Provide training and resources to match technology development

–Support of change management QAT

–Develop documentation

–Need on-line equipment information

–Identify location of equipment

–Documentation and training

Define/standardize corporate guidelines	A, B, C M1–M3	Provide documentation and education	B, A, C M1–M2	Methodology documentation and coordination	C, A, B W, M1–M3

Driving Forces

Help Desk QAT Opportunities for Improvement

More trained coverage:
  Seven-to-24 trained help

Split help desk:
  One or two front-line people for the easier questions
  Two people for harder and longer problems (one on one with
    customer)

Different log package:
  Fixit on-line data base (building eight central dispatch)
  Outside vendor
  Historical and on-line log

Training and documentation:
  All data center staff
  All networks and equipment

Help Desk QAT Results

Force field analysis driving forces—20 items
Responsibility breakdown:

Management actions	13 items	65%
Management /worker actions	6 items	30%
Worker actions	1 item	5%
	20 items	100%

Result comparison

	Help desk QAT	Typical QAT
Management	73%	85%
Worker	27%	15%

Help Desk Flowchart
Level I

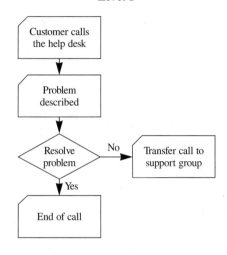

Help Desk Flowchart
Level II

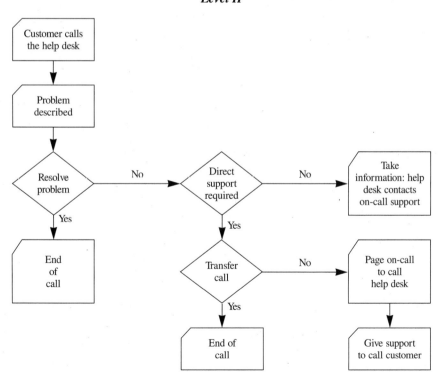

Appendix D
Process Evaluation

Presentation Outline

Introduction of team members

Brief history of team

Mission statement

Current process flowchart

Recommendations for improvements

Proposed process flow

Comparison of processes and cost of quality

Proposed customer/supplier agreement

Conclusions

Questions and answers

Mission Statement

To define a consistent tape initialization process through effective and ongoing cross-functional participation that clearly identifies respective customer/supplier roles and relationships, while exposing quiescent improvement opportunities.

Cross-Functional Media Label and Initialize Process*

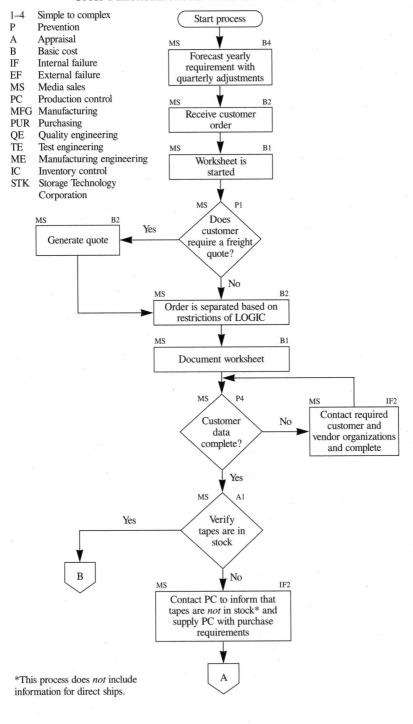

1–4   Simple to complex
P   Prevention
A   Appraisal
B   Basic cost
IF   Internal failure
EF   External failure
MS   Media sales
PC   Production control
MFG   Manufacturing
PUR   Purchasing
QE   Quality engineering
TE   Test engineering
ME   Manufacturing engineering
IC   Inventory control
STK   Storage Technology
        Corporation

Start process

MS   B4
Forecast yearly requirement with quarterly adjustments

MS   B2
Receive customer order

MS   B1
Worksheet is started

MS   P1
Does customer require a freight quote?

MS   B2
Generate quote

Yes

No

MS   B2
Order is separated based on restrictions of LOGIC

MS   B1
Document worksheet

MS   P4
Customer data complete?

No

MS   IF2
Contact required customer and vendor organizations and complete

Yes

MS   A1
Verify tapes are in stock

Yes

B

MS   IF2
Contact PC to inform that tapes are *not* in stock* and supply PC with purchase requirements

No

A

*This process does *not* include information for direct ships.

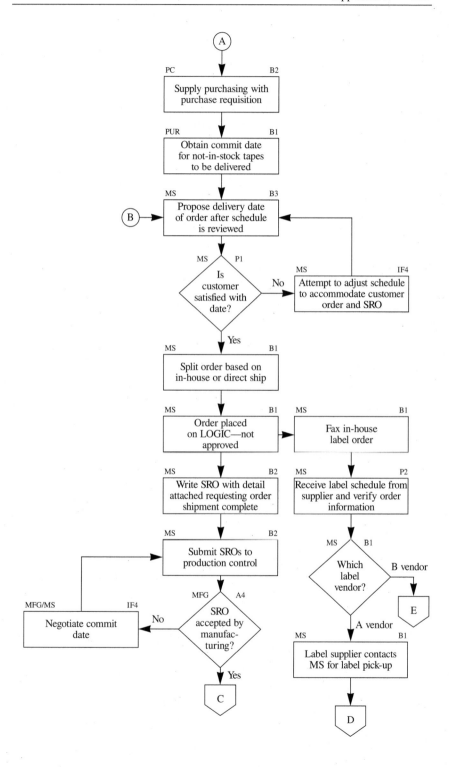

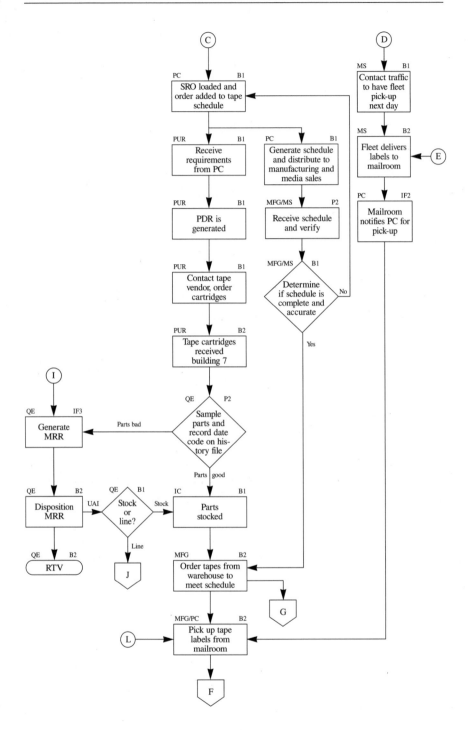

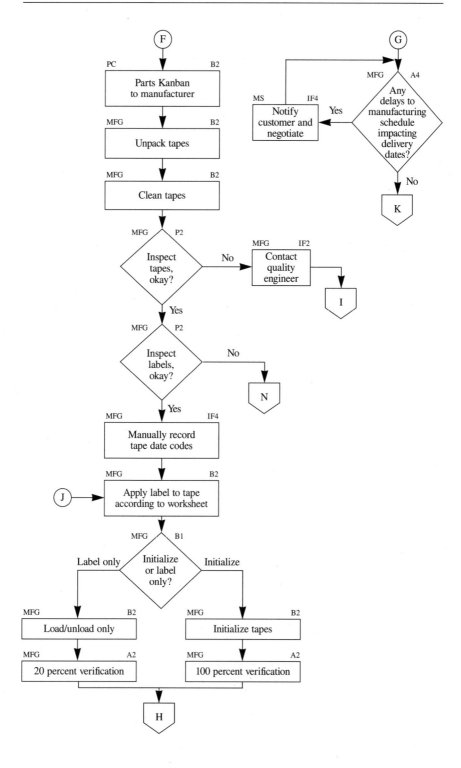

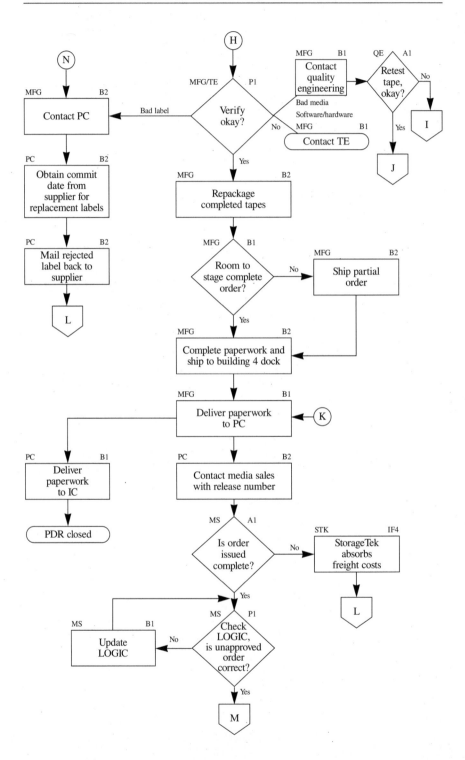

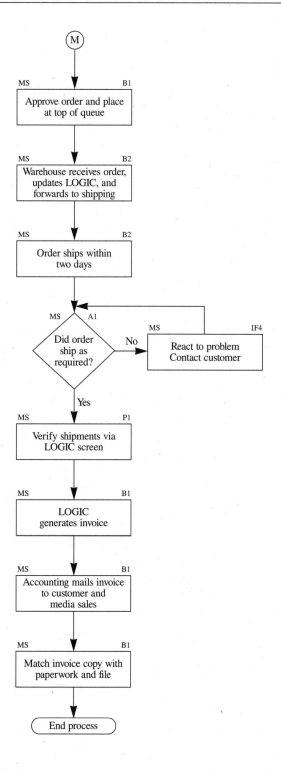

Recommendations for Improvements

1. Provide manufacturing with an on-line EMC2 terminal and a telephone.

   • Provide direct communication for all departments associated with the process.

   • Schedule and confirm orders with manufacturing via EMC2.

   • Make changes to schedule, that is, reprioritization, stop-line notification, and so on, via EMC2.

   • Track defective labels.

2. Manufacturing to provide media sales with a 90-day build schedule by week including sick days, vacation days, and holidays.

   • Simplify acceptance procedure.

3. Media sales to input tape cartridge requirements via an on-line SRO system.

   • Direct line to purchasing, eliminating the hand carrying of our requirements to PC, PC to management, then PC to purchasing.

   • Required resource will be acquisition of a 132-column terminal or equivalent.

4. Provide adequate room in the Longmont facility for tapes to be staged taking into consideration multiple order processing. (Quantity not yet determined.)

   • Staging facilities for this number would allow orders to ship complete rather than in partials.

   • Freight charges will be more accurate.

5. A customer/supplier agreement be written to allow media sales the ability to schedule orders (based on the quantity supplied by manufacturing) without the SRO sign-off by management. Media sales would secure management approval if order requirements exceed the agreed-upon schedule limitations.

   • Review quarterly.

6. Form a team to address recording and tracking of date code information from cartridge to customer.

7. Meet with marketing management to discuss forecasting accuracy and impact on manufacturing due to a fluctuating schedule.

8. Form a team to develop a product return policy.

   • No procedures currently exist.

9. Label suppliers to deliver direct to mailroom and plan for direct delivery to Longmont facility.

10. Manufacturing to have written procedures that are updated regularly.

    • Procedures to outline rules responsibilities and integration of the PC functions.

11. Label delivery on a set schedule.

    • Label and replacement label on a set schedule.

    • Meeting with label vendors to discuss requirements.

    • Zero defects from label suppliers.

    • Commit versus schedule.

12. Empower the group to establish measurements in the process and also to continue working through the QIP.

Proposed Customer/Supplier Agreement

Manufacturing

   • Will supply media sales with a 90-day manufacturing commitment, by week, taking into account vacations and sick time, scheduled holidays, and machine capacity. This information will be used to schedule orders and make external customer commitments.

Media Sales

   • Will secure the approval of manufacturing management if the schedule exceeds the volume committed by manufacturing.

Recommendations
Pareto—Number of Boxes Affected

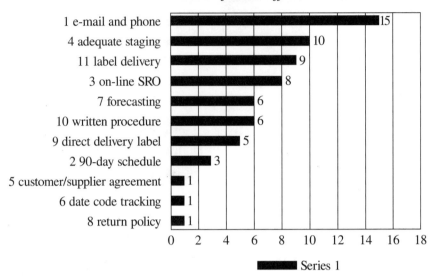

Series 1

Current Process
Cost of Quality

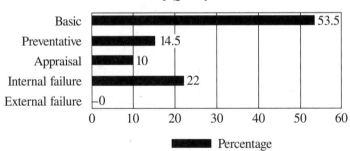

Percentage

New Process
Cost of Quality

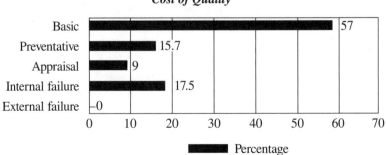

Percentage

- Will not adjust the schedule within the week of production without manufacturing management approval; any schedule changes for the next week will be made by Thursday morning the week prior to production.
- Will supply a purchase requisition for tape cartridges (parts internal to manufacturing) within a 10-working-day period and for accessory items (that is, cleaning cartridges, cleaning cartridge labels, and so on) that are not ordered via SRO.
- Will supply a yearly forecast to be reviewed quarterly.

Purchasing

- Will be the focal point for all contract issues between StorageTek and cartridge/label suppliers.
- Will supply, in writing, any policy and procedure changes affecting media sales and/or manufacturing.

All Groups

- Will communicate efficiently and effectively.
- Will empower teams to continue cycling through the quality improvement process for opportunities.
- Will put forth their best effort to ensure that our customer/ supplier relationship is a "partnership"—a benefit to all functional areas involved, not a liability.

Appendix E
SQA/EVT
Quality Action Team

Brainstorming Session (Issues/Problems)

- No project owner (to resolve issues)
- Too many projects/low resources (compromise testing)
- Demotivating test process (testing task not manageable)
- Unclear testing charter (functional versus environmental) (EVT versus CPAT)
- Customer/supplier agreement (development)
- Customer requirements (interaction with customers, feedback)
- Stable testing development inputs (timely manner, complete)
- No SQA activities
- Motivation/demotivation
- MBOs versus accountability/responsibility (personal MBOs versus company's MBOs)

Effect: Software development process does not produce products that meet or exceed (int/ext) customer requirements.

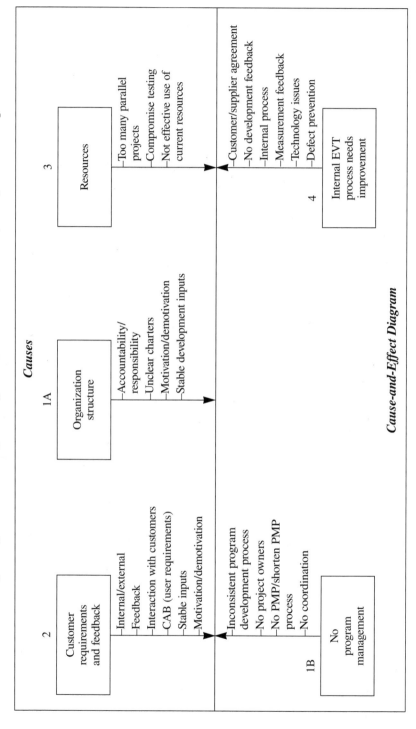

Causes

1A — Organization structure
- Accountability/responsibility
- Unclear charters
- Motivation/demotivation
- Stable development inputs

3 — Resources
- Too many parallel projects
- Compromise testing
- Not effective use of current resources

4 — Internal EVT process needs improvement
- Customer/supplier agreement
- No development feedback
- Internal process
- Measurement feedback
- Technology issues
- Defect prevention

2 — Customer requirements and feedback
- Internal/external
- Feedback
- Interaction with customers
- CAB (user requirements)
- Stable inputs
- Motivation/demotivation

1B — No program management
- Inconsistent program development process
- No project owners
- No PMP/shorten PMP process
- No coordination

Cause-and-Effect Diagram

1A. Software engineering organizational structure is functionally inadequate.

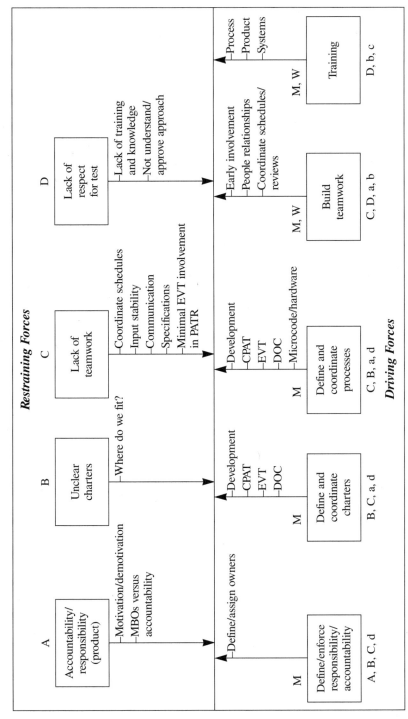

1B. Program management is inconsistent and ineffective.

Restraining Forces

A	B	C	D
No program ownership	PMP	No process coordination	Project estimation and scheduling
—Accountability/ responsibility —Lack of authority —Accessibility —Status meetings —Coordination	—Shortened —None —Not followed	—Undefined —Inconsistent	—Inaccurate —Lack of skills —Coordination —Missing functional areas
—Meeting leader (training)	—QA to ensure process is followed	—See 1A.C —Marketing	—Coordinate functional areas —Data collection —Training
M	M	M	M
Assign ownership	Enforce use of PMP	Coordinate and communicate processes	Develop estimation and scheduling techniques
A, B, c, d	B, c, d	C, a, b, d	D

Driving Forces

2. Little or no direct customer requirements input or testing feedback.

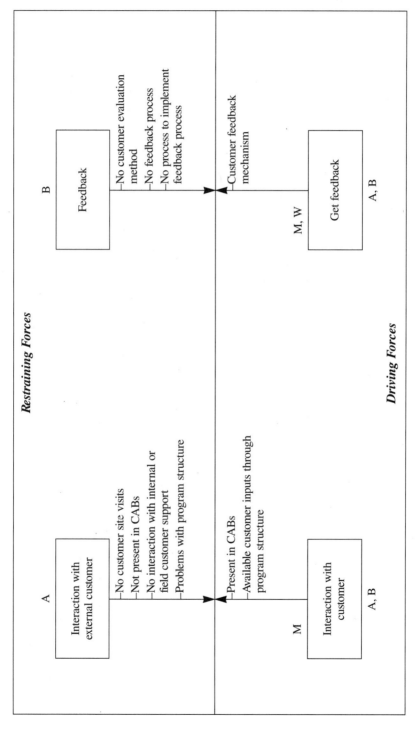

3. Inadequate resources.

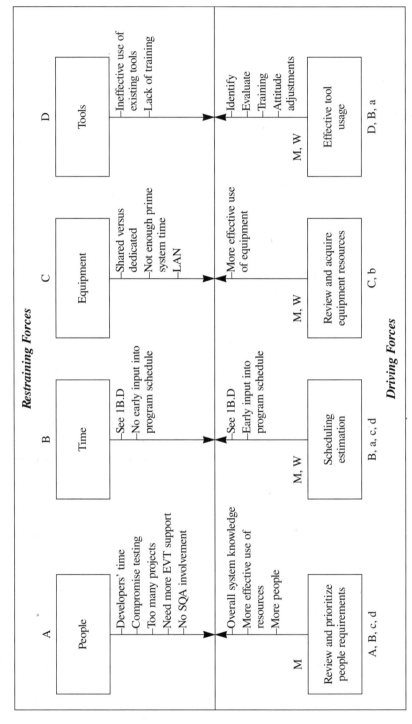

Restraining Forces

A — People
- Developers' time
- Compromise testing
- Too many projects
- Need more EVT support
- No SQA involvement

B — Time
- See 1B.D
- No early input into program schedule

C — Equipment
- Shared versus dedicated
- Not enough prime system time
- LAN

D — Tools
- Ineffective use of existing tools
- Lack of training

M — Review and prioritize people requirements
- Overall system knowledge
- More effective use of resources
- More people

A, B, c, d

M, W — Scheduling estimation
- See 1B.D
- Early input into program schedule

B, a, c, d

M, W — Review and acquire equipment resources
- More effective use of equipment

C, b

M, W — Effective tool usage
- Identify
- Evaluate
- Training
- Attitude adjustments

D, B, a

Driving Forces

4. Internal S/W EVT process needs enhancement.

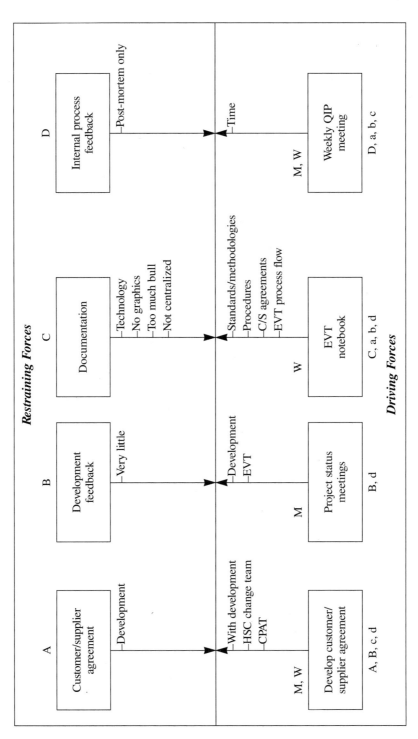

Summary of Driving Forces

Define and enforce accountability and responsibility

- Provide accountability/responsibility (product/organization)
- Promote teamwork
- Assign program ownership
- Clarify charters

Improve project scheduling

- Accurate schedules
- Acquire scheduling skills
- Coordinate schedules
- Include all functional areas
- Schedule concurrent projects

Identify and provide adequate resources

- People
- Time
- Equipment
- Efficient use of resources

Identify and provide training

- System product
- Tools
- Test methodologies

Define and coordinate charters/processes

- Coordinate/communicate engineering processes
- Develop customer/supplier agreement

Establish interaction with customers

- Obtain direct customer communication and testing feedback

Define/enforce use and evolution of engineering processes

- Use PMP
- Follow and review PMP

Results

Force Field Analysis Driving Forces—19 Items

Responsibility Breakdown:

Management actions	10 items	95%
Management/worker actions	8 items	
Worker actions	1 item	5%
Total	19 items	100%

Appendix F
Electrical Development Process
Quality Action Team

Initial Brainstorm Session

- Electrical development process does not yield quality products
- Component quality and availability
- Schedules
- Test process
- Lack of continuity (womb to tomb)
- Lack of skill sets (resources)
- Management directions
- Inconsistent corporate strategy
- Tools—administration (not coordinated)—no process
- Level of support from support/service groups
- Committee (task forces) versus teams
- Lack of standards/guidelines/procedures

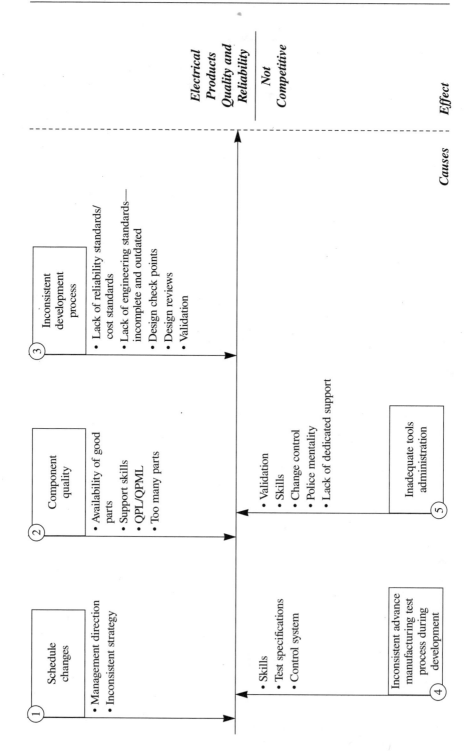

Problem 1: Schedule Changes Too Frequent

Driving Forces

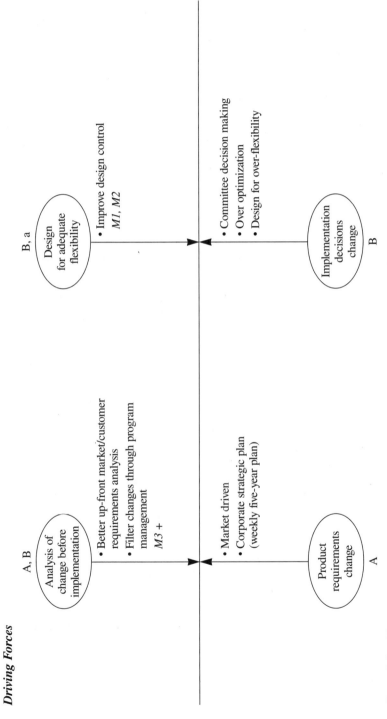

Restraining Forces

Problem 2: Quality of Components Too Low

Restraining Forces

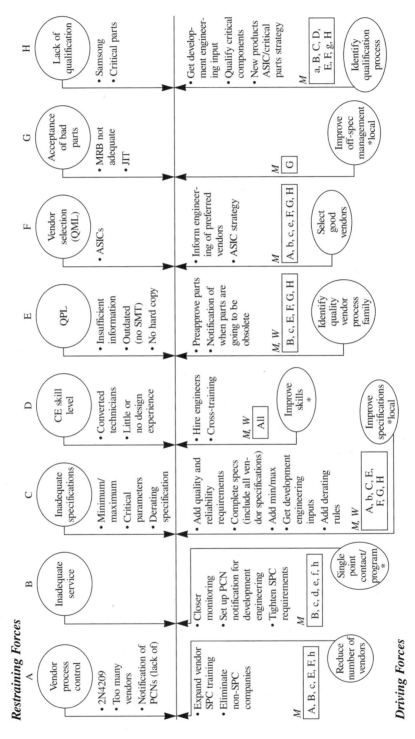

Driving Forces

Problem 3: Inconsistent Development Process

Restraining Forces

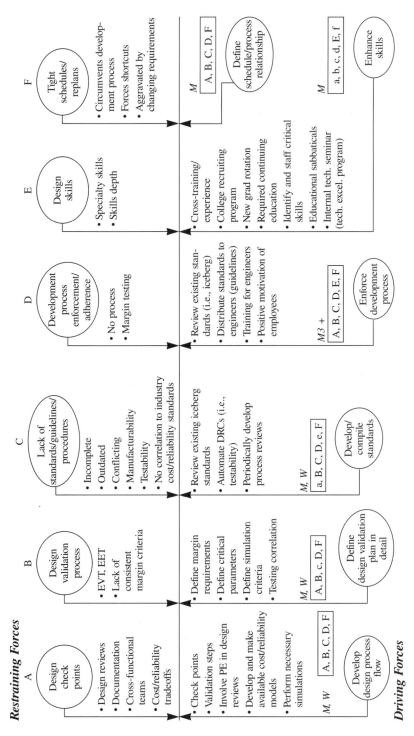

Driving Forces

Problem 4: Inconsistent Advanced Manufacturing Test Process

Restraining Forces

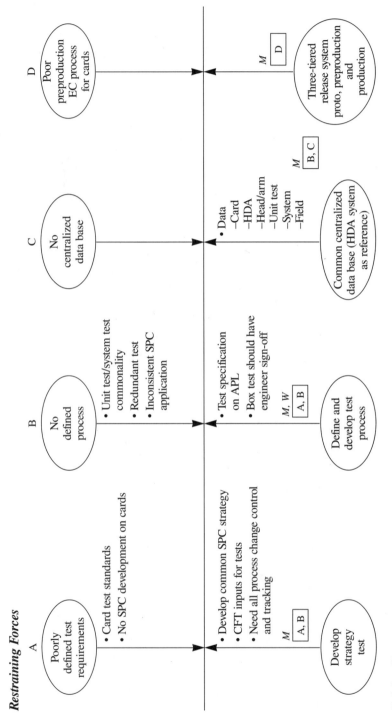

Driving Forces

Problem 5: Inadequate Tools Administration

Restraining Forces

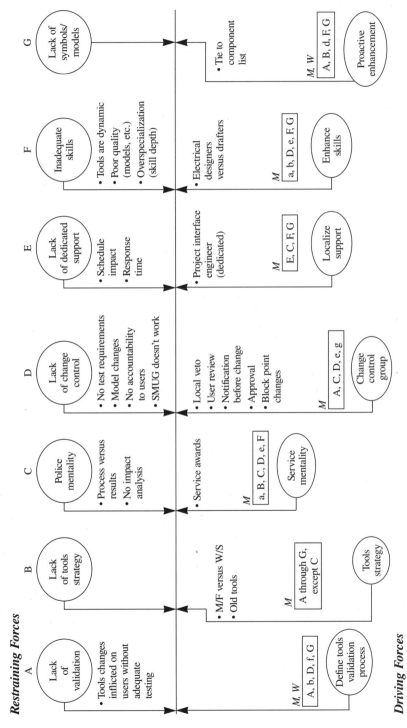

A — Lack of validation
- Tools changes inflicted on users without adequate testing

M, W — A, b, D, f, G
Define tools validation process

B — Lack of tools strategy
- M/F versus W/S
- Old tools

M — A through G, except C
Tools strategy

C — Police mentality
- Process versus results
- No impact analysis
- Service awards

M — a, B, C, D, e, F
Service mentality

D — Lack of change control
- No test requirements
- Model changes
- No accountability to users
- SMUG doesn't work
- Local veto
- User review
- Notification before change
- Approval
- Block point changes

M — A, C, D, e, g
Change control group

E — Lack of dedicated support
- Schedule impact
- Response time
- Project interface engineer (dedicated)

M — E, C, F, G
Localize support

F — Inadequate skills
- Tools are dynamic
- Poor quality (models, etc.)
- Overspecialization (skill depth)
- Electrical designers versus drafters

M — a, b, D, e, F, G
Enhance skills

G — Lack of symbols/models
- Tie to component list

M, W — A, B, d, F, G
Proactive enhancement

Driving Forces

Summary

- Design for flexibility
- Single point of contact for component engineering
- Improve component specifications
- Improve component engineering skill sets
- Improve off-specification management
- Analyze design change before implementing
- Develop/design process flow
- Develop/compile standards
- Enhance/develop engineers skill set
- Define and develop advanced manufacturing test access
- Develop proto EC system
- Localized design tools support
- Need tools strategy
- Need change control group to tools

Electrical Design QAT

Typical QAT Results

Management actions	85%
Worker actions	15%

Electrical QAT Results

Management actions	76%
Worker actions	24%

Appendix G
Just Say No
Quality Action Team

The Just Say No to E&O team started in October 1990. Several departments and functions have been involved in the following work.

The most valuable result of the team's efforts has been the elimination of walls between organizations and the acceptance of the importance of controlling the inventory. All of the individuals operate in functions that are in some way related to achieving the corporate strategy of 6.8 inventory turns. Eliminating excess and obsolete materials will be instrumental in streamlining our inventory processes. There were several causes of this extra material—most of which this team cannot be a direct influence on changing. The following plans represent the items the team believed could be influenced.

Mission Statement
To identify the improvement opportunities in the E&O process that will help reach the inventory turn goal and will help us surpass the industry standard for excess inventory levels (below 5 percent).

Recommendation 1
Develop a notification between customer services and MLC that will provide a more efficient method of communication, to ensure accurate counts and costing, and establish proper effectiveness.

Activities
- Understand the current process flow.
- Identify process owners and responsibilities.

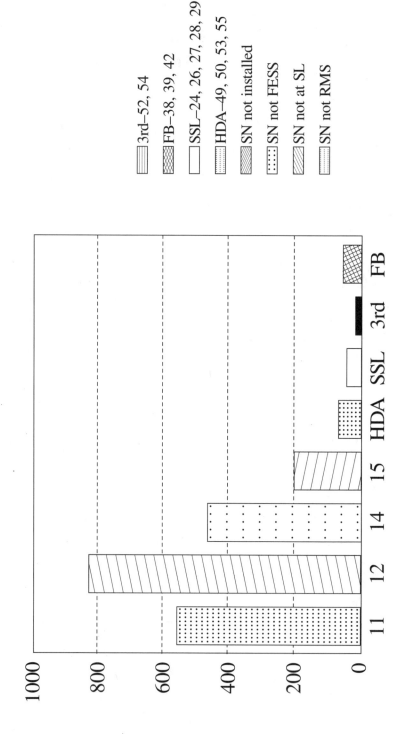

- Develop an e-mail communication form.
- Establish customer/supplier agreements specific to the form.
- Obtain management input on training deployment.
- Set implementation date.

Recommendation 2

Develop a communication vehicle that promotes a better understanding and more immediate awareness of EC activities so that material can be dispositioned efficiently and effectively.

Activities

- Understand the process flow and address weaknesses.
- Identify roles and responsibilities.
- Develop new process flow.
- Produce an e-mail router.
- Establish customer/supplier agreements specific to routing.
- Obtain management input on training deployment.
- Set implementation date.

Other Recommendations

1. Develop a more efficient/effective process flow for part transfer notices.
2. Develop a training procedure and process that eliminates the inconsistencies that cause excess.
3. Prevention of ISRs back to stock with no requirements. (QAT currently working this issue.)
4. Improve visibility of actual material requirements to buyers.
5. Develop a policy limiting economic buys to a specific time frame.
6. Improve the current SRO process.
7. Develop customer/supplier agreement among purchasing and its customers.

Recommendations for the Clearing of Material on ECs

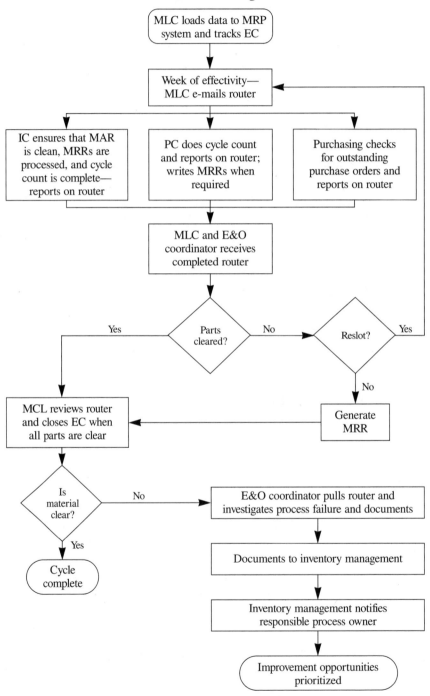

Name of customer organization: Machine level control

Name of process: MLC/customer services logistics EC part number count notification

Customer/supplier agreement (Agreement will be discussed monthly to integrate improvements and to address customer concerns.)

1. MLC will initiate e-mail requesting that customer services logistics reviews part numbers in EC.

2. Customer service logistics will respond within 24 hours with counts of the part numbers affecting them and provide average weekly usage, and if there is an open schedule.

3. MLC will use data to arrive at appropriate effectivity.

Name of customer process: MLC excess part number router.

Customer/supplier agreement (Agreement will be discussed quarterly by management to integrate improvements and to address customer concerns.)

1. Our group will actively participate in the router process, clearing material and signing off.

2. MLC will initiate e-mail router one week before effectivity.

3. Purchasing and production control will respond to router within two working days.

4. Inventory control will respond by Monday of the effectivity week.

5. Offsite inventory control management will report any consistent deviations to the appropriate process owner.

6. Management will ensure that personnel are given the procedure and that there is adherence to the process.

7. E&O coordinator will provide on request a chart of monthly EC-related excess proposed.

Appendix H
Sales Maintenance Invoicing Tasks
Process Improvement Team

CE/FFA

The cause-and-effect diagram identifies the number one quality problem or the *effect*. In this case it is a breakdown between application systems and procedures, result in excessive rework and customer dissatisfaction. Major causes are then identified which resulted in this effect.

A force field analysis has also been prepared for each of the major causes on the cause-and-effect diagram. The force field analysis examines the cause and identifies restraining forces—the situations and events that keep the problem at its current level. To counter the restraining forces, driving forces are provided which identify problem resolutions or opportunities for improvement. The document includes a force field analysis for the following:

- National account process
- Invalid/incorrect customer invoicing
- System interface problems
- Inadequate communication and training
- Complexity of the process

Cause and Effect

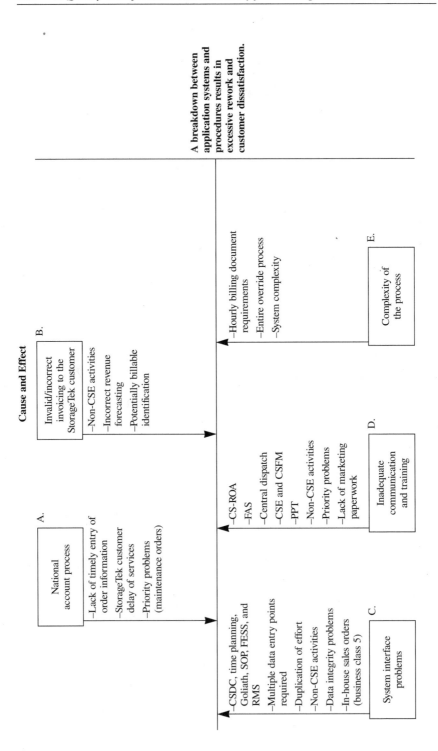

A breakdown between application systems and procedures results in excessive rework and customer dissatisfaction.

A.
National account process

–Lack of timely entry of order information
–StorageTek customer delay of services
–Priority problems (maintenance orders)

B.
Invalid/incorrect invoicing to the StorageTek customer

–Non-CSE activities
–Incorrect revenue forecasting
–Potentially billable identification

–Hourly billing document requirements
–Entire override process
–System complexity

E.
Complexity of the process

–CS-ROA
–FAS
–Central dispatch
–CSE and CSFM
–PPT
–Non-CSE activities
–Priority problems
–Lack of marketing paperwork

D.
Inadequate communication and training

–CSDC, time planning, Goliath, SOP, FESS, and RMS
–Multiple data entry points required
–Duplication of effort
–Non-CSE activities
–Data integrity problems
–In-house sales orders (business class 5)

C.
System interface problems

Force Field Analysis

A. Problem statement: Established procedures for processing national service accounts (NSA) are outside the scope of the standard sales order process, leading to inefficiencies within interfacing systems and processes.

Restraining Forces

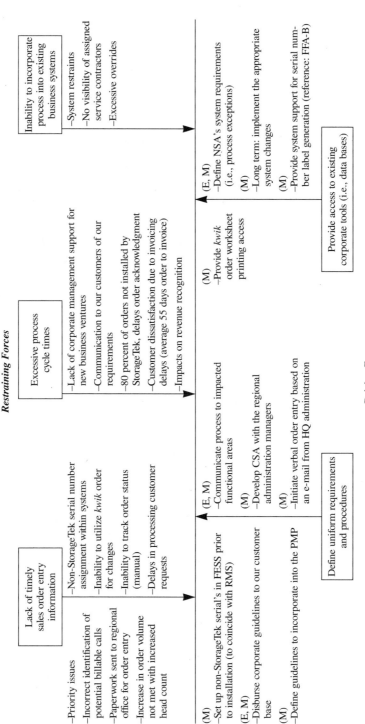

Lack of timely sales order entry information

–Non-StorageTek serial number assignment within systems
–Inability to utilize *kwik* order for changes
–Inability to track order status (manual)
–Delays in processing customer requests

–Priority issues
–Incorrect identification of potential billable calls
–Paperwork sent to regional office for order entry
–Increase in order volume not met with increased head count

Excessive process cycle times

–Lack of corporate management support for new business ventures
–Communication to our customers of our requirements
–80 percent of orders not installed by StorageTek, delays order acknowledgment
–Customer dissatisfaction due to invoicing delays (average 55 days order to invoice)
–Impacts on revenue recognition

Inability to incorporate process into existing business systems

–System restraints
–No visibility of assigned service contractors
–Excessive overrides

(E, M)
–Communicate process to impacted functional areas
(M)
–Develop CSA with the regional administration managers
(M)
–Initiate verbal order entry based on an e-mail from HQ administration

(M)
–Provide *kwik* order worksheet printing access

(E, M)
–Define NSA's system requirements (i.e., process exceptions)
(M)
–Long term: implement the appropriate system changes
(M)
–Provide system support for serial number label generation (reference: FFA-B)

(M)
–Set up non-StorageTek serial's in FESS prior to installation (to coincide with RMS)
(E, M)
–Disburse corporate guidelines to our customer base
(M)
–Define guidelines to incorporate into the PMP

Define uniform requirements and procedures

Provide access to existing corporate tools (i.e., data bases)

Driving Forces

Force Field Analysis

B. Problem statement: A failure to integrate application systems and procedures result in incorrect/invalid invoicing to the customer.

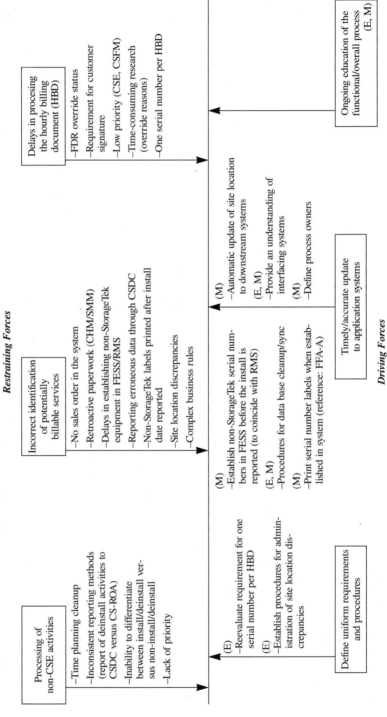

Restraining Forces

Delays in processing
the hourly billing
document (HBD)

–FDR override status
–Requirement for customer
signature
–Low priority (CSE, CSFM)
–Time-consuming research
(override reasons)
–One serial number per HBD

Incorrect identification
of potentially
billable services

–No sales order in the system
–Retroactive paperwork (CHM/SMM)
–Delays in establishing non-StorageTek
equipment in FESS/RMS
–Reporting erroneous data through CSDC
–Non-StorageTek labels printed after install
date reported
–Site location discrepancies
–Complex business rules

Processing of
non-CSE activities

–Time planning cleanup
–Inconsistent reporting methods
(report of deinstall activities to
CSDC versus CS-ROA)
–Inability to differentiate
between install/deinstall ver-
sus non-install/deinstall
–Lack of priority

Driving Forces

Ongoing education of the
functional/overall process
(E, M)

(M)
–Automatic update of site location
to downstream systems
(E, M)
–Provide an understanding of
interfacing systems
(M)
–Define process owners

Timely/accurate update
to application systems

(M)
–Establish non-StorageTek serial num-
bers in FESS before the install is
reported (to coincide with RMS)
(E, M)
–Procedures for data base cleanup/sync
(M)
–Print serial number labels when estab-
lished in system (reference: FFA-A)

(E)
–Reevaluate requirement for one
serial number per HBD
(E)
–Establish procedures for administration of site location discrepancies

Define uniform requirements
and procedures

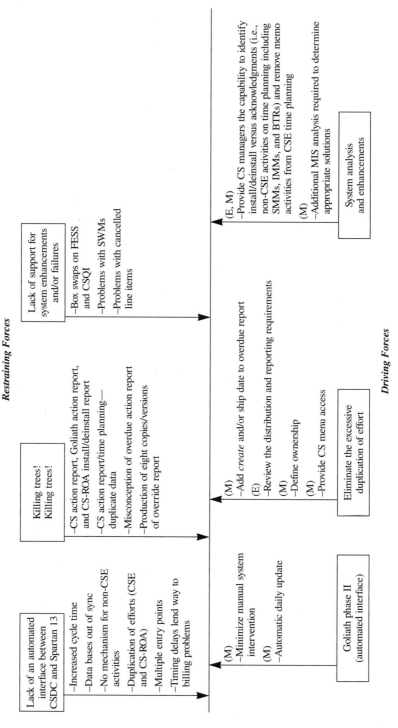

Force Field Analysis

C. Problem statement: Due to the interfacing requirements of multiple systems, a breakdown is occurring, resulting in excessive rework.

Restraining Forces

Lack of an automated interface between CSDC and Spartan 13

–Increased cycle time
–Data bases out of sync
–No mechanism for non-CSE activities
–Duplication of efforts (CSE and CS-ROA)
–Multiple entry points
–Timing delays lend way to billing problems

Killing trees!
Killing trees!

–CS action report, Goliath action report, and CS-ROA install/deinstall report
–CS action report/time planning—duplicate data
–Misconception of overdue action report
–Production of eight copies/versions of override report

Lack of support for system enhancements and/or failures

–Box swaps on FESS and CSQI
–Problems with SWMs
–Problems with cancelled line items

Driving Forces

Goliath phase II (automated interface)

(M)
–Minimize manual system intervention
(M)
–Automatic daily update

Eliminate the excessive duplication of effort

(M)
–Add *create* and/or ship date to overdue report
(E)
–Review the distribution and reporting requirements
(M)
–Define ownership
(M)
–Provide CS menu access

System analysis and enhancements

(E, M)
–Provide CS managers the capability to identify install/deinstall versus acknowledgments (i.e., non-CSE activities on time planning including SMMs, IMMs, and BTRs) and remove memo activities from CSE time planning
(M)
–Additional MIS analysis required to determine appropriate solutions

Force Field Analysis

D. Problem statement: Failure to achieve an effective implementation/continual education and communication program, results in excessive rework and customer dissatisfaction.

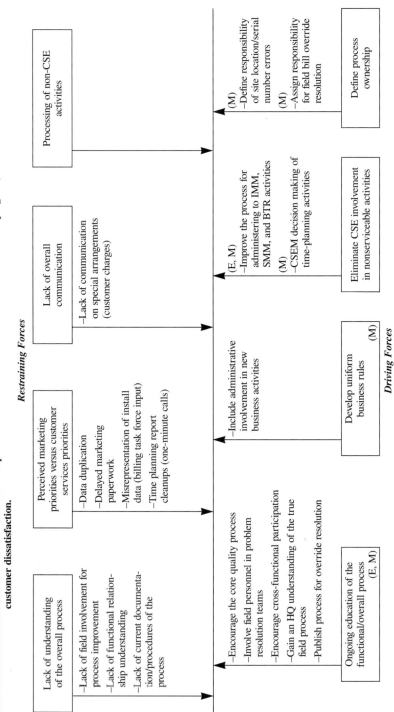

Force Field Analysis

E. Problem statement: A complex overall process has developed due to changes to business procedures and systems.

Restraining Forces

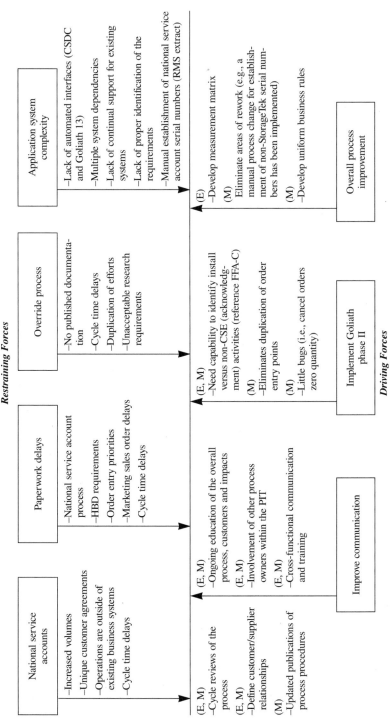

National service accounts	Paperwork delays	Override process	Application system complexity
–Increased volumes	–National service account process	–No published documentation	–Lack of automated interfaces (CSDC and Goliath 13)
–Unique customer agreements	–HBD requirements	–Cycle time delays	–Multiple system dependencies
–Operations are outside of existing business systems	–Order entry priorities	–Duplication of efforts	–Lack of continual support for existing systems
–Cycle time delays	–Marketing sales order delays	–Unacceptable research requirements	–Lack of proper identification of the requirements
	–Cycle time delays		–Manual establishment of national service account serial numbers (RMS extract)

(E, M)
–Cycle reviews of the process

(E, M)
–Define customer/supplier relationships

(M)
–Updated publications of process procedures

| Improve communication |

(E, M)
–Ongoing education of the overall process, customers and impacts

(E, M)
–Involvement of other process owners within the PIT

(E, M)
–Cross-functional communication and training

| Implement Goliath phase II |

(E, M)
–Need capability to identify install versus non-CSE (acknowledgment) activities (reference FFA-C)

(M)
–Eliminates duplication of order entry points

(M)
–Little bugs (i.e., cancel orders zero quantity)

| Overall process improvement |

(E)
–Develop measurement matrix

(M)
Eliminate areas of rework (e.g., a manual process change for establishment of non-StorageTek serial numbers has been implemented)

(M)
–Develop uniform business rules

Driving Forces

Force Field Analysis Results

Typical Results

Management   =   85%

Employee   =   15%

SMIT-PIT Results

Driving forces = 49

Management actions	= 55	=	93%
Employee actions	= 4	=	7%
Totals	59	=	100%

Major Improvement Opportunities

- National service accounts
  - Initiate verbal order entry (FFA-A)
  - Provide *kwik* order worksheet printing (FFA-A)
  - Improve timeliness of third-party label generation (FFA-A, B)

- CSRs to align systems with current business practices (FFA, E)

- Implement Goliath phase II install/deinstall download (FFA-C, E)

- Provide MIS analysis for non-CSE activities
  - Provide CSFMs capability to identify non-CSE activities (FFA-C, E)
  - Move memo activities from CSE time planning to CSFM planning (FFA-C, D)

- Educate and communicate (FFA-All)

- Eliminate duplicate efforts (FFA-C, E)

- Automate update of site locations to downstream systems (FFA-B, D)

Appendix I
Information Systems
Quality Action Team

IS QAT
Problem Statement

Problem statement evolved from two issues:

I. Seventy-one percent of IS employees state there is little or no documented, well-communicated process for an employee to address real or perceived quality issues.

II. The following factors prevent IS employees from addressing or resolving quality issues:

1. Deadlines
2. Apathy
3. Fear
4. Budget
5. Trust
6. Risk
7. Been turned down before
8. No direction
9. Too many changes in direction
10. Name dropping
11. Solutions not clear with cost/benefit
12. No QAT formed by individuals (it was always perceived it had to be management directed)
13. Perception management has no time
14. Perception there is low management participation in QAT/QRTs
15. Employees do not understand what management is doing
16. Management does not understand what employees are doing

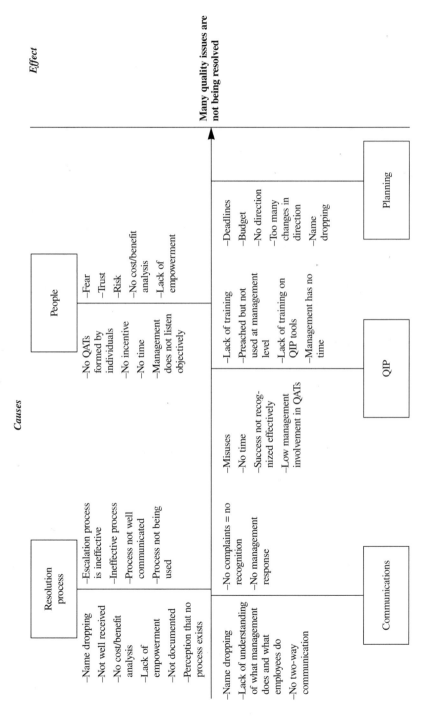

Is QAT Cause-and-Effect Diagram

Causes

Effect

Many quality issues are not being resolved

Resolution process
- Name dropping
- Not well received
- No cost/benefit analysis
- Lack of empowerment
- Not documented
- Perception that no process exists

- Escalation process is ineffective
- Ineffective process
- Process not well communicated
- Process not being used

People
- Fear
- Trust
- Risk
- No cost/benefit analysis
- Lack of empowerment

- No QATs formed by individuals
- No incentive
- No time
- Management does not listen objectively

Planning
- Deadlines
- Budget
- No direction
- Too many changes in direction
- Name dropping

QIP
- Lack of training
- Preached but not used at management level
- Lack of training on QIP tools
- Management has no time

- Misuses
- No time
- Success not recognized effectively
- Low management involvement in QATs

Communications
- No complaints = no recognition
- No management response

- Name dropping
- Lack of understanding of what management does and what employees do
- No two-way communication

Many Quality Issues Are Not Being Resolved
Force Field Analysis

1. The current IS quality resolution process is ineffective.

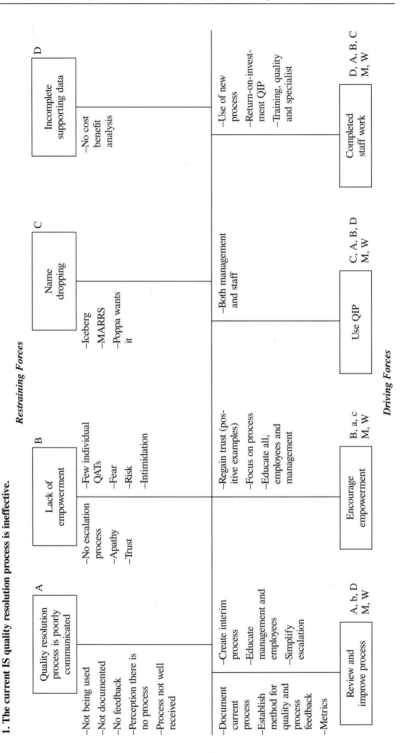

Restraining Forces

Driving Forces

Many Quality Issues Are Not Being Resolved
Force Field Analysis

2. People are not addressing quality issues effectively.

Restraining Forces

A — Fear
- Poor reviews
- Lousy work assignments
- Process not working
- Management view is negative
- Repercussion
  - Fear of incompetence
  - Peer pressure
  - Intimidation
  - Escalation
  - Lack of trust
  - Risk

B — Apathy
- Skepticism
- Give up
- Multiple processes
- Why bother
- Lack of consistency
- No incentives

C — Lack of time
- Poor planning
- Too much work
- Unrealistic expectations
- Dictated schedules
- No individual participation on QAT
  - No cost/benefit analysis
  - No/few department-level PICs

D — Management failure
- No incentives
- Inconsistency
- Lack of objective listening
- No support
- No empowerment
- Fear of repercussion
  - Quality is a hobby
  - Failure to educate people

Driving Forces

Build trust — A, B, D M, W
- Two-way trust building
- Management participation
- Constructive criticism
  - QIP should be the norm, not the exception
  - Encourage empowerment
  - Recognize
  - Encourage use of resolution process

Improve communication — A, B, C, D M, w
- Publicize success
- IS quality newsletter
- (See "Communications Is Ineffective" FFA)

Improve planning — C, a, b, D M
- Time management
- Involve employees in planning process
- More effective budget process
- Follow focused direction
  - Let employees know what they can expect
  - Communicate goals and objectives
  - Coordinate resources with projects
  - Support department PICs

Teamwork at all levels — D, A, B, C M
- Understand what staff does
- Provide training
- Manage upper-management expectations
  - Practice what we preach
  - Empower people
  - Effective use of team goals

3. Use of QIP is inconsistent.

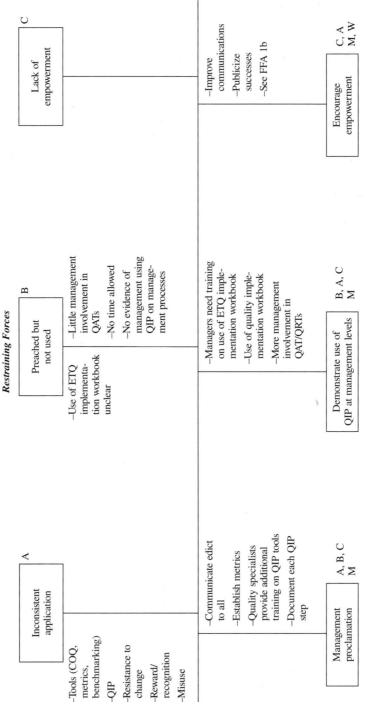

**Many Quality Issues Are Not Being Resolved
Force Field Analysis**

Restraining Forces

A — Inconsistent application

–Tools (COQ, metrics, benchmarking)
–QIP
–Resistance to change
–Reward/recognition
–Misuse

B — Preached but not used

–Use of ETQ implementation workbook unclear
–Little management involvement in QATs
–No time allowed
–No evidence of management using QIP on management processes

C — Lack of empowerment

Driving Forces

Management proclamation — A, B, C / M

–Communicate edict to all
–Establish metrics
–Quality specialists provide additional training on QIP tools
–Document each QIP step

Demonstrate use of QIP at management levels — B, A, C / M

–Managers need training on use of ETQ implementation workbook
–Use of quality implementation workbook
–More management involvement in QAT/QRTs

Encourage empowerment — C, A / M, W

–Improve communications
–Publicize successes
–See FFA 1b

4. Communication is ineffective.

Many Quality Issues Are Not Being Resolved
Force Field Analysis

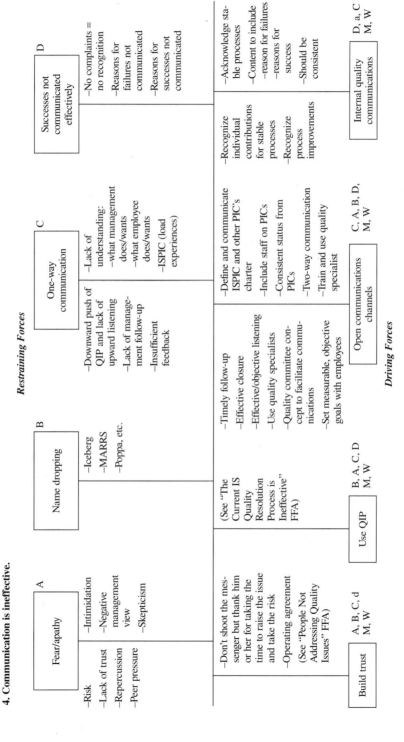

Restraining Forces

A	B	C	D
Fear/apathy	Name dropping	One-way communication	Successes not communicated effectively

A — Fear/apathy
- Risk
- Lack of trust
- Repercussion
- Peer pressure
- Intimidation
- Negative management view
- Skepticism

B — Name dropping
- Iceberg
- MARRS
- Poppa, etc.

C — One-way communication
- Downward push of QIP and lack of upward listening
- Lack of management follow-up
- Insufficient feedback
- Lack of understanding:
  - what management does/wants
  - what employee does/wants
  - ISPIC (load experiences)

D — Successes not communicated effectively
- No complaints = no recognition
- Reasons for failures not communicated
- Reasons for successes not communicated

Driving Forces

Build trust	Use QIP	Open communications channels	Internal quality communications

Build trust
- Don't shoot the messenger but thank him or her for taking the time to raise the issue and take the risk
- Operating agreement

(See "People Not Addressing Quality Issues" FFA)

A, B, C, d
M, W

Use QIP

(See "The Current IS Quality Resolution Process is Ineffective" FFA)

B, A, C, D
M, W

Open communications channels
- Timely follow-up
- Effective closure
- Effective/objective listening
- Use quality specialists
- Quality committee concept to facilitate communications
- Set measurable, objective goals with employees
- Define and communicate ISPIC and other PIC's charter
- Include staff on PICs
- Consistent status from PICs
- Two-way communication
- Train and use quality specialist

C, A, B, D,
M, W

Internal quality communications
- Recognize individual contributions for stable processes
- Recognize process improvements
- Acknowledge stable processes
- Content to include
  - reason for failures
  - reasons for success
- Should be consistent

D, a, C
M, W

Many Quality Issues Are Not Being Resolved
Recommendations

Management must consistently express its commitment to ETQ by stating:

• All IS employees will use the QIP as a standard mode of operation.

• Management will support and allow time to use QIP.

• More management will participate in QAT/QRTs.

Many Quality Issues Are Not Being Resolved
Recommendations (continued)

Communicate IS Quality Issues

Content

1. Recognize individual and team contributions for process improvements.

2. Acknowledge stable processes.

3. Publish:
   - Reasons for processes succeeding.
   - Reasons for processes failing.

4. Process improvement updates:
   - Define and communicate all PIC charters and process flows.
   - PIC decisions and impacts.
   - QRT/QAT status.

Many Quality Issues Are Not Being Resolved Recommendations (continued)

Communicate IS Quality Issues

Methods

1. Information exchange

2. Status reports

3. Staff meetings

4. IS project workbook

5. ETQ implementation workbook

6. Corporate publications

7. All-IS staff meetings

Many Quality Issues Are Not Being Resolved Recommendations (continued)

Encourage Training and Education

1. Listening skills

2. Assertiveness training

3. How to give and receive feedback

4. Team building

5. Time management

6. Conflict management

7. IS QIP workshops:
   - Metrics
   - Cost/benefit analysis
   - Return on investment
   - Use of quality implementation workbook

Many Quality Issues Are Not Being Resolved

Recommendations (continued)

Improve IS Working Environment

1. Set measurable, objective goals with employees.

2. Ensure clear understanding of goals.
   - Individual
   - Team
   - IS
   - Corporate

3. To drive fear and mistrust out of the workplace:
   - Management must change assumptions about employees.
   - Employees must change assumptions about management.

4. Establish IS operating agreement.

Many Quality Issues Are Not Being Resolved

Recommendations (continued)

Establish IS Operating Agreement

☑ Show respect for others.

☑ Participate in two-way communication. Listen to others and express opinions and concerns.

☑ Keep criticism constructive.

☑ Keep focus on process.

☑ Realize accountability for our own actions.

☑ IS mission, objectives, and goals determine our priorities.

☑ Don't shoot the messenger.

Many Quality Issues Are Not Being Resolved Recommendations (continued)

Proposed Quality Review Process

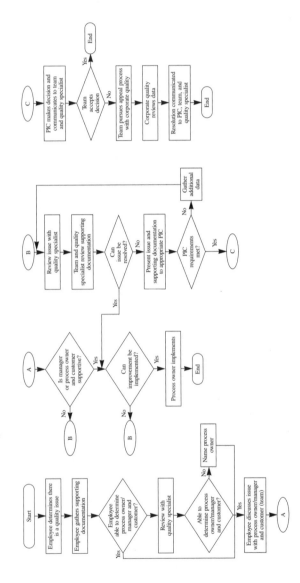

Many Quality Issues Are Not Being Resolved
Recommendations (continued)

Train 10 Quality Specialists to Be Used as Internal Consultants in Supporting Implementation of ETQ Throughout IS

1. Selections to be made from IS through structured interviews.

2. Managers must commit to supporting quality specialist activities as number one priorities over other work assignments.

3. Form a quality committee comprised of quality specialists.

4. Provide formal training for quality specialists.

5. Act as a liaison between management and staff.

6. Maintain regular communication with employees, management, quality officer, and corporate quality consultant.

Many Quality Issues Are Not Being Resolved

What's Next?

	Start	End	Owner
1. Open systems team will prototype selected QAT recommendations.	5/21/92	ongoing	Karen Smith
2. QRT be formed to:			
• Publish and communicate quality review process.	6/17/92	7/31/92	process support
• Interview and select quality specialists.	6/17/92	8/1/92	
• Begin training of quality specialists.	6/29/92	10/2/92	
• Establish and communicate IS operating agreement.	7/1/92	8/1/92	
3. Question and answer table be added to the IS information exchange.	7/1/92	ongoing	ISPIC
4. Add quality segment to monthly status report and publish via e-mail to all MIS managers.	7/1/92	ongoing	process support
5. Regular and structured staff meetings to include: • Project status. • PIC decisions and impacts. • Process status.	7/1/92	ongoing	managers
6. Communicate and deploy key IS processes to all IS employees.	8/3/92	ongoing	ISPIC

Many Quality Issues Are Not Being Resolved

What's Next? (continued)

	Start	End	Owner
7. All managers set measurable, objective goals with employees and report status until 100 percent complete. Develop a job-related skills and personal career path plan.	7/1/92	12/31/92	managers/employees
8. Communicate contents and availability of IS project workbook	7/1/92	ongoing	process support
9. Communicate purpose and content of ETQ implementation workbook to managers.	7/1/92	ongoing	corporate quality
10. Communicate purpose and content of ETQ implementation workbook to staff.	9/1/92	10/1/92	quality specialist
11. Add recognition segment to quarterly all-IS employee meeting.	Q3	ongoing	Rich Nortnik
12. All IS QATs, QRTs, and PICs document and communicate charters, process flows, and decisions.	7/1/92	9/1/92	direct reports

QAT Operating Agreement

Start on time

Stop on time

Be relaxed

Keep process focus

Use parking lot concept (10-minute maximum discussion)

Consensus

Have fun

Confidentiality

Appendix J
Direct Connection
Quality Action Team

Mission Statement

To promote teamwork and open communication between manufacturing and product procurement to meet internal and external customer needs.

Problem Statement

The lack of communication and awareness with the direct delivery process has created potential and actual part shortages on the manufacturing floor.

Quality Improvement Process

Step 1: Document Process Flows and Identify Process Ownership

Direct Delivery Kanban Triggering

Operational Procedure

Overview

Once the kanban sizes are established, the request confirmation form is used as the means by which the StorageTek buyer analyst notifies supplier of kanban needs. Manufacturing communicates the need to the material analyst who then notifies the buyer analyst. (Commonly referred to as kanban *trip* or *trigger.*)

Procedure

Responsibility	Action
Manufacturing associates	1. Place kanban card in pick-up location when trip point is reached.
Purchasing material analyst	2. Complete the request/confirmation form, one vendor per form based on visual trip point or predetermined schedule consumption. Routes form to buyer analyst for fax to supplier. A. If working on a weekend, ensure extra kanban are requested.
Purchasing buyer analyst	3. Determine type of purchase order. A. If blanket order, create blanket release (per procedure PUR0166). 4. Fax direct delivery request form to supplier.
Material distribution	5. Audit and complete a systems receipt of the kanban. (Reference material receipt procedure DTS0110.)
Line stocker	6. Stock material on build line and place kanban card in designated area so that it is available for tripping when identified trip point is reached.

Direct Delivery Kanban Triggering

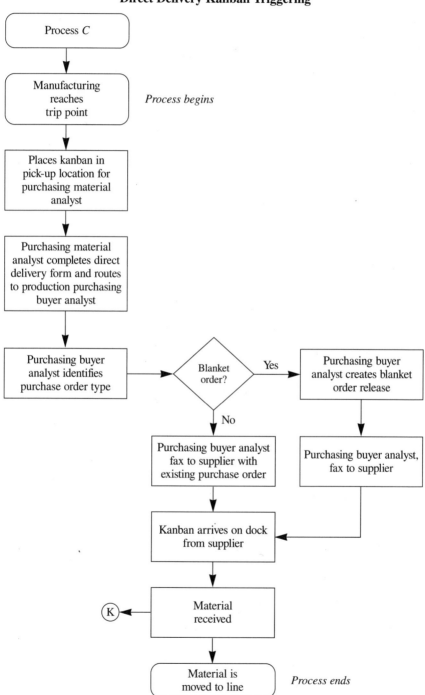

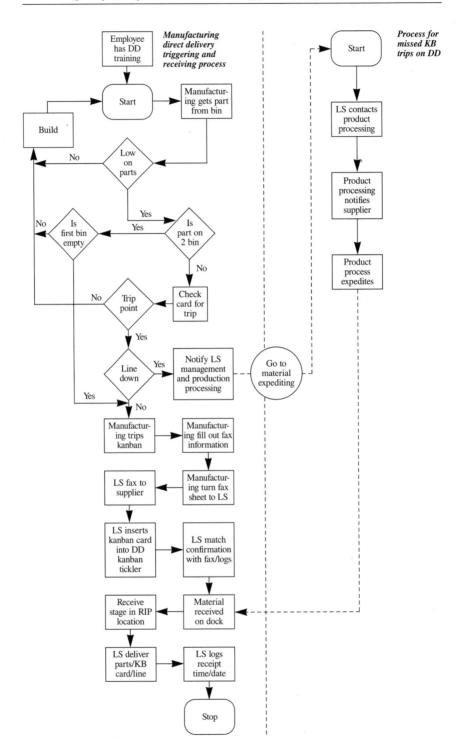

Quality Improvement Process

Step 2: Identify Customer Requirements and Establish Effective Measurements

Customer	Requirements	Supplier	Target Value
Line stocker	Pull packing slip/box count and move parts to staging area within four working hours of delivery.	Receiving	Four hours
Line stocker	Kanban card to line stocker or in order bin at trip point.	Manufacturing	Trip quantity
Line stocker	Immediate verbal notification of possible line down situations to included p/n, description, quantity, and reason (missed trip, quality, delivery, schedule).	Manufacturing	Immediate
Line stocker	Fill out fax correctly. (quantity, p/n, supplier, time, date, and initials) *No ditto marks*	Manufacturing	Accuracy
Production processing	Immediate verbal notification of possible line down situations to include p/n, description, quantity, and reason (missed trip, quality, delivery, schedule).	Manufacturing	Immediate
Manufacturing	Answer kanban trip flags within 15 minutes	Line stocker	15 minutes

Customer	Requirements	Supplier	Target Value
Manufacturing	Upon need the parts and card will be moved from the dock or staging area to the line with packaging material removed when applicable.	Line stocker	upon need
Manufacturing	Continuous education and communication on direct delivery process.	Manufacturing manager P/P management	ongoing
Manufacturing	Formal training on direct delivery process.	Manufacturing manager P/P management	30 days from hire

Quality Improvement Process

Step 3: Identify Cost of Quality

Cost of Quality Categories (Direct Connection QAT)

Basic costs—Costs associated with performing first-time, essential activities that produce revenue for the company.

Appraisal—Costs incurred to determine whether or not requirements have been met.

Prevention—Costs expended to prevent a failure to meet requirements; these costs are incurred to ensure that the employee does the job right the first time.

Internal failure—Costs to fix products or services that do not meet requirements. These failures are discovered before the goods or services are delivered to the customer.

External failure—Costs to fix products or services that do not meet requirements. These failures are discovered after the goods or services are delivered to the customer.

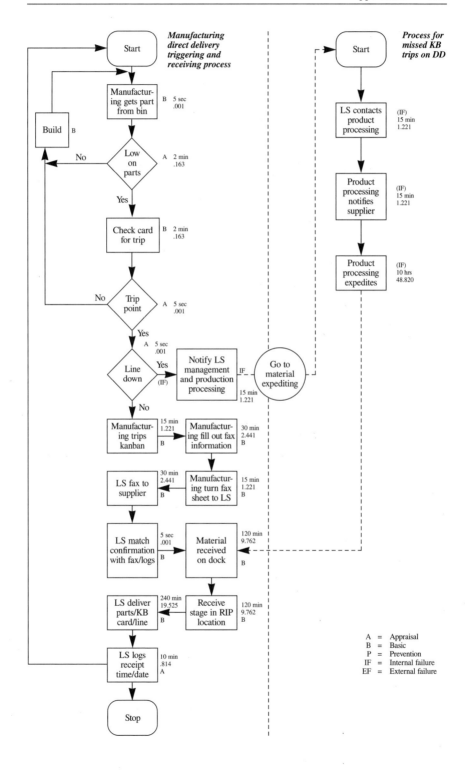

Manufacturing direct delivery triggering and receiving process

Start

Manufacturing gets part from bin — B 5 sec .001

Build — B

Low on parts — A 2 min .163

No

Yes

Check card for trip — B 2 min .163

Trip point — A 5 sec .001

No

Yes

A 5 sec .001

Line down — Yes → Notify LS management and production processing — IF 15 min 1.221 (IF)

→ Go to material expediting

No

Manufacturing trips kanban — 15 min 1.221 B

Manufacturing fill out fax information — 30 min 2.441 B

LS fax to supplier — 30 min 2.441 B

Manufacturing turn fax sheet to LS — 15 min 1.221 B

LS match confirmation with fax/logs — 5 sec .001 B

Material received on dock — 120 min 9.762 B

LS deliver parts/KB card/line — 240 min 19.525 B

Receive stage in RIP location — 120 min 9.762 B

LS logs receipt time/date — 10 min .814 A

Stop

Process for missed KB trips on DD

Start

LS contacts product processing — (IF) 15 min 1.221

Product processing notifies supplier — (IF) 15 min 1.221

Product processing expedites — (IF) 10 hrs 48.820

A = Appraisal
B = Basic
P = Prevention
IF = Internal failure
EF = External failure

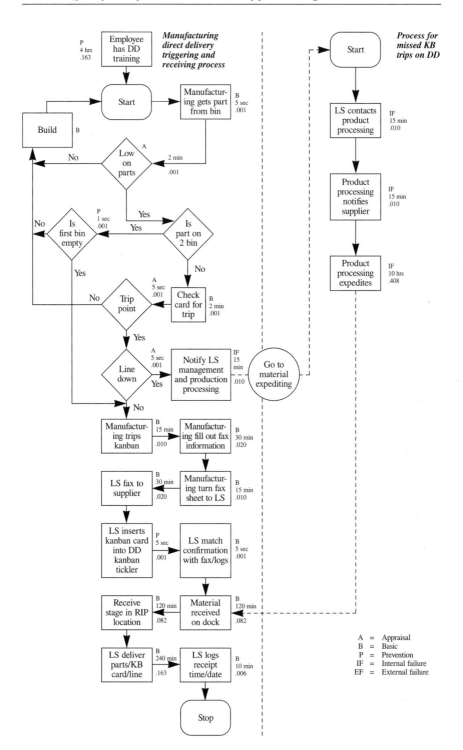

Manufacturing direct delivery triggering and receiving process

Process for missed KB trips on DD

A = Appraisal
B = Basic
P = Prevention
IF = Internal failure
EF = External failure

Quality Improvement Process
Step 4: Identify and Prioritize Improvement
Opportunities

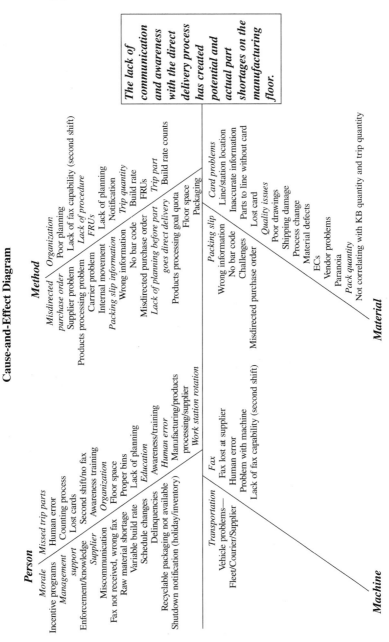

Cause-and-Effect Diagram

The lack of communication and awareness with the direct delivery process has created potential and actual part shortages on the manufacturing floor.

Quality Improvement Process
Step 5: Organize and Develop Improvement Teams

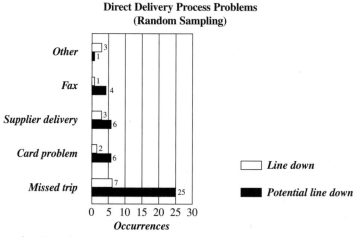

**Direct Delivery Process Problems
(Random Sampling)**

April to November

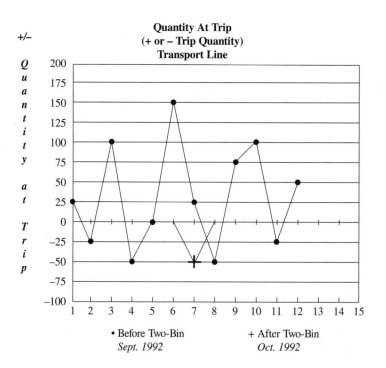

**Quantity At Trip
(+ or – Trip Quantity)
Transport Line**

• Before Two-Bin   + After Two-Bin
Sept. 1992   *Oct. 1992*

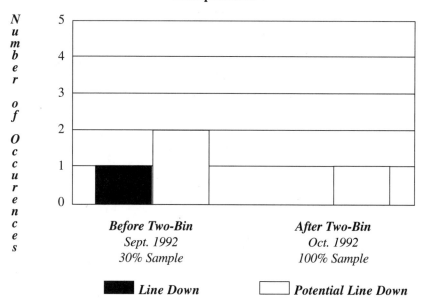

Two-Bin Results
Transport Line

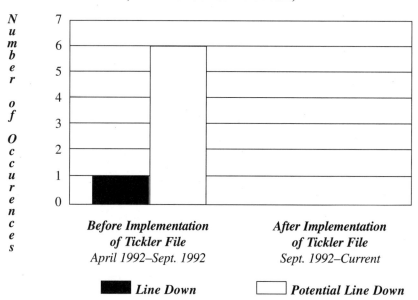

Card Problems
(Card Not Put Back With Part)

Quality Improvement Process
Step 6: Present Improvement Plans to Management
Suggested Solutions

Implemented Solutions	In-Process Solutions	Possible Solutions
Two-bin process instruction sheet	Implemented two-bin system where applicable	Consistency on cards on all three lines
Bin for direct delivery cards by day for line stockers	Implement manufacturing management on direct delivery approval form	Incentive programs put in place
Instruction sheet for 48/72-hour turnaround from suppliers	Implement training program for new hires and as refresher course	Recyclable packaging material
Readjust kanban quantities	Direct delivery handbook (to be coordinated with class listed above)	Put all pink kanban boards in central location on each line in numerical order
Implement seven steps	Customer/supplier agreements put in place	Implement direct delivery approval form
	Remark/enlarge staging area for line stockers	Update 48/72-hour turnaround from suppliers
		Review direct delivery goals corporatewide

Two-Bin Kanban System

- *Do not* use parts from bin 2 until bin 1 is empty. Bin 2 holds just enough parts to build while the supplier fills the request for parts and the line stocker moves the parts to the line. If you use bin 2 before bin 1 is empty you may go line down.

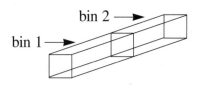

- Turn in kanban card when bin 1 is empty. This is the trip point.
- Once your have turned in the kanban card move all of the parts in bin 2 to bin 1. You should *not* have any parts in bin 2 until the line stocker puts the parts on-line from the fax that was just sent to the supplier.
- Now the whole process starts over again.
- If a trip point is missed, contact the line stocker immediately! If the line stocker is notified he or she can contact purchasing, and the parts can be expedited before the line goes down.
- If you have any questions contact one of the line stockers.

Kanban/Direct Delivery Turnaround

There is a 48-hour turnaround time for all supplier deliveries (excluding PIKE TOOL*) on supplier working days (Monday–Friday).

Order Times

All direct delivery parts ordered A.M. will be received from supplier within 48 hours of order time.

All direct delivery faxes ordered P.M. will not be received by supplier until the following morning, therefore add 1 day to delivery time.

Orders for direct delivery on Friday (P.M.), Saturday, or Sunday will not be received by suppliers until Monday morning.

Note: PIKE TOOL has a 4-day turnaround time for orders on supplier working days (Monday–Friday).

Louisville Warehouse Turnaround

Up to 24-hour turnaround from Louisville 7 (maxi) and Louisville 5 (mini) if ordered A.M.; up to 36 hours if ordered P.M.

Ordering for weekend should be done on Thursdays to compensate for turnaround times.

Delivery times from Louisville 5 and 7 to Longmont (building 10) are currently set at 9:30 A.M. and 2:30 P.M., Monday through Friday.

Direct Delivery Turnaround

All Suppliers Excluding PIKE TOOL

Day	Monday	Tuesday	Wednesday	Thursday	Friday
Ordered A.M.	Weds.	Thurs.	Fri.	Mon.	Tues.
Ordered P.M.	Thurs.	Fri.	Mon.	Tues.	Weds.

Any kanban turned in to be faxed on Saturday or Sunday will not be received by the supplier until Monday morning.

PIKE TOOL

Day	Monday	Tuesday	Wednesday	Thursday	Friday
Ordered A.M.	Thurs.	Fri.	Mon.	Tues.	Weds.
Ordered P.M.	Fri.	Mon.	Tues.	Weds.	Thurs.

Any kanban turned in to be faxed on Saturday or Sunday will not be received by the supplier until Monday morning.

Quality Improvement Process
Step 7: Implement Plans and Monitor/Measure Results

Step 8: Maintain the Solution(s)

Step 9: Reward and Recognition

Requests to Management

In order for this team, along with the 44XX and 2511 subteams, to continue to improve the direct delivery process, it needs management support. This list contains the requests along with the person(s) the team believes can help in that area.

- Two-bin process instructions (ISO 9000 certification)
- Turnaround time instructions (ISO 9000 certification)
- Continued support for purchasing of new ESD bins (manufacturing/product procurement management)

Action Plan

Action	Responsibility	When	Status
Two-bin implementation including purchasing bins	Subteam/manufacturing	ongoing	
Direct delivery approval form	QAT/inventory planning	2nd quarter 1993	
Direct delivery procedure for implementation	QAT/inventory planning/ manufacturing/production purchasing/industrial engineering	2nd quarter 1993	
Direct delivery training course with handbook	QAT	1st quarter 1993	
Customer/supplier agreements	QAT/manufacturing	Jan. 1993	
RIP/LOC staging area	Receiving		
Direct delivery instruction by part number for turnaround time	QAT/subteam	1st quarter 1993	
Incentive programs	Products processing/ manufacturing management		
Two-bin instruction sheet posted	QAT		complete
Bin for direct delivery cards	QAT		complete
Adjust kanban quantities	QAT/subteam		complete
Seven step	Subteam/manufacturing		complete

- Replacement of all non-ESD bins (manufacturing/product procurement management)
- Approval of new direct delivery/dock-to-stock approval form (direct delivery steering committee)
- Direct delivery training and manual (manufacturing/product procurement management)
- Implementation of the customer/supplier agreements (manufacturing/product procurement management)
- Implementation of incentive programs (manufacturing/product procurement management)
- Review corporatewide direct delivery goals (direct delivery steering committee, manufacturing/product procurement management)

Appendix K
Customer Services Quality
Invoicing Team Excellence

Project Selection

- **Customer dissatisfaction**
  - –Invalid invoices
  - –Untimely invoices

- **Internal audit**
  - –Negative revenue impact
  - –Lengthy cycle time

- **Decentralization requirement**

- **Application systems incompatibility**

Excellence Through Quality
Nine-Step Process

CSQI

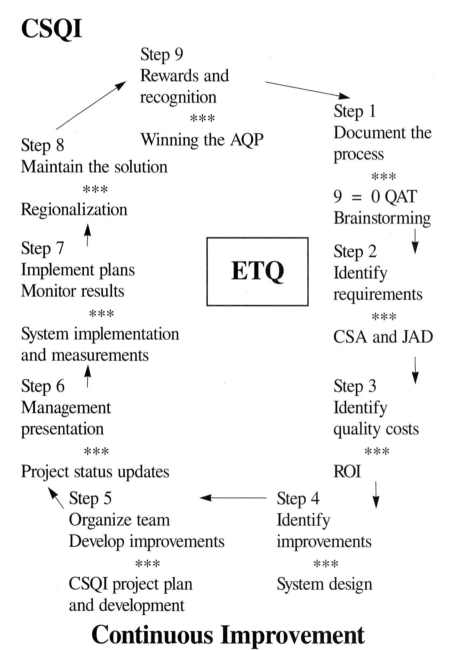

Step 9
Rewards and
recognition
***
Winning the AQP

Step 8
Maintain the solution
***
Regionalization

Step 7
Implement plans
Monitor results
***
System implementation
and measurements

Step 6
Management
presentation
***
Project status updates

Step 5
Organize team
Develop improvements
***
CSQI project plan
and development

ETQ

Step 1
Document the
process
***
9 = 0 QAT
Brainstorming

Step 2
Identify
requirements
***
CSA and JAD

Step 3
Identify
quality costs
***
ROI

Step 4
Identify
improvements
***
System design

Continuous Improvement

Seven-Step
Problem-Solving Process

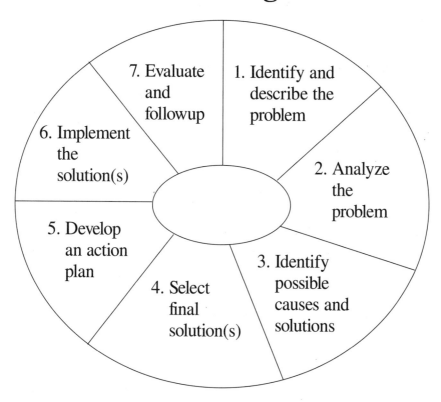

Project Selection

Techniques

- Nine-step quality improvement process
- Seven-step problem-solving process
- Customer surveys
- Brainstorming sessions
- Analysis of process metrics

Project Selection

Stakeholders

- StorageTek customer
- Headquarters' billing administrators
- Regional billing administrators
- Customer services engineers
- Accounts receivable representatives

Project Selection

Organizational Goals

- Improved cycle time
- *BBB* bond rating
- StorageTek quality policy: Customer satisfaction is our number one priority

Root Cause Analysis
Cause-and-Effect Diagram

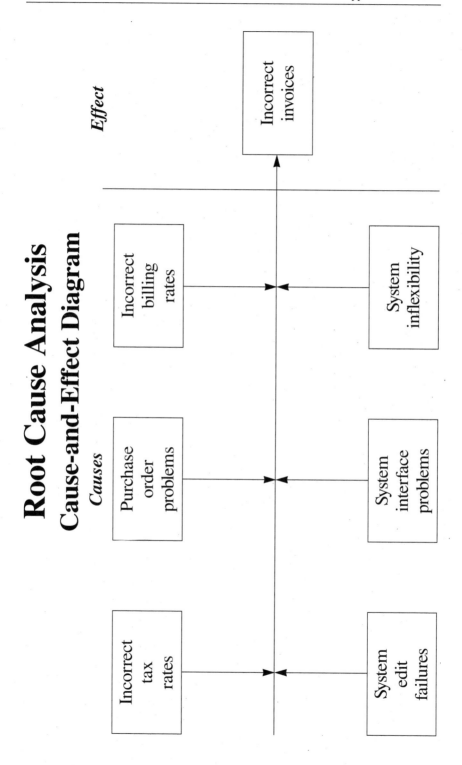

Root Cause Analysis

Analysis Techniques

- Brainstorming sessions
- Understand the process
- Develop process flows
- Identify cost of quality
- CE/FFA

Root Cause Analysis

Force Field Analysis

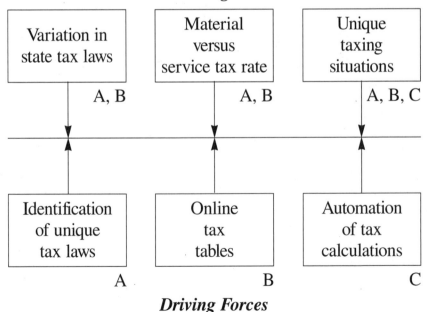

Restraining Forces

Variation in state tax laws	Material versus service tax rate	Unique taxing situations
A, B	A, B	A, B, C

Identification of unique tax laws	Online tax tables	Automation of tax calculations
A	B	C

Driving Forces

Data Gathering

Techniques

- Documenting the process

- Measuring cost of quality

- Utilizing recommendations from *other* quality action teams

- Joint application design session (JAD)

Data Gathering

System Requirements

Joint Application Design (JAD)

- Piloted JAD methodology

- $5,000 cost savings

- Addressed requirement for business changes/system flexibility

- Involved all customers/suppliers

Data Gathering

Invoicing Process Flow

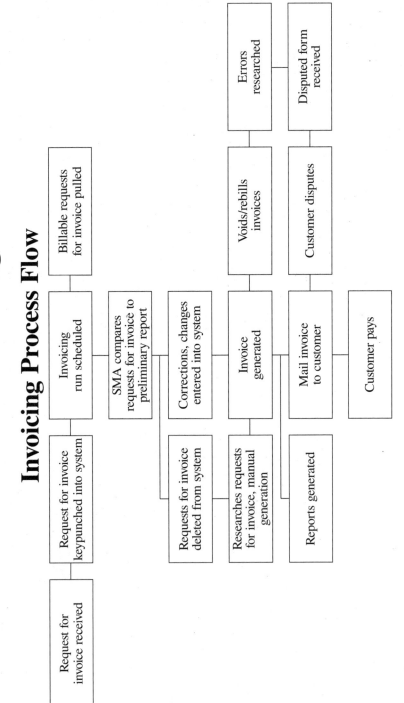

Joint Application Design (JAD)

Participants

- Regional billing administration
- Special maintenance billing
- Information systems
- Customer services
- Logistics
- Tax
- Field administration support
- Customer services marketing
- Internal audit
- Central dispatch
- Product performance tracking (CSDC)
- Printer operations
- Orders administration

Solution Development
Selection Criteria

- Customer satisfaction
- Decentralization
- Stakeholder buy-in
- Improved cycle time
- Invoice accuracy
- Cost

Solution Development
Expertise

- Knowledge of StorageTek business processes (current and future)
- Knowledge of new methodologies
- Knowledge of tax laws
- Systems design and development

Solution Development
Expertise

Developed StorageTek Business Rules

- Based on customer services directives
- Alignment with StorageTek customer maintenance contracts
- Compliance with taxing jurisdictions

Solution Development
Project Plan

System implementation

3/92

3/92

Unit/system test

Programming

Report layouts/requirements
8/91

Validate/document prototype
4/91

Database design
3/91

Design/validation of program specs
10/91

Dec. 1990

March 1992

Solution Development

The CSQI Solution

Root Cause

• Process failures

Solution

• Eliminated manual intervention

• Automated manual tasks

• Provided system interfaces

• Automated PBIs

Solution Development

The CSQI Solution

Root Cause

• System failures

Solution

• Modular program design

• Simplified code

• Business practice alignment

• On-line data access

Solution Development

Benefits

• Improved cycle time

• Improved invoice accuracy

• Increased customer satisfaction

Implementation

Project Agreement

- Stakeholder involvement through *all* phases
- Complete management commitment
- Customer/supplier agreement (CSA)

Implementation

Tracking Techniques

- CSQI process measurement report
- Total revenue detail report

Report Development

- CSQI process management report
- Total revenue detail report

Metrics

- Cycle time
- Disputed invoices

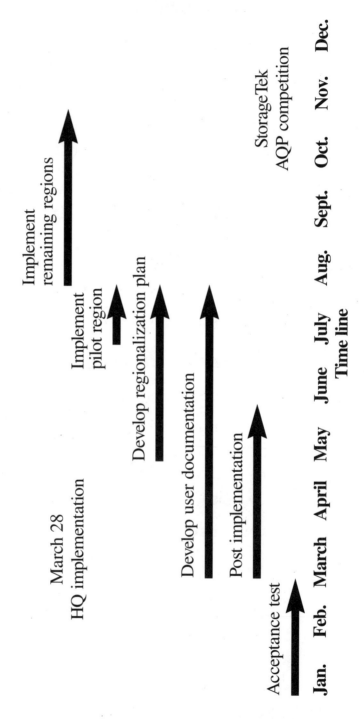

Implementation Plan

Customer Services Quality Invoicing System

Implement
remaining regions

Implement
pilot region

Develop regionalization plan

March 28
HQ implementation

Develop user documentation

Post implementation

Acceptance test

StorageTek
AQP competition

Jan. Feb. March April May June July Aug. Sept. Oct. Nov. Dec.

Time line

Implementation
Tracking Techniques

Project name: CSQI

Reviewer's name: Consensus rating from all reviewers (13)

Evaluation criteria	Project	User	Consulting
Product met customer requirements	3.7		
Adherence to schedule/budget	3.7		
Business goals and objectives met	3.7		
Effectiveness of change control process	3.4		
Communication		3.6	3.5
Planning and organizing		3.4	3.6
Adherence to standards/methodology		3.6	3.6
Promote teamwork		3.7	3.7
Creative problem solving		3.6	3.6
Knowledge of business		3.6	3.7

Overall Rating of 3.7 = Extremely Satisfied

Implementation Plan

Communication of Results

- CSQI announcement letter

- StorageTek news article

- Monthly report generation
  –Process measurement
  –Financial

Conclusion

CSQI System Benefits

- Improved cycle time

- Improved invoice accuracy

- Increased customer satisfaction

Bibliography

Deming, W. Edwards. *Out of the Crisis.* Cambridge, Mass.: MIT Press, 1982.

Gryna, Frank M. "The Quality Director of the '90s." *Quality Progress* 24 (May 1991): 53.

Imai, Masaaki. *Kaizen: The Key to Japan's Competitive Success.* New York: Random House Business Division, 1986, 18.

Juran, Joseph M. "Strategies for World-Class Quality." *Quality Progress* 24 (March 1991): 81–85.

Price, Frank. *Right Every Time: Using the Deming Approach.* New York: Marcel Dekker, 1990.

Scherkenbach, William W. *The Deming Route to Quality and Productivity: Road Maps and Roadblocks.* Washington, D.C.: CEEPress Books, 1986.

Stratton, A. Donald. *An Approach to Quality Improvement That Works: Implementing Quality Improvement in the 90s.* Milwaukee, Wis.: ASQC Quality Press, 1991.

Index